LIGHTNING IN A BOTTLE

The Sox of '67

By Herbert F. Crehan
With James W. Ryan

Branden Publishing
Company--Boston

Library of Congress Cataloging-in-Publication Data

Crehan, Herbert F., 1943-
    Lightning in a bottle : the sox of '67 / by Herbert F. Crehan with
James W. Ryan.
      p. cm.
    Includes bibliographical references and index.
    ISBN 0-8283-1968-5 (paper--1st printing)
    ISBN 0-8283-1967-7 (cloth--2nd printing)
    1. Boston Red Sox (Baseball team--History.
 I. Ryan, James. W.
 II. Title.
GV875.B62C74 1992
796.357'64'0974461--dc20   91-32388
                CIP

BRANDEN PUBLISHING COMPANY
17 Station Street
Box 843 Brookline Village
Boston, MA 02147

DEDICATION

This book is dedicated to Daniel H. Farquhar who took me to my first Red Sox game on Father's Day in 1951. The last thing he probably needed was another kid to keep an eye on. The thing I most needed on that day was a father substitute.

It is also dedicated to the memory of my mother, Ruperta S. Crehan, who suffered with me through rain delays, Don Buddin errors and Pinky Higgins. She is missed.

These two special people are perfect symbols of the unique love affair that Red Sox fans have with their team. These fans are the Red Sox every bit as much as Tom Yawkey is the Red Sox, Ted Williams is the Red Sox and Carl Yastrzemski is the Red Sox.

-H.F.C.

1997

Merry Christmas, George!! Love, Dan

TABLE OF CONTENTS

FOREWORD

This book is really a love letter. It is a love letter to the team that has played such a large part in my life: the Boston Red Sox.

It is a book written by a lifelong Red Sox fan for other lifelong Red Sox fans. It is for the "true believers" who plan their vacations around the Red Sox schedule, who mark their seasons by the opening of spring training and the last game of the World Series.

It is *not* written for the professionals who are more concerned about escalators to the Six Hundred Club than the aisles leading to the most distant bleacher seats. It is *not* written for professionals who defame the proud name Red Sox by typing "Bosox" to save a few seconds on their stories. Most of all, it is *not* written for the casual followers who think that Sammy White is the name of an old bowling alley in Boston's Brighton section.

My first trip to a Red Sox game, over 40 years ago, was a rather auspicious beginning. My father and I started out from Braintree, Massachusetts, to make our way to Fenway Park via public transportation. It was quite an adventure for a six-year old. Since it was an arduous trek, nothing would do but a stop at a local watering hole in Quincy. After watching my father down a prodigious amount of beer, I got my first clue that our journey was not to be a success. Through the smoke-filled barroom air I could see from the grainy nine-inch TV screen that the game had started without us. Perhaps I should have realized at that moment that the Red Sox were fated to break my heart.

This book is written to recall the wonder of that special Red Sox year, 1967. Those Red Sox were special for many reasons. First, their American League pennant ended over twenty years of frustration for their fans. In addition, their success was a complete surprise. Having finished ninth, twenty-six games out of first place the year before, the Red Sox opened the season as a 100-1 shot to win the pennant.

The 1967 Red Sox were also special because they saved a proud and venerable franchise from oblivion. Younger fans who are accustomed to attendances of 30,000 plus fans may be surprised to know that the 1966 Red Sox drew 811,172, an average of just over 10,000 per game. To put that in perspective, nearby Suffolk Downs, arguably the ugliest horse track in America, drew 978,210 patrons the same year.

Tom Yawkey's pockets were deep, very deep indeed, but they were not bottomless. While it is incomprehensible to imagine that he would ever have abandoned the franchise, who knows what cost-cutting measures would have followed if attendance continued to lag.

But the 1967 Red Sox completely caught the imagination of Bostonians and attendance soared to over 1,700,000. The following year attendance grew to better than 1,900,000 and the trend has continued to the point where fewer than 2,000,000 in attendance would be a disappointment. The Red Sox are one of the most successful franchises in professional sports, but they came within an eyelash in 1967 of sliding into oblivion.

The Boston Red Sox are indeed New England's team. Few teams have a true regional following -- six contiguous states -- in the same sense that the Red Sox do. If you doubt it, check out the number of buses from Maine, Vermont and Connecticut double-parked behind the center field wall for a Sunday afternoon game.

But this regional loyalty is always at risk. At risk to the TV and radio waves invading our territory from such alien cities as New York. Perhaps as 1967 approached this regional phenomenon was at risk but the "Impossible Dream" team preserved this loyalty. Not even the Boston/Milwaukee/Atlanta Braves (America's team: perhaps they'll move to your city next!) can threaten the Red Sox' stranglehold.

It is fascinating to reflect on the fact that the '67 Red Sox soared like a meteor in the evening sky and, just as quickly, the magic disappeared. When the eight everyday players featured in this book took the field and were joined by Jim Lonborg on the mound, the average age was only twenty-four years. Given their spectacular finish and the chemistry of the team, they appeared a dynasty in the making. But the 1968 Red Sox finished a disappointing fourth, seventeen and one half games out of first place. In late 1969, Dick Williams, who was considered a near genius in 1967, was summarily dismissed by the front office.

The best way to relive the excitement of the 1967 Red Sox is to look at it through the eyes of the ten men -- the eight everyday players and the two pitchers -- who were most responsible for their success. Not just what they did, but how they got there and what they are doing now. A Russ Gibson, who grew up in nearby Fall River and who travelled the fifty miles to Fenway via ten years of back roads in the minor leagues. A Mike Andrews and a Jim Lonborg, who both grew up 3,000 miles from Fenway but who have made Boston their home and who contribute significantly to their communities. A George Scott, who grew up poor in Greenville, Mississippi, played fourteen years in the big leagues and now struggles vainly to find a job in organized baseball.

Nineteen sixty-seven was a year which will never be equalled again in Red Sox history. All of the factors converged. An entire region -- New England -- was starved for baseball success. A major city -- Boston -- was struggling for racial harmony. For a brief moment in time, you could stop for dinner in Berlin, New Hampshire, and know the Red Sox would be on TV. You could walk down Massachusetts Avenue in Boston and hear Ned Martin in stereo.

It was special. They were special. It is time to relive it.

PROLOGUE

It was the bittersweet year of 1967, a quarter century ago in a time and place hardly remembered. A wornout winter had given way to a cruel April. Americans were becoming grimly aware that the war in Vietnam was evolving inexorably into a national nightmare. Few then, however, could begin to comprehend the true cost.

Happily, on the homefront, the baseball season was about to get underway with all its hype and fanfare and lofty dreams of glory to be played out on manicured diamonds across the breadth of land. As always, the national pastime would serve as a national panacea to shield the citizens from any unpleasantness. In most minds, the boys of summer promptly took precedence over the boys of battle.

But in Boston, as on so many opening days, there was little joy, less to shout about and lots of lethargy. The betting world had listed the lowly Red Sox as a 100-1 longshot to win their first American League pennant since 1946. The odds truly translated into no shot at all.

No matter, Governor John A. Volpe tossed out the first ball to open the Red Sox season at Fenway Park on a raw, brisk Wednesday, April 12, 1967. Before 8,234 never-say-die fans Boston squeezed out a 5-4 win over the Chicago White Sox. Innings earlier Volpe had already fled the premises for the warmth of his State House office.

Despite the initial victory, none of the fans filing out of the park believed for a moment that it portended a championship year for the hometeam. Obviously, there wasn't any fatuous talk about the 1967 Red Sox finally realizing the "Impossible Dream" of winning their first league pennant in twenty-one years.

Who could be so foolish to consider such a possibility? How could anyone realistically suggest it? These were the Boston Red Sox. The Red Flops, The Consistent Chokers. How many times had the faithful seen them go to the well only to draw another empty bucket? Or even forget to bring the bucket? It would be silly to contemplate a league title for this team. Don't even think about a World Series title! Why risk an anxiety attack or a complete stoppage of the heart?

The Red Sox team unfailingly is comprised of the original Heartbreak Kids. How many times do you have to ask for a date and be rejected before you understand your love is unrequited? No diehard fan can ever forget the New Haven bartender who told sports columnist, Peter Gammons, after the Red Sox blew another playoff series, "They killed our fathers and now the sons of bitches are coming for us!"

Gammons, a long-suffering Boston loyalist along with his brother, Ned, attested in writing that his father assured him before he died in 1981 that "the Red Sox will win in your lifetime." They did, indeed, win several league flags since, but the World Series title has remained out of reach.

Whether a playoff series or a World Series, the Red Sox repeatedly take their fans up the mountain only to desert them like an insensitive gigolo just before the summit. When it looks like they are in an unbeatable situation, they again create a way to break our hearts that goes beyond our wildest imaginations.

Remember game six of the 1986 World Series when there were two outs and none on in the bottom of the tenth and the Red Sox had a 5-3 lead over the Mets in Shea Stadium? Only one out away from their first World Series championship since 1918 and yet they found a way to let the Mets win and break their fans' hearts. Right Bill Buckner?

Incredibly though, hope burns eternal in the collective breast of Boston loyalists, but it was only a flickering ember at the season opener in 1967. In that year, that April 12, they wouldn't have given a drop of lamp oil that the hometeam would finally ignite and finish higher than fourth place.

Sadly, most fans thought that spot would be nothing to complain about. Just the year before the Red Sox had finished in ninth place, half a game out of dead last. Boston fans were consoled somewhat because the 1966 last place finishers were the despised New York Yankees, the pinstriped nemesis that consistently shattered Boston's aspirations to achieve the "Impossible Dream".

Quixotically, however, whether they win or lose, the Red Sox are envisioned in baseball mythology as a proud, venerable and ill-starred major league franchise -- whose franchise is the six-state New England region but whose following is truly national.

Much of their national popularity through the years is due to the lengthy lineup of heroic and colorful players of star vintage who have worn Boston's flannels. They've had far more than their share of superstars going all the way back to the days of the legendary, Cy Young, the pitching and hitting feats of Babe Ruth, and continuing into the era of feisty Jimmy Foxx.

The litany of standouts extends without letup through Ted Williams, Carl Yastrzemski and into the present day to Roger Clemens. Everyone of them is a Hall of Famer or a future Hall of Famer. Invariably, about all of them has been just as controversial off the field as on it.

But blessed as they have been with an abundance of individual stars in eight decades, they appear cursed in their constant failure to capture a World Championship. Strangely, this dichotomy in their history and the split personality of their achievements only adds to the folk tale appeal of the team in the national psyche.

The Red Sox haven't won a World Series since 1918. That makes them big losers, right? No, wrong. The fact is that Americans find that statistic incredibly transfixing. They can't take their minds off of it. All those years, they think, and how many more do you figure the Red Sox can extend it without winning a World Series title? Go for it, guys. Let's see how far you can run out the streak of futility without winning. Those Red Sox are our kind of guys, right?

Forever in their memory, "Billy Buck" is frozen for the ages in a time warp where he watches in cool disdain as a routine groundball flashes between his black hightops in that sixth game of the 1986 World Series. The nation loved it; there would be another day of baseball. Mike Torrez loved it too. Finally, after eight years, he was off the hook for giving up the homer to Bucky Dent, allowing the Yankees to triumph 5-4 over the Red Sox in the second ever American League playoff.

Despite the lack of World Series pennants after 1918, the earlier Red Sox were in fact a near dynasty in the game, tracing their genesis back to late 19th century teams known variously as the Plymouth Rocks, Speed Boys, Boston Puritans and Boston Pilgrims. They became the Red Sox in 1907 when new owner, John I. Taylor, of the *Boston Globe* family first had them wear red stockings.

While they had been an American League franchise since 1901, Taylor renamed them the Red Sox after a one-time famous team of that name in the National League. Why start from scratch with an unfamiliar name when you had one that evoked memories of greatness from an earlier age?

In the first eighteen years of the twentieth century, the Red Sox went on to win the American League pennant six times. It may be of some consolation to Boston fans to remember that during this same period the huffy New York Yankees failed to win the top gonfalon even once.

Contemporary Red Sox fans may be even more amazed to know that their baseball team chalked up an outstanding World Series record in this time span. In the very first World Series in 1903, the Red Sox routed the highly favored New York Giants five games to three. The pompous Giants were so humbled by this experience at the hands of the upstart Red Sox from the junior circuit that they refused to participate in the 1904 World Series when the Bostonians repeated as American League champions.

(Perhaps if the New Yorkers could have squinted into a crystal ball and viewed the carnage of 1946, 1967, 1975 and 1986 they would have shown up to play and taken their chances at the hands of the parvenus from Boston!)

After a dry spell of some eight seasons, the Red Sox went on to represent the American League four more times in World Series held between 1912 and 1918. On all four occasions, the Red Sox emerged victorious to gain the hearts and minds of fans in a bizarre love-hate relationship that extends into our own day. Whatever, at that time the Red Sox, with six pennants tucked in their belts and boasting a perfect 5-0 World Series record, could easily claim to be the strongest franchise in major league baseball.

These glory years took on added lustre in 1912 when the Red Sox opened Fenway Park. The team's popularity had soared with each new title and the old Huntington Field ballpark could no longer accommodate the throngs who wanted to watch their hometown boys strive for immortality. Northeastern University occupies the site now.

Never one to overlook an opportunity to add to the family treasury, Taylor personally supervised the construction of the new ballpark. Naming it was no problem. "It's in the Fenway section, isn't it? Then name it Fenway Park," he ordered.

With the passing years, Fenway Park has come to rank equally with the Red Sox and its star players in the creation of the mystique and national interest which are focused yearly on the Boston franchise. Invariably, anyone who views Fenway Park on television vows to visit it someday. Those who do stare in fascination at the mix of obtuse angles as though they were the staunch pillars and vaulted ceilings of a medieval cathedral.

Author John Updike, who has been a Red Sox fan since his boyhood in Pennsylvania, once described Fenway Park "as a lyric little bandbox of a ballpark." The less literary refer to is as Friendly Fenway. To more than one visiting manager it has been a House of Horrors. More than a few left-handed pitchers have been heard to curse it as "that #$%¢&@! excuse for a ballpark." To the natives, it's just plain old Fenway like " . . . I'm goin' over to Fenway to see the game."

Anyway you look at it, Fenway Park's dimensions are as eccentric and albeit as lovable as a maiden aunt. Put it down mostly to the fact that the only available parcel of land for the park ended abruptly at Landsdowne Street which was squeezed like a rolled carpet flat against the former Boston & Albany Railroad tracks.

Mention Fenway Park and any fan anywhere immediately thinks first about the formidable left field wall -- the famed Green Monster -- that looms thirty-seven feet in height with a twenty-three-foot high screen atop the length of it. Its huge size tricks the eye of the uninitiated into believing left field is closer to home plate than right field. In fact, though, the right field line is actually thirteen feet closer, 302 feet versus 315 feet to left.

If that seems a bit bizarre, consider the fact that straight-away right field is 380 feet from home plate. Anyway you look at it, it takes a very strange angle to get from 302 feet down the line to 380 feet in dead right. Every rightfielder who has ever chased a ball around that section of the right field line can attest to the vagaries of that angle!

No one can deny that the period of 1912 to 1918 represented the Red Sox' "salad days". In those distant days they produced four league pennants and world championships and a dazzling jewel of a ballpark. Then when it seemed there was no way they could top these achievements, they introduced the greatest baseball player of all time to their mesmerized fans -- George Herman "Babe" Ruth. The Babe was nineteen years old, hardly more than a man-child with a prodigious appetite and toothpick-shaped legs, when he joined the Red Sox in 1914. He had little more than time for a quick look-see about the ballpark before he was shipped off to the Providence farm club for further seasoning. But he was back before the 1914 season ended to begin a career which remains unique in baseball history.

When fans think about Babe Ruth, they instantly focus on his 714 home runs -- a major league record which remained untouchable until Hank Aaron eclipsed it in 1974. And who can forget the Babe's slugging average of .600, his 2,056 walks and his home run percentage of 8.5 -- all lifetime marks that established the standards for these categories.

What should always be remembered, although many fans tend to overlook it, is that Ruth as a member of the Red Sox, was perhaps the finest left-hand pitcher in the major leagues from 1915 to 1918. In 1915, his first full year in the majors, Ruth posted a record of 18-8 with a sparkling earned run average of 2.44. The very next year, he boosted his pitching record to 23-12, with a league leading ERA of 1.75.

Even more spectacular was Ruth's pitching in the World Series. Between the 1916 and 1918 Series, he put together a chain of twenty-nine and two-thirds consecutive innings of shutout baseball. His lifetime ERA for post-season play stands at a remarkable 0.87 -- the third best mark in the sport's history.

Ironically, despite the awesome records he chalked up as a pitcher, his prowess as a batter could not be ignored. Ruth batted .325 performing strictly as a pitcher in 1917. Inevitably by 1918, he started twenty games as a pitcher that year and played several fielding positions in seventy-two additional games.

The results were 66 RBIs plus a league-leading slugging average of .555 and home run totals of eleven. If that home run output of eleven appears puny by later Ruthian standards, consider that the total home runs hit by the Red Sox that year was fifteen!

By 1919, the Babe's metamorphosis from pitcher to batter was almost complete. He pitched in seventeen games but started 115 games in the field. With the huge increases in at-bats, the Babe banged out a record-setting total of twenty-nine home runs. His total almost doubled the major league record of sixteen set eighteen years earlier by Ralph Seybold of the Philadelphia Athletics. To put Ruth's accomplishments in perspective, it is equivalent to some major leaguer setting a new standard by hitting 110 home runs.

Contemporary Red Sox fans probably are having difficulty reading about all the wonderful things that happened to the old Red Sox. The modernists can't be faulted for believing that it's too good to be true. These are the Red Sox after all -- they just couldn't go on their winning way without bringing some catastrophe on themselves. A shot in the foot? A self-inflicted wound of some sort? Guess what? That's just what they did!

The first faint outlines of the inevitable self-destruction of the team were glimpsed on the horizon in 1916 when Harry Frazee purchased the Red Sox from Joseph Lannin who had picked up the franchise earlier from the Taylor family. The play was the obsession for Frazee, but unfortunately it was the kind acted out on Broadway theater stages and not on baseball playing fields. Ultimately, Frazee's longing for the bright lights of old Broadway would plunge the Boston franchise into a decline that would extend for some fifteen years.

Still, it must be reported that the first few years of Frazee's stewardship were relatively tranquil. The Red Sox won the league pennant in 1918 and triumphed over the Chicago Cubs by a margin of four games to two in the World Series. In the following year, with the nation at peace after World War I, the initial leaks in Frazee's financial dike were spotted. Unfortunately, he had no time to plug the holes because his repertory of Broadway offerings was on a losing streak that would have embarrassed even the New York Mets of the early 1960s.

Frazee's overwhelming need to finance a new musical, "No, No Nanette," unleashed the flood that was to inundate the Red Sox. He saw the solution to his problem right at Fenway Park -- his star players! The Yankees would pay cash in hand for them.

Ernie Shore and Duffy Lewis, magical names to Boston fans, shortly took the train to New York. Within a year Carl Mays was put aboard the train at South Station for the five-hour trip to Gotham.

And so that's the way it went for a while. The treacherous Frazee would forward key ballplayers to New York, and the Yankees would send cash back to Boston. Quickly though, the cash would be shipped back to New York to invest in Frazee's losing Broadway productions. In retrospect, the process was sort of a forerunner to the Trump Shuttle.

Frazee's ultimate betrayal of his team's loyal following, depriving the scenario of any tinge of humor it might have exuded to that point, came on January 6, 1920. On that crepe-framed day, one that was burned indelibly into the memory of fans alive then, Frazee accepted the symbolic thirty pieces of silver by selling Babe Ruth to the New York Yankees for $125,000.

Red Sox fans reeled in shock. The Yankees! Washington, Chicago, Philadelphia, perhaps even St. Louis -- if Frazee was hurting that bad. But Ruth to the pinstriped primadonnas?! Visions of Judas and Benedict Arnold danced in their fevered brains. If Frazee had been spotted on a Boston street that day he undoubtedly would have been tarred and feathered like a Tory of old. A scarlet 'T' branded on his forehead would have been too good for the traitor.

From a contemporary perspective, even Joni Mitchell's song, "They Took Paradise and Put Up a Parking Lot," doesn't begin to point up the enormity of Frazee's travesty on that day.

Ruth's legendary exploits in his Yankee uniform through the 1920s and into the early 1930s need no recounting here. It's too painful for any Boston fan to even think about them. Suffice it to say that behind Ruth's big bat the Yankees went on to dominate major league baseball. Indeed, the Babe provided the inspiration and heart, the guts and the sinew the Yankees had been patiently seeking to become the strongest franchise in all of professional sports.

Ruth's departure from Boston clearly signalled the end of a many-splendored era. For almost two decades, the Red Sox had set a vaunted pace for major league baseball, chalking up record after record and winning one pennant after another. But now the Babe truly was gone and the golden years of the Boston Red Sox waned to a faint yellow and then a dull white . . . until the dark ages enveloped the franchise.

Now if this book was about the highlights of the Red Sox in the 1920s and early 1930s, the reader would be at the Index by this point. The team's lowlights would take a little longer to digest, but even they were deadly predictable. The high point of this era probably occurred when Harry Frazee sold the club in 1923. Those of a less gentler nature might say it occurred when the playboy socialite died in his Park Avenue apartment in 1929.

Whatever, by the time of the sale, the damage to the Red Sox already had been done. From 1920 to 1932, the Boston franchise was to finish in fifth place twice, in seventh place twice, and in eighth place (last place in those days) nine times. In that period, nine managers tried their hand at the helm, but the talent just wasn't there for any of them to succeed.

In 1932, when the Depression began to wrap its tentacles tightly around the nation's economy, only 182,000 (fool)hardy fans found their way to Fenway Park. Sadly by this time, the lovely, cozy park was beginning to deteriorate.

Bob Quinn, the new owner of the Red Sox, by all accounts had good intentions but little more money than Frazee. Even Quinn was reduced to trying to raise cash by selling off his ballplayers. But there was little demand for them because the ones of value had been disposed of by the "Butterfly of Broadway." Times were so bad that in 1926, when the wooden bleachers in the left field corner burned to the level of the playing field, Quinn simply had his groundskeepers rope off the section.

Just when the Red Sox' fortune appeared to be at its darkest, a southern Prince Charming dug into his very deep pockets and came up with the right sum to purchase the Boston franchise from Quinn. The new owner was Thomas Austin Yawkey. It was February 1933 and the start of a new era: the unforgettable Yawkey Years.

No man in Red Sox history was to have a greater effect on the team than Yawkey. He was to own the club for forty-five years and place his stamp of integrity, sensitivity and loyalty on anyone and everything connected with the ball club.

Still, there was little, if any, dancing in the streets of Boston or elsewhere in the region when Yawkey bought the club. For one thing, the Red Sox no longer had the huge following they knew in their dynasty days. Then again, the streets were clogged with unemployed men looking for work or selling apples for a nickel apiece. Bottomline, baseball was a welcome diversion during the grim days of the Depression but it didn't figure in any way as a top priority.

At that time, Yawkey was a relatively young man of thirty-four; few men of his age even dreamed of owning a major league baseball club. Money though was not a problem for Yawkey. He was extremely wealthy. From his uncle Bill Yawkey he had inherited several million dollars. He also probably picked up a lot of good tips about baseball from the same uncle who once had owned the Detroit Tigers. Where money follows money, he subsequently gained another inheritance in the tens of millions of dollars from his grandfather who had built his fortune in the lumber business. Obviously, the effects of the Depression were not felt in the Yawkey manse.

Fortunately, Yawkey had not picked up the Boston franchise to preside over its further decline and quickly proved that he was more than willing to put his money where his mouth was located on his ruggedly handsome face. With a deep and opened purse, he acquired Lefty Grove, one of the premier left-handed pitchers of the time. With little haste, he followed up that acquisition with the purchase of another stellar pitcher, Wes Ferrell.

In 1934, Yawkey planked down the unheard of sum of $250,000 to obtain the services of Joe Cronin, the player-manager of the Washington Senators. (Cronin would go on to manage the Red Sox from 1935 to 1947, move up to general manager, and later become the president of the American League.) The very next year, Yawkey shelled out another $150,000 for Jimmy Foxx, the Athletics' great home run hitter.

After laying out close to $1,000,000 on these and other deals, Yawkey had the personal satisfaction of seeing his troops begin to edge up in the standings. Miracle of miracles, in both 1938 and 1939 the Red Sox fought and clawed their way through their schedule to finish second behind the Yankees.

But the really big news in 1939, putting aside the outbreak of World War II, the New York World's Fair and the commendable Red Sox climb to new prominence, was the debut of the greatest hitter of the past fifty years: Theodore Samuel Williams. While Yawkey was to become the most significant figure in Red Sox history, Williams is far and away the franchise's dominant ballplayer.

Teddy Ballgame. What John Wayne would have loved to have been in real life. The only icon ever needed to evoke the team's image. As a rookie, a brash one at that, he was tabbed as the "Splendid Splinter," the stuff of legends and myths. With his peerless eyesight, knotted arms and wrists, and remarkable sense of timing, he hammered the ball relentlessly to define the franchise from 1939 through 1960.

Williams was only twenty years old when he broke in as a rookie in 1939, but he hit .327, chalked up thirty-one home runs and garnered a league-leading 145 RBIs. Just two years later he became the first major league player since Bill Terry in 1930 to finish the season batting over the .400 mark. His 1941 batting average of .406 has not been equalled to this day and, with each passing year and the changes in the game, it becomes less likely that there will ever be another .400 batter.

Because of the batting records he set right from his start in the majors, Williams contributed to the persona of the team as a good-hitting but a poor-pitching unit. With their red hot bats, the Red Sox led the league in hitting from 1940 to 1942, but they still couldn't finish any better than second place. By then the U.S. had also become embroiled in the Big War and baseball had to take a back seat in the public's mind. By 1943 most of the able-bodied players, including Teddy Ballgame who joined Marine Corps aviation, had gone off to do their bit for God and country. In this war, the national pastime would have to wait for the veterans to return to regain the respect and glory of old.

Then it was 1946 and World War II was over and the boys were coming home from the Pacific and Europe and points in between and even farther afield. It was a time of optimism in the land. Everyone felt that prosperity was at hand. There was nowhere to go but up. No one felt this more strongly than the new generation of Red Sox fans. Their veterans had returned to Fenway Park and pennant fever permeated April's breezes.

Tom Yawkey's checkbook couldn't buy enough stars to bring the franchise a first place finish, but the money he had generously lavished on the club's farm system was about to pay dividends. Along with Williams, other home-grown talent like Bobby Doerr at second base, Johnny Pesky at shortstop and Dom DiMaggio in center field had become established as stars before enlisting in the war effort. The fans' expectations rose to new heights when the pitching staff led in tandem by Dave "Boo" Ferriss and Tex Hughson rounded into top form.

On paper at least, the 1946 edition of the Red Sox had assumed the proportions of a juggernaut in the public's eyes and for most of that season they acted accordingly. After putting together a fifteen-game winning streak in April and May, the Red Sox never looked back. Ferriss went 25-6, Hughson chipped in with 20-11, and Ted Williams hit .342 along with thirty-eight homers. The pennant was clinched September 13 by Williams' only lifetime inside the park home run.

Deep in the atavistic psyche of many Red Sox fans is the uncontestable belief that the Boston team has been cursed -- fatally. This conviction goes back to Harry Frazee who treacherously sold Babe Ruth to the Yankees and his soul to the devil, thus inflicting such a whammy on the Red Sox that they never, ever, will win another World Series.

The genesis of this folk tale can be traced to the seventh game of the Red Sox-St. Louis Cardinal series in 1946. With the score tied 3-3 at the bottom of the eighth inning and with Enos "Country" Slaughter on first base, Harry "The Hat" Walker lined sharply into left center. Slaughter took off like a skittish greyhound and dashed right through the third base coach's stop sign. Shortstop Johnny Pesky took the relay from the outfield, appeared to hesitate a second, and Slaughter slid under his throw to the plate -- scoring the game and series-winning run.

Right here, several things should be made very clear about Johnny Pesky who was born John Paveskovich. First, no single person has been more devoted to the Red Sox. He has been associated with the Boston franchise for more than fifty years as a player, coach, manager, broadcaster and assistant to the general manager.

Second, Pesky has been known as the man who let Enos Slaughter score all the way from first base on a single when, in fact, Walker's hit went into the scorebook as a double. Third, since Pesky had his back to the plate, it was the responsibility of the second baseman to inform him where he should throw the ball. Doerr shouted for Pesky to "go home" but could not be heard above the roar of the crowd.

And if you can't buy into any of this theorizing about the Red Sox curse, who knows what extraterrestrial bogeyman could have intervened once more in their impossible dream.

Although the Boston fans were very disappointed by the loss of another World Series, they were cheered by the fact that the hometowners appeared to be positioned to dominate the American League for many seasons to come. If they had known that they would have to wait more than twenty years for the team's next World Series, they might not have been so patient.

In 1947, the Red Sox fell to third place but rebounded to tie the Cleveland Indians for first place the following year, leading to the first playoff game in American League history. Unfortunately, none of the Red Sox frontline pitchers were rested enough for the game and Denny Galehouse, 8-8 for the season, was pounded by the Indians and their player-manager, Lou Boudreau, for a final score of 8-4. With this loss went the hopes for a "subway series" with the Boston Braves who had edged out the Cardinals to take the National League flag.

In 1949, the outcome proved to be more painful than the experience of the previous year. After trailing the Yankees all year, the Red Sox went to New York needing only one game to emerge victorious. (Hear the echo? "Went to New York needing . . .") The Yankees reached a little deeper into their bag of tricks, guts and willpower and came up with two victories, 5-4 and 5-3, to win the pennant by one game.

The near-miss in 1949 would prove to be an omen signalling the beginning of the end for the post-World War II Red Sox "dynasty." The club led the league in hitting in 1950 -- but the pitching, the perennial team soft spot, just wasn't there. Bobby Doerr retired after the 1951 season, Pesky was traded in 1952, Williams was recalled for service in the Korean War, and Dom DiMaggio was hounded into permanent retirement by new manager Lou Boudreau's fixation with the immortal Tommy Umphlett.

In retrospect, the Red Sox of the fifties were a reflection of the times. They were about as respectable and exciting as the "I Like Ike" presidential administration. Their outfield of Williams, Jimmy Piersall and Jackie Jensen was about as flashy and successful as Ford's "Better Idea" -- the hardtop convertible. The Red Sox of that era achieved third and fourth place finishes with the same intensity as students of the era strived for a gentlemanly C.

Perhaps the most significant development for the Red Sox came at the tail end of the fifties when Pumpsie Green became the first black player to wear Boston's flannels. Volumes could (and perhaps should) be researched and written about the Red Sox' inability to develop players of color in the same proportion as other baseball franchises. Certainly, it has been documented that the team passed on signing Jackie Robinson in 1945.

There have been suggestions that there is a direct correlation between Boston's failure to sign black players in any numbers and its lack of success in achieving a World Championship. Truly, the Red Sox have been at least as ineffectual at finding and developing pitchers as they have been at finding and developing black players. A genuine cynic easily could observe that if there were more outstanding black pitchers around, the Red Sox would be buried even deeper in the pack of also-rans.

Despite their lack of pennants and titles in the fifties, the Bostonians drew reasonably well at the gate. You could put it down partly to the fans' dream for a return to the success of the late 1940s, and partly to the absence of competition for the fans' dollars after the Braves packed their duffel bags and departed for Milwaukee in 1953. The main reason though, deep down and rarely voiced, was the fact that Bostonians and New Englanders just plain love baseball and are crazy about their Red Sox.

Few too could turn their backs and cold-shoulder the stars the team continued to introduce front and center stage. Jimmy Piersall was a show unto himself. Jackie Jensen was the only athlete to play in the Rose Bowl, the East-West Shrine Game, the major league baseball all-star game and the World Series. Dubbed the "Golden Boy," Jensen was Bo Jackson before Bo was born. And if any other act failed, there was always Ted Williams. No one, no one, ever left the park -- even when the Red Sox were down five or six runs -- until the Big Guy had his last at-bat.

Few things, if anything, last forever and so it was with the Williams era as the decade turned into the sixties. Williams, who had celebrated his forty-first birthday during the 1959 season, hit below .300 for the first time in his career that year, winding up with an abysmal .254 mark. The figure was a tip-off to the self-styled experts who agreed among themselves that Williams was finished and should retire forthwith before embarrassing himself further.

Teddy Ballgame though was made of sterner stuff than his critics and hung on to prove them wrong in 1960 by batting .316 and stroking twenty-nine four-baggers. In his last at-bat, with a flair for the dramatic that characterized his long career, Ted homered into the right field bullpen. When journeyman, Carroll Hardy, replaced him in left field in the following inning, another epoch in the Red Sox saga had ended.

Williams' impact on the game can best be illustrated by one maneuver that he brought unwittingly about. Since the game was first played in the mid-19th century, both infielders and outfielders have played within reasonable distances and parameters of the standard fielding positions. That held as a truism until one ballplayer, Ted Williams, forced fielders by his hitting prowess to radically depart from their normal fielding positions. The famed shift, introduced by Cleveland manager, Lou Boudreau, in 1946, moved all of the fielders except the third baseman and the leftfielder to the right of second base.

Certainly other batting stars have been recognized by opponents who tailor defensive alignments against them, but only Williams brought about a wildly different configuration in defensive maneuvers, one that lasted fifteen years in response to his peerless hitting.

Just as Williams' star was setting over Fenway Park, another budding star appeared in the form of Carl Yastrzemski, not too long off a potato farm on Long Island. Entering the majors in 1961, the twenty-one-year-old leftfielder was quickly dubbed "the new Williams" by newshungry sportswriters. The only problem though was that he was not "the new Williams," rather he was the young Yaz.

Yaz was five inches shorter than Williams and thirty or so pounds lighter and any way you cut it suffered in comparison to Ted. Yaz had been gifted with an athlete's eye-hand coordination and balance; Williams had borrowed God's own swing and improved upon it. Williams was lithe and natural; Yaz was compact and choppy. A svelte waltzer versus a rough two-stepper.

It was not of his making but Yaz immediately had to deal with a media pack determined to fill the Williams' void and eager to do it under the glare of TV lights. While he shared an intensity, a work ethic and a total dedication to the game with Williams, Yaz had a far more difficult struggle in the beginning of his career.

At one point early-on, an SOS was dispatched to Williams who generously returned to tutor his heir apparent. Ted scrutinized Yaz's batting style, provided him with a few hitting tips, urged one and all to be patient with the budding star and returned without a backward glance to his favorite pastime -- salmon fishing. Yaz progressed to .296 in 1962 and earned his initial batting crown in 1963 with an average of .321.

While Yastrzemski's offensive statistics improved, the team's achievements were decidedly lackluster. From 1961 to 1966, the team finished sixth, seventh, eighth (twice) and ninth (twice). Except for the Herculean efforts of reliever Dick Radatz during most of this period, the team may well have finished in the International League.

As in the past, the gradual emergence of future stars produced by the minor league system served to provide the fans with some bright spots through some overcast years. Local boy, Tony Conigliaro, burst upon the Red Sox scene as a nineteen-year-old rookie in 1964, taking the town by storm with a batting average of .290 and twenty-four home runs. Rico Petrocelli, making his debut in 1965, quickly laid claim to the "shortstop of the future" role. Pitcher Jim Lonborg joined the club that same year, and while his freshman record of 9-17 was a disappointment, there was no question about the promise of the righty's arm and his native intelligence.

In 1966, two additional future stars appeared in Boston flannels. George Scott displayed a golden touch around first base and contributed twenty-seven home runs to the cause. Joe Foy showed himself to be a steady third baseman as a rookie, chipping in with fifteen home runs and sixty-three RBIs.

In that same year, Jose Santiago and John Wyatt were acquired from Kansas City to give additional strength to the starting pitching rotation and bullpen, respectively. The acquisition of Lee Stange from Cleveland during the 1966 season provided further stability to a struggling corps of starting pitchers.

As the 1966 season drew to a close, there was some reason for optimism about the future. It was mostly based on the fact that a nucleus of regulars was beginning to take shape as a team, and further top prospects were on the way to Boston from the Toronto farm club. It could be said that the team had bottomed out in 1966 and now was headed for much higher rungs on the league's ladder of success.

There was, however, no getting around the fact that the Red Sox had finished ninth in 1966, twenty-six games out of first place. Moreover, fans were staying away in droves and Fenway Park was beginning to look a little ragged around the edges and in few other familiar places. The only consolation for the true believers rested on the fact that the Red Sox had finished a half-game ahead of the Yankees. Take that Harry Frazee! The dismal season was highlighted in September by the firing of Boston manager Billy Herman who left Boston grumbling and cursing that Yaz was impossible to manage.

In an effort to demonstrate how serious management was about sharply boosting Boston's prospects, Dick Williams, who had a reputation for wearing iron underwear and sleeping on a bed of nails, was named manager. Sarcastic and outspoken, Williams wasted no time in spring training in putting the fear of God into his players. He was the boss and they were the employees and they'd do exactly what he told them.

Tom Yawkey had always pampered his ballplayers, permitting the Red Sox to obtain the title of baseball's "country club." The new iron-fisted manager quickly put a stop to that attitude. They were going to be winners under his aegis and no one was going to goldbrick it. Anyone who couldn't handle the demands of the new regime could pack his bag and leave. Anyone! Rising star or not!

About that period, Williams said, ". . . if I was going down, I was going to go down my way. I made up my mind to run that club the way I wanted and the way it should have been done." And that's exactly what he did and why he was a great manager then and for many years to follow.

Williams' predecessors had been from the old school, the one of soft knocks. They numbered Billy Herman, Johnny Pesky, Mike Higgins and Billy Jurges. Good decent guys from a long line of traditional baseball men who could be counted on by management not to rock the boat, but rather to just go along and make the conventional moves.

Williams though wore a different school tie, one from the school of hard knocks and thought nothing of standing up in the boat to rock it all over the place. As a player, Williams had parlayed average major league skills into a thirteen-year pro career. He mixed that ingredient with versatility, diligence and, most of all, hard work to remain a viable force in the game. Always in his locker, ready for use, were a first baseman's mitt, a fielder's glove and a catcher's mitt; he came to play. And to be sure he did, he was the first player in the clubhouse every game day.

When questioned about his early-bird habit, Williams replied candidly, "I want to make sure no one gets here ahead of me to take the uniform out of my locker."

At the age of thirty-seven in 1967, Williams was the youngest manager in the American League and he was determined to succeed at any cost. Fresh from two championship seasons with the Red Sox Triple-A club in Toronto, Williams had only known victory in his brief two-year managerial career.

When pressed by the media about his commitment to win, he said, "Ever since I can remember, there isn't anything I wouldn't do to be a success in baseball."

As the Red Sox team's new manager, Williams made it very clear that he was not about to share his authority with anyone else, especially his ballplayers. Within two weeks of assuming his duties, he announced that the Red Sox would not have a captain in 1967. With this piece of news, the media sniffed blood because the incumbent captain was Carl Michael Yastrzemski. Anxious for a genuine controversy, the press beat a hasty beeline to Yaz's home in Lynnfield, Massachusetts.

The bait was tossed to Yaz but he refused to bite. It wasn't his style. As he told Will McDonough, a young reporter then for the *Boston Globe*, "Happy is not the word. Relieved is a better word. To be honest, I never wanted to be captain. Now that I'm not, I feel like a weight has been taken off my shoulders."

When the press next bounced Yaz's comments off Williams, the manager reacted succinctly, "There's only one boss here and I'm it."

Tough new manager or not, the so-called experts were very gloomy about the Red Sox' prospects for the year. Las Vegas, as previously noted, had established them as a 100-1 shot to win the pennant. The consensus about the 1967 team was as follows: a few promising young players; a potentially great outfield; but no pitching staff and how can you win without good pitching? Overall prediction: the 1967 Red Sox should show some improvement over 1966 and given a few breaks and a lot of luck, a shot at fourth place!

About that Boston pitching staff, a *New York Times* spring training report described the Red Sox hurlers as "what may be the most unimposing staff in the majors." The story then went on to nominate such promising rookies as Russ Gibson, Mike Andrews and Reggie Smith for starting roles respectively as catcher, second base and centerfield. (In fact, the trio did indeed go on to make significant contributions to the team during the 1967 season.) In typical *Times'* style, the article concluded, "If by some unlikely miracle the Red Sox get good pitching, they could raise ructions." While *Times'* reporters are always literate, they sometimes even turn out to be prescient.

One Red Sox pitcher who fully intended to bring about as much ructions as possible was third-year starter Jim Lonborg. As a Stanford University graduate, he probably even knew what the word meant. Lonborg stood a lanky six-foot five inches in height and had recorded a disappointing 19-27 win-loss statistic in his initial two years with Boston, but he had learned and matured and tempered his pitching skills in the heat of those dual seasons.

Obviously intelligent and a gracious person both on and off the field, Lonborg had quickly earned the nickname of "Gentleman Jim." But, in honing his craft, it soon became apparent to Lonborg that baseball was not truly a gentleman's game and that he would have to pitch inside to keep the hitters honest.

In spring training of 1967, Lonborg tipped a reporter to "keep count of how many batters I hit this year." To underline the truth of his new strategy, he began keeping a running total by placing a mark for each hit batsman on the back of his glove, in the manner of an Old West gunslinger. By season's end he would have scratched nineteen "notches" on his glove and boosted his strikeout total from 131 to 246.

Lonborg was not the only Red Sox player who reported to spring training camp with an upbeat attitude and a determination to achieve the best possible season for the team. Carl Yastrzemski, coming off a .278 season, was of the same frame of mind as Lonborg, anxious to put aside the labels of an underachiever and a clubhouse lawyer.

Under the keen scrutiny and direction of Gene Berde, a physical fitness instructor from Boston's North Shore, Yaz had worked out all winter. Berde had challenged Yaz to push his body conditioning to the outer limits of its capabilities, permitting him to report to camp in the best shape of his career.

While he was optimistic about the season and the Red Sox' prospects, he was less optimistic about his own prospects, especially at bat. Yaz told the press, "I'll never do what Frank Robinson has done in Baltimore. I don't have the capabilities to hit home runs like that. I have limitations and there isn't anything I can do about that."

Fortunately for the Red Sox, Yaz turned out to be a much better slugger than he was a forecaster. During the upcoming 1967 season he would outhit Robinson by fifteen points (.326 vs. .311), out homer him forty-five to thirty, and drive in twenty-seven more runs (121 RBIs vs. 94). For one season at least, Frank Robinson was no Carl Yastrzemski.

For Red Sox fans in New England, the opening of spring training is an annual rite of passage to be greeted warmly. Whatever else, it's a sign that winter's frigid reign is about to give way to spring's welcome succession. Truly, if you were shoveling a foot of new snow in Concord, New Hampshire, on February 25, 1967, the radio report that "twenty-four pitchers and four catchers reported to rookie manager, Dick Williams, today in Winter Haven, Florida . . ." surely made the task seem more bearable.

Even more dramatic than the gradually changing new weather was the switchover in the climate of the training camp under Williams. To veterans and rookies alike, Williams immediately demonstrated that he was a taskmaster and that he was organized. In Williams' lexicon there was no such thing as "downtime." If you weren't involved in a skill session, then you'd better be found in one of the ongoing volleyball games. The message was loud and clear: the country club days of yore were no more.

Williams' acumen was also readily demonstrated in his crafty choice of coaches, the all important drill sergeants needed by any officer to whip the men into quick compliance to orders. To counter-balance his stern and gruff manner of dealing with the troops, Williams selected Eddie Popowski as his third base coach because he was well aware that Popowski had developed a solid rapport with most of the Red Sox youngsters while coaching them in the minors.

In another choice of coaches to offset his snarly martinet style, Williams named Bobby Doerr as hitting instructor and first base coach. One of the most respected gentlemen in the game, Doerr provided a link to the last Red Sox pennant winners in 1946 when he was one of the best second baseman in the league. To those who always seek further motivations for one's actions, Williams was well aware that Popowski was too old to succeed him and that Doerr had turned down the job in the past.

Williams' pitching coach, Sal Maglie, had always played with a winning team and communicated a "meanness" in taking on opponents that was just the tonic for Jim Lonborg and the other young pitchers on the staff. He rounded out his lineup of assistants by selecting Al Lakeman to serve the yeomen duty as the bullpen coach. As a group, not one of the coaches was a Williams' crony; rather they were four professionals who had a specific role to play in forging the 1967 Red Sox team.

As the team began to shuffle through the placid Grapefruit League schedule, it became immediately clear that Williams intended to establish a winning attitude. Traditionally, the Red Sox treated spring training games as meaningless exhibitions to bring in a little cash to pay the overhead until the opening of the regular season. Winning was not a priority and Boston hadn't produced a winning spring training record in years.

All this quickly changed under Williams' reign. Veteran observers were amazed to learn that golf no longer was the major topic of conversation: baseball had taken its place. Williams used the training games to get a good look at all his players, but simultaneously he was willing to pull out all the stops to win.

In a contest with the Detroit Tigers on March 19, he had one catcher, Bob Tillman, squeeze home another catcher, Russ Gibson -- with the bases loaded! In risking this toss of the dice, the Red Sox snatched a 7-6 victory from the befuddled Tigers.

It is a baseball axiom that the pitchers are always ahead of the batters in spring training. But in the spring of 1967 there was a big exception to this rule in the person of twenty-two-year-old Tony Conigliaro, already a three-year veteran in the major leagues with 84 home runs to his credit. Tony C. was hitting a blistering .600 when he took a John Wyatt fastball to his left arm during batting practice. No matter, Conigliaro bounced back from this injury and put together his best spring ever. Everyone was in agreement that he was coming up on his finest season ever with Boston.

At twenty-four years of age, Rico Petrocelli was another young veteran who was displaying many of the signs of emerging stardom as he headed into his third year as starting shortstop for the Red Sox. Because he had been shy and reticent in the past, many experts felt that he wasn't tough enough to reach true stardom. But Williams with his eagle eye for talent went out of his way to make Rico feel more confident at his position and at the bat, going so far as to appoint him leader of the infield. In response, Rico developed quality leadership ability and a more powerful bat.

In sharp contrast to his sensitive handling of Petrocelli, Williams seemed to go out of his way to treat George Scott as his personal whipping boy. Tony Horton was given a shot at Scotty's first base job. George was ordered to play third base. Then he was dispatched to the outfield. There was even talk of making George into a catcher. The "Boomer" went for the bait: he sweated his tail off and fought to curb his urge to swing for the fences on every pitch. By the end of spring training, he was right where Williams all along had intended him to be -- at first base as a starter.

The infield was pretty well set with Scott at first, Rico at short and Joe Foy at third. Mike Andrews appeared to have the lock on second base but he had injured his back lifting weights earlier and would miss the season opener. As it turned out, Reggie Smith opened at second and filled the gap there for six games.

Afterwards, Reggie would return to his natural position in center field for 144 games and enjoy an outstanding rookie year both in the field and at bat. With all-star Carl Yastrzemski in left and Tony C. in right, the outfield definitely was the Red Sox strong suit in the hand they prepared to play.

As the dust of spring training slowly dissipated, the outlines and form of the pitching staff began to take shape. Gentleman Jim clearly was the ace. Jose Santiago, a four-year major league veteran, appeared to have a chance to be the number two man. Lee Stange and Darrell Brandon were shaping up to be the other two obvious choices as starters. John Wyatt, who had been in Williams' doghouse for hitting Tony C. in batting practice earlier, was showing a lot of good stuff in a relief role.

As for the rest of the staff, its makeup was difficult to discern because of the thick clouds that still engulfed it. Was Peter Magrini the answer to the relief chores? How about the wiry, twenty-one-year-old left-hander Billy Rohr? Had he tamed his tendency to wildness? Could mercurial Jerry Stephenson provide badly needed assistance in the relief department? What about Dave Morehead? There were still as many questions as answers.

As spring training wound down and the Red Sox prepared to move north, the catcher's job was still up for grabs. The top contender for the position was rookie Russ Gibson. With ten solid years in the minors, Williams was hopeful that Gibson's strength behind the plate could probably overcome the negative of a light bat. Also fighting for the spot were Mike Ryan and Bob Tillman.

Elsewhere, Dalton Jones brought a hot bat off the bench and utility man George Thomas was ready to take any position at any time. Jose Tartabull could be counted on to play a credible outfield and George Smith was hopeful that he could come back from an injury to provide infield depth.

As the Red Sox took the field at Chain O' Lakes Park on April 8, they brought with them a 13-12 spring mark. Pulling out all the stops from his bag of managerial skills, Williams produced a 6-2 win over the Tigers. This was offset by a 4-3 loss to the Tigers the following day; still the team headed home with a winning record for the first time in years.

The record was in line -- barely -- with the one predicted for the 1967 Red Sox. "We'll win more than we lose," Williams had repeatedly been quoted. At the time it was a very optimistic prediction for a manager taking over a ballclub that had won seventy-two and lost ninety the year before.

No matter the previous season's record, opening day at Fenway Park is one of pomp and circumstance, high hopes and high jinx, flags and fanfare and all amidst dreams of pennants past and championships future. Traditionally, the crimson and white uniformed Harvard College band entertains before the start of the game. Likewise the governor of the Commonwealth throws out the first ball and is always roundly booed for his effort. From out of nowhere, ten thousand dandies appear, never to be viewed at another game all year. A funny thing though happened to this unique group in 1967: they reappeared for the first game of the World Series in October.

Where the weather in New England is as unpredictable as the Red Sox, no one was upset when Arctic air forced a twenty-four-hour postponement of opening day. The ten thousand dandies were not ones to worry; they simply took an extended lunch hour.

The weather on April 12 was cold and raw but the Sox -- Red and White -- managed to complete it. Jim Lonborg pitched the way the ace of the staff is expected to pitch and Rico Petrocelli contributed four RBIs to the 5-4 victory. Any optimism about a rosy season was dampened the next day when the Bostonians reverted to form and committed five errors. Williams, who had stressed the fundamentals of the game all spring, was beside himself after the 8-5 loss. Welcome to Fenway, Dick!

On Thursday night as the Red Sox headed for New York by bus to provide the opposition on opening day at Yankee Stadium, several facts seemed quite apparent. Undoubtedly, Williams was going to have his hands full delivering on his 1967 prediction. That, as a young club, the Red Sox would be subject to ups and downs and five error games -- such glitches fitted the profile. And if, as Williams proclaimed, pitching was ninety percent of the game, the Red Sox were only fifty percent of the way there.

But beneath all of the predictions, the youthful makeup of the ballplayers and the dearth of starting pitchers, there was one hard and fast fact that was not apparent to anyone at the time -- no matter what they claimed or boasted later. The fact was that the 1967 Boston Red Sox were a team that could catch lightning in a bottle and make faint hearts weak with suspense. Although only a tentative signal, the first flash of lightning would bedazzle the faithful the very next day within the cavernous confines of the House That Ruth Built, Yankee Stadium.

CHAPTER ONE

Boston Red Sox vs. New York Yankees

Friday, April 14, 1967

Russ Gibson, one of the most heralded school boy stars in the history of sports-crazy Fall River, Massachusetts, played his first major league game when the Red Sox met the Yankees in New York. It was the third game of the season for the Red Sox but the home opener for the Yankees, who sent their ace pitcher, Whitey Ford, to the mound to ensure an initial victory before the home crowd of some 14,375. Gibson, who had labored in the Red Sox minor league system for a decade as a catcher, was teamed with Billy Rohr, a twenty-one year old rookie lefty, who was also appearing in his first major league game. To Gibson, then twenty-seven, the years of striving were about to pay off by placing him within one hit of catching a no-hitter in his major league debut.

Friday, April 14, 1967, dawned sharp and clear in New York City. The sun's ray fought with the lingering cold of winter to produce a typical spring baseball day in the Northeast.

The weather may have been typical but the events of the day would be anything but. For rookie catcher Russ Gibson and rookie pitcher Billy Rohr just waking up in the Biltmore Hotel in Manhattan was an adventure. The fact that they would both be making their major league debut at Yankee Stadium that afternoon seemed quite implausible.

Gibson had learned late Thursday that he was going to catch for Rohr against the Yankees shortly after manager, Dick Williams, finished castigating the team in the clubhouse for its 8-5 loss to Chicago. Williams was particularly upset because his players had committed five errors and gave up five unearned runs in the top of the ninth. Third baseman, Joe Foy, caught a lot of the steam for his two errors. The loss put the Red Sox at 1-1 for the early season.

"Dick came over to me after the meeting and told me that I was going to catch the next day. This was after Mike Ryan had caught for the team in the first two games against Chicago. The next day meant the Yankees in New York. I could only say, 'Great!' The fact was that I couldn't wait to get into the lineup and see major league action."

Actually Gibson was glad that Williams hadn't started him in Boston because the few days off helped to settle him down and shake off any nervousness about playing in the majors.

"Dick was smart that way, the way he handled his players. He had a lot of confidence in me. Knew how I played and I had all that experience from the minors, but still he let me unwind by sitting out our first two games. To tell you the truth, I was glad that I didn't catch the opener at Fenway. All the hometown crowd, the family and friends who'd be up from Fall River; I'd probably have been very nervous. Yeh, I really was glad."

For Fall River native Gibson, it was a dream that seemed impossible just two short years earlier. Not that he lacked the tools to do the job behind the plate at the major league level. That was never in doubt. Sure you would like to see a little quicker bat and a bit more power. But Russ Gibson could call a game with any of them and he could handle pitchers. That was a given.

Two years earlier in 1965, Gibson had been a victim of the Red Sox depth chart at catcher. He was invited to spring training with the major league club coming off an outstanding year at the Red Sox Triple-A club in Seattle. He had batted a solid .276 with seventeen homers and anchored a young pitching staff for 130 games behind the plate. After eight years of riding buses in the bushes, Gibson was more than ready for "the show".

The newly-married Gibson put on a show of his own in Florida. Still a few months shy of his twenty-sixth birthday, he was in his prime and he showed it with his defensive ability and with his bat. Surely the top brass on Jersey Street couldn't ignore his performance.

But ignore it they did. Six foot four Bill Tillman had batted .278 in 131 games for the Red Sox the year before and he was pencilled in at number one before spring training even started. Mike Ryan, another local boy, from Haverhill, Massachusetts, was two years younger than Gibson, a little bigger than him and the brass wanted to see what he could do in the Bigs. Besides, the new manager in Toronto, Dick Williams, was only thirty-five years old and could benefit from the presence of a seasoned veteran. And if Russ Gibson was anything, he was an organization man to the core. Ryan would go north to Boston and Gibson would go farther north to Toronto.

It's a long ride from central Florida to Toronto, Ontario. And it's even longer when you've just sent your new bride home alone. Home as in Fall River, Massachusetts, just an hour drive from Fenway Park, home of the Boston Red Sox. Your home team.

To get to Toronto from Florida you have to go through North Carolina and if you're Russ Gibson you think about 1959-61 in Raleigh and Winston-Salem. As you head further north into Pennsylvania and New York you think about Corning, New York, in 1957 and York, Pennsylvania, in 1962. Certainly Toronto is a lot closer to Fenway than Seattle was in 1963 and 1964. But in April of 1965 the locals would be much more interested in hockey star Frank Mahavolich of the Toronto Maple Leafs than the arrival of journeyman catcher, Russ Gibson.

A five-day car ride gives a man a lot of time to think. Especially if you've already logged as many miles on the highway over eight years in the minors as your average Greyhound bus driver. In a very short time Gibson had gone from the dead of winter in Fall River to the false spring of Winter Haven, Florida. As the seasons reversed themselves again and he headed back to the lingering winter in Toronto, Gibson had come to a difficult conclusion.

Two years later, Gibson was standing in the lobby of the Biltmore thinking about the game with the Yankees that afternoon. He could look around and see veterans like Carl Yastrzemski, Rico Petrocelli, and Tony Conigliaro who thrived on the limelight of New York. He could look over and see fellow rookies, Mike Andrews and Reggie Smith, who had been teammates on last year's championship Toronto club. And he could see rookie manager, Dick Williams, who had been his manager and mentor in Toronto for the past two years. In some ways, Williams was the man who was most instrumental in Gibson's starting assignment that day.

When Gibson arrived in Toronto in April of 1965, he reported directly to manager Williams' office. Almost the first words out of his mouth were, "If I can't make it to the majors after eight years in the system and the spring I had, I think it's time to hang them up." Williams responded with, "Look, I'm new at this job and I need some help. I want you to stay here as a player-coach. I expect that my time will come in Boston and if I can, I'll take you with me. Take a few days off to play golf and then come back and let's get to work."

Gibson played a little golf -- you can get some good drives off when the ground is still frozen -- and thought it over. He came back and helped Williams and Toronto to two consecutive championships. Now he was getting ready for Opening Day in Yankee Stadium and he knew he had made the right decision.

Gibson never talks about his first game in the majors without recalling a humorous anecdote. "All those years in the minors, Corning, Lafayette, Waterloo . . . Raleigh and Winston-Salem, York and then on to Seattle and Toronto . . . no matter where we went to play, it was almost always by way of bus. Every type of bus you can imagine. Now, finally, I'm in the big leagues, the majors, and I'm imagining that wherever the team goes, it'll be first class and by air. So what happens? When I'm told that I'm to catch the next day in New York against the Yankees, the Red

Sox take a chartered bus at night to go down to the big town. Boy, what a letdown. It's 1967 and we're going to New York for their season opener and there I am back in the bus, for Pete's sake!"

When the Red Sox went out to Yankee Stadium Friday, Gibson, a husky six-footer with hands like bear paws, felt calm and confident, ready to do the job. It was his first major league start, but the Red Sox were away from home and as always puffed up to do battle with their traditional foes, the pinstriped Yankees.

"It didn't bother me that I was going to catch because we were in New York and I'd be more relaxed, at least that's what I thought until I walked into Yankee Stadium. As soon as I came out of the dugout and could see the size of the field, all I could think was, 'God, this is unbelievable!' They had all the plaques of the great Yankees . . . Ruth, Gehrig, DiMaggio, all those guys and the size of it. And all the fans who were out for the opener. It was beautiful! Fantastic! But it's like everything else, believe me. I'm a pro and as soon as the National Anthem was over, I knew I had a job to do and looked forward to it."

Gibson knew his pitcher, Billy Rohr, would be subject to the jitters. Like Gibson, it was his first major league start. Russ, though, had ten years playing time in the minors against many top caliber players who had gone up to major league teams, so he wasn't so overawed by big leaguers and the crowd.

Rookie southpaw, Billy Rohr's route to the majors was much less bumpy and had almost no u-turns. Rohr had been a high school phenomenon at Bellflower High School in Garden Grove, California. His portfolio in his senior year included three no-hit games. The Pittsburg Pirates signed the seventeen-year-old Rohr for $40,000 immediately after graduation. Serious money in those days.

Rohr and Gibson took very different paths through the minors. Gibson reported directly from graduation to Corning, New York, in the New York/Pennsylvania league. He got four hits in his first two games and was told to report to Lafayette in the Midwest League. Corning wanted to use someone else as their catcher.

Rohr reported to Kingsport, Tennessee, in the Appalachian League and was told that he was too valuable to pitch in games. His routine was to pitch batting practice and then watch from the stands. The Pirates were trying to hide him. The Red Sox weren't fooled. When the Pirates failed to protect him by putting him on their expanded major league roster, the Red Sox snapped him up for $8,000. It would appear that Pittsburg paid $32,000 to provide Kingsport with a batting practice pitcher! Strange places these major leagues.

While Gibson had to work his way up the minor league rungs over ten years, Rohr was assigned immediately by the Red Sox to their Triple-A farm club in Toronto. Once again, the system's depth chart had come into play. The pitching-thin Red Sox were ready to throw any strong, young left-handed arm into the breach. Rohr showed a great deal of promise in Toronto but he was a long-shot to stick when he arrived in Winter Haven in the spring of 1967. A strong showing in Florida and Dick Williams' belief in his potential had earned him the starting nod for opening day in Yankee Stadium.

"I could tell from his initial practice throws that he was nervous and it was up to me to settle him down. Hey, he was just this tall, skinny kid . . . part Indian, Cherokee, if I remember . . . and it was just a matter of talking to him. Billy had shown a lot of good stuff in spring training and he and I had talked about the batters we'd be facing and how he should pitch to each one. I went out to talk to him. 'Just put 'em between the lines, Billy, and we'll take each out as it comes along.'"

Gibson reminded Rohr, whose best pitches were a fast sinking ball and sharp curve, that Yankee Stadium was a great park for him to pitch in, particularly where it was his first major league start. Even 400 foot fly balls could be caught for easy outs, a fact Dick Williams was well aware of when he assigned Rohr to pitch against the Yankees.

Gibson recalled, "Billy's ball moved a lot. He had a sharp curve that came in on the hitter and a fastball away. In fact, the ball moved so much that it looked like it was right over the plate.

But by the time you took a cut at it, swung away that is, it was down and away. Billy, that day, once he got his rhythm, had them hitting a lot of ground balls, ones our guys could easily scoop up."

Gibson had one edge over the typical rookie debuting in New York. As a teenager, he had been a three-sport start at Durfee High in Fall River, Massachusetts. Sports consumed this old New England town -- they still do -- and Russ was the super star of his era. He quarterbacked the football team, turning down several football scholarships to join the Red Sox immediately after graduation. Gibson was a sparkplug on the Durfee High basketball team leading them to the New England schoolboy championship in his junior year. But his first love was baseball and his natural position was behind the plate.

In the fifties, the Hearst Corporation sponsored an all-star series throughout the United States starting at the local level. This culminated in a national all-star game bringing the 50 best high school ball players in the U.S. together. Gibson excelled at all regional levels and three hits at Fenway Park earned him a trip to the Nationals. The game was played at the old Polo Grounds in New York and Gibson was on the receiving end of three innings of shutout baseball thrown by Mike McCormick, who went on to a distinguished career with the San Francisco Giants.

If Gibson was a little nervous, Rohr was nearly a basket case. Rohr had sought to prepare for his moment of glory by switching roommates from catcher Bob Tillman to staff ace Jim Lonborg. Lonborg took him out for dinner to go over the Yankee hitters. According to Lonborg, "We were there for two hours, and for an hour and three quarters, he didn't say a word. I talked and he just listened."

Rohr took a sleeping pill but he was up and about at 7:00 a.m. the next morning. "We talked about their hitters some more, had breakfast, then went to the park. I knew he was nervous," said Lonborg.

Rohr's teammates sensed his nervousness. Pitcher Dennis Bennett quipped, "If he gets by the first inning he'll be okay. But he's a nervous wreck right now."

The opening day crowd was small by New York standards: only a shade over 14,000 fans. But there was an ample mix of celebrities. Jacqueline Kennedy was there with her eleven--year-old son, John Jr. Quincy-born movie star, Lee Remick, was there. The late Tony Conigliaro sent her a note before the game suggesting that if she wanted to date a real star she should meet him after the game.

The 1967 Yankee team will not go down in the annals with the 1927 Yankees, or the 1936 team or even the 1961 Yankees. There were no Ruths, no DiMaggios, not even a Phil Rizzuto. But there were some decent bats in the lineup. Tom Tresh and Joe Pepitone could still swing a bat. Ellie Howard was nearing the end of a distinguished career, but as he would later dramatically prove, he could still get around and the sight of No. 7, Mickey Mantle, pinch-hitting in the eighth inning would strike fear in the heart of Russ Gibson.

"Alright, Billy-baby, settle down. Easy out there. Just keep it between the lines," Gibson yelled through his mask to his battery mate atop the mound. Despite his nerves, Rohr got the Yankees one, two, three in the first inning and began to relax because by then the Red Sox had a 1-0 edge off Reggie Smith's lead-off homer.

Once the game began, the only real sign of nervousness from Rohr was the rapidity with which he pitched. Gibson remembers "every pitch was right at my target . . . I didn't even have to move. His control was unbelievable and his fastball was really sinking. They couldn't do anything with him."

Gibson could sense his pitcher settling down as he retired the first ten Yankees in the giant stadium before walking a man. "Yeh, he was still a little nervous, but you could almost see the wave of confidence taking over him," Gibson recalled. "He was remembering what Jim Lonborg had told him about the hitters and the stuff about them that we'd discussed before the game and between each inning as we went along. 'Course because you got 'em out with one type of pitch one time, didn't mean that you'd call for the same pitch against him every time. You sort of have to pitch them a little different every time. If you get a hitter out on fastballs, you can't throw him ten of them in a row. He gets the big picture and soon will hammer one away. No, you have to mix it up."

Gibson has some success at the plate as well. Facing the wily veteran, Whitey Ford, Gibson was prepared for anything in his first at bat. Gibson remembers that "Whitey's ball moved a lot. I got one that I could handle and lined it right up the middle." Not a bad start for a guy who was ready to give up the game two years earlier.

Gibson was too concerned about keeping his pitcher under control to think about his own situation. "Fact was I really wasn't nervous, especially after a couple of innings of play. Sure it was the Yankees and we were on their home turf, but it was easy for me by then. I began to think of it as any other ballgame where I always wanted to win. When we got the lead on Reggie's homer, and I got a hit my first time at bat it helped a lot. Meanwhile, Billy was just pitching a hell of a ballgame."

Rohr had the ability to throw the ball where he wanted it to go. "It was unbelievable," Gibson recalled, "I couldn't believe it for a kid like that in his situation. He had such good control. The only pitch that got away that I can remember is the one in the ninth."

After five innings, both teams and the fans became aware of what was transpiring. With each succeeding inning, the tension built in the stands. As is baseball tradition, no one on the Red Sox bench mentioned even the words "no-hitter." Gibson concentrated on going over the hitters between innings. It was a tight game and there was no time to focus on individual glory, just the task of winning the game.

Rohr entered the sixth inning without anything against him even resembling a basehit. And he was nursing a slim 1-0 lead. To pitch a no-hitter you need outstanding "stuff" and a great deal of luck. There is more than one pitcher in the Hall of Fame who never put that combination together. But Rohr was working so quickly that it appeared the game would soon be over. And he was about to catch a bit of luck.

The first ball hit hard off of Rohr was a line drive from the bat of Horace Clarke. It was a solid smash, but it went on a line to Carl Yastrzemski. A portend of more good fortune to come later.

There was even greater drama in the sixth inning. Bill Robinson was pretty much a journeyman ballplayer, but he could hit some. And hit one he did in the sixth. Hit one right at Rohr. Hit one right off Rohr. Baseball is the game that has benefitted the most from the instant replay. Plays of multiple dimensions happen in a flash and given the game's elegant pauses, there is time to freeze-frame the action and figure out what really happened.

Picture Rohr's eighty-five miles an hour fastball reaching Robinson in a second. Imagine Robinson's bat responding in milliseconds. His line drive goes directly back at Rohr with twice the speed of the pitched ball. It careens directly off Rohr's shin and in less than one second it has been redirected to Joe Foy at third base. Foy grabs it and fires it to George Scott at first base and Robinson is out by an eyelash. Less than five seconds have elapsed from the time the ball has left Rohr's hand. Miraculously, it seems Rohr's flirtation with immortality has been preserved. Such is the perfection of baseball's dimensions and the combinations that are played out.

Gibson was already headed for Billy who was dancing around the mound in pain. Right behind him came Williams and trainer Buddy LeRoux. Elsewhere in the stadium, the crowd roared its appreciation for the great out.

Williams recalled later that he "asked the kid to roll down his stocking. He was on television. He has the skinniest legs you ever saw. I knew he was hurt. I was thinking of taking him out but I left him in."

"I had mixed feelings on my way," Gibson said. "I was happy for Foy's great play but also very concerned for Billy. That ball had ricochetted like a cannonball off his leg. But he sort of waved us off. Kept saying he was okay. Williams was not completely convinced. He thought maybe Billy should come out because he might hurt his arm by favoring his leg. Billy said it wouldn't be a problem. He wanted to stay in. Dick cautioned me to let him know immediately if Billy began to favor his leg and he'd have to pull him."

After taking a few pitches, Billy signalled that he was okay to pitch. The crowd gave him a big hand while Gibson scrutinized his pitching performance.

"He looked good to me. Far as I was concerned he was tossing better pitches than before that grounder hit him. I told Dick that when we came off the field and he left him in."

From Rohr's perspective, it was the ultimate "bang-bang" play. He told Cliff Keane of the *Boston Globe* after the game, "I never saw the ball come back at me. It hit my leg and it hurt. I looked and saw Joe Foy take the ball by third base with his bare hand and he threw out the runner."

When a pitcher goes five innings without a hit, everyone gets interested. You're past the half-way point. When a pitcher reaches six innings without a hit, everyone gets serious. Only nine more outs to go: a very manageable number. Two-thirds of the way there.

Gibson said that he first became a believer in a Rohr no-hitter after that sixth inning. "I think everybody by then was having thoughts about such a possibility. You just had to know it was a possibility, but no one said a word about it. We just kept going along through the seventh and eighth innings and Billy just kept setting them down."

There was a certain amount of tension on the Red Sox bench but after all these were all professional athletes not schoolboys. Their primary focus was on squeezing out a victory. Gibson recalls being very aware of the no-hitter in progress, but he was more concerned about being on the right side of a tight 1-0 lead.

He continued to go over the hitters with Rohr and to urge him to bear down. The ultimate pros find a no-hitter in progress to be a distraction. Their only interest is in putting a "W" on the board.

When the Red Sox failed to score in the top of the seventh, the New York crowd rose for the traditional home seventh inning stretch. While they were Yankee fans, their sentiments were clearly with Rohr as he marched to the mound and towards history. Rohr faced the meat of the Yankee order and he dispatched them just as quickly as if he were still pitching for Bellflower High School against a local nine. Three up, three down and only six to go.

This was getting very serious. Gibson had to shift his attention from the eighth inning Yankee lineup to his turn at bat. He would leave young Mr. Rohr in the capable hands of pitching coach, Sal Maglie.

Catchers will tell you that they don't hit for higher averages because they have to concentrate so much on the defensive part of the game. Yankee pitcher Whitey Ford had Gibson's full attention on this at bat, however. Gibson knew that Whitey remembered he had thrown him his best pitch on his first at bat and had been burned with a hit. He figured Ford would try something else so he went up "thinking curve". Curve him Whitey did and Gibson touched him for his second hit.

Perched on first base, Gibson had to be glowing. He had toiled ten years in the minors to get to this place. Now two hours into his first game he's hitting .500 -- off of Whitey Ford, no less -- and catching a no-hitter. Which direction is Cooperstown anyway?

Reggie Smith failed to advance Gibson who represented a cushion for their 1-0 lead. Young third baseman, Joe Foy, a native of the Bronx, stood in against Ford. No respecter of future Hall-of-Famers, Foy sent a Ford delivery smartly into the left field bleachers. The Red Sox bench, sensing victory, jubilantly welcomed local boy made good Foy. With a three-run margin, the tension was eased a little.

There is a lot of evidence that it is "easier" to pitch a no-hitter in a tight ballgame than a blowout. For example, in the American League there were twelve no-hitters thrown during the 1960's. Nine of the twelve games were settled by a margin of four runs or less and eight of them were two-run margins or less. In a close game, the pitcher has to bear down on each and every hitter. There is no margin for error. With a lead of five runs or more, a pitcher may look to "save" a little for his next start and give up a few.

Rohr appeared to be ideally positioned as he took the mound in the bottom of the eighth inning. With a three-run lead, he could go for the "perfect pitch". If he cut it too fine a bases empty home run would still leave him with a two-run lead. Not only that but he was working to the lower-third of the Yankee batting order.

With shortstop John Kennedy due up to the plate, catcher Gibson was startled by the loudest roar from a crowd that he had ever heard. He looked beside him to see a large number seven and the most imposing looking hitter he had ever seen. The legendary Mickey Mantle had been announced as a pinch hitter. Mantle wasn't huge -- 5' 11 1/2" -- by any standard, but he looked as if he had been carved from clay and fitted with Yankee pinstripes. If anyone could put an end to Rohr's epoch effort, Mantle could. But twenty-one-year-old native Californians are not awestruck by New York legends -- at least not young Mr. Rohr. Mantle, whose days of terrorizing American League pitching were several years behind him, flied out routinely to Tony Conigliaro in right field. Another major threat had passed and Gibson breathed a sigh of relief.

As Rohr walked off the mound at the end of the eighth inning, reality began to set in everywhere in Yankee Stadium. The reality to the fans that he was only three outs away from immortality. The reality among his teammates that the kid might just do it. Nowhere was reality more in evidence than in the Press Box. Reporters were flipping through record books to see if any rookie had ever pitched a no-hitter in his first game. Phone calls were made back to the sports desks in New York and Boston. Someone said, "How about Bobo Holloman?" That turned out to be wrong. Holloman had pitched a no-hitter for the St. Louis Browns in 1953 but he had made one previous three-inning relief appearance. No one had a nominee, not even the most senior reporter, but no one had a definitive answer either.

Dick Williams was interested in Rohr's no-hitter but he was much more concerned about getting an insurance run or two. After all this was his New York debut as a manager and he had promised that his 1-1 team would win more than they would lose. This wasn't the Yankees-Red Sox of *The Summer of '49* -- the teams had finished one-half game apart in tenth and ninth places respectively in 1967 -- but this was an important game to his young team.

"Then there we were at the top of the ninth," Gibson recalled, "and all our guys went down in rapid fire order. But it was okay because we led 3-0. And Billy and I looked at each other and without a word we walked up from the dugout. Boy, for a kid, he sure had a serious expression on his face. It was strange; everyone was standing to watch Billy go to the mound but no one was cheering. It was like no one wanted to do anything that might snap the no-hitter, even the Yankee fans."

Gibson reviewed the three Yankee hitters due up in the top of the ninth. The three best Yankee hitters. Tom Tresh, batting in the third spot, was only about a .250 hitter but he had power. He had hit twenty-seven home runs in 1966 and he was good in the clutch. Tresh could be the one to stop it. Joe Pepitone was worrisome. He was another .250 hitter with power and he was unpredictable. He might strike out or he might hit one into the right field bleachers. Joe was a problem. Elston Howard was a cause for concern as well. Although Howard was thirty-eight years old, he had been a tough out for thirteen years in the big leagues. He had hit .313 as recently as 1964 and he had the experience of playing under pressure in forty-seven World Series games. Ellie was a real threat. Three tough outs: all pitchable but not one sure thing in the bunch.

Standing tall and thin atop the mound, the young Boston lefty looked about like some imperial potentate on his lowly subjects, checking to be sure all eight were positioned to his taste. Each in turn gazed back at him as though he was some demi-god who was about to perform a magical feat that would bring them all lasting fame.

"Their leftfielder, Tom Tresh, was first up for New York," Gibson said. "I give Bill the signal for his fast sinking ball and he lets it go and Tresh catches it clean and hard on his bat and it takes off like a rocket to left over the heads of the infielders. I cursed. There was no way that ball was going to be caught. It was a white blur on a course to rip right over Yastrzemski's head. There goes the no-hitter!"

Yaz, however, wasn't buying it. While the crowd groaned, he took off like a shot towards the fence on a line with the white blur that was headed right for the space far above him. He was running all out when he leaped like a yearling deer into the air to spear Tresh's ball with his splayed glove.

Yaz came to earth with a thump and absorbed the impact by going into a full somersault. The crowd held its breath! Did he have the ball? He rose triumphantly to hold the ball safely in his glove for all to see. It was a catch for the record book and all the more so in such a game. The cheers from the crowd seemed to swell in their numbers.

Three to nothing, Boston. Last of the ninth. One out. Now only two outs away from an historic no-hitter. The thunderous roars and applause was not only for Yaz but mostly for Rohr's working no-hitter which he had saved. The genie was out of the bottle. The forbidden word was being spoken: NO-HITTER! All hoped that they'd see history happen right before them that day.

"Billy was more relaxed, looking good," Gibson said. "The grim look had faded with Yaz's spectacular catch. He was beginning to believe that he might just pull off the unthinkable -- a no-hitter in his first major league game. We were working very good, getting the pitches right down the middle."

The next batter up for the Yankees was rightfielder Joe Pepitone, who hit a fastball in the air to right field. Tony C. hardly had to extend himself to make the catch. The crowd again sundered the air with their whoops of delight. A historic moment lay ahead and they would be part of it for the ages.

With two outs in the bottom of the ninth and losing 3-0, catcher Elston Howard, a solid, muscular slugger who had gone zero for three at bats, prepared to face young Billy Rohr. Before he got to the plate, Williams hurried to the mound to caution Rohr to watch his first pitch, "Howard's a dangerous batter on the first pitch."

Now there wasn't a sound to be heard but the encouraging chatter of the Red Sox players as they hovered expectantly about their positions in anticipation of Rohr's initial pitch. The count went to two and two on fastballs and the stadium was set to explode. The unthinkable was going to become reality. Get ready for it!

Rohr would up, all arms and legs whirling about, and threw his next pitch. "It was a strike! Right on!" Gibson said. "It was the final out of the game. Then, I couldn't believe it."

But believe it he had to. The umpire, Cal Drummond, called Billy's toss a ball to bring the count to three and two. Gibson though to this day says he will go to his grave convinced that the umpire blew the call. "It was that close between our rookie battery and the veteran batsman. He obviously felt that he had to give it to Howard."

Gibson only mildly contested the call. "I knew Billy was thinking three and two and that he really wanted to get on top of the curve ball and get it over good to put Howard away. Up to the ninth we hadn't thrown a curve at him. Billy figured it was time to toss one up. It fooled Howard, making him swing in the dirt for it. Now with the three and two count we figured it was time to throw him another one."

Rohr appeared so confident on the mound that Gibson never went out to speak to him at any time during the ninth. "His control was just that good. We had Howard to three and two and agreed on the second curve. Billy would up and threw the ball but I knew immediately that he held it too tight and it sort of squirted out on him. What the hell! One pitch that hung a fraction too long!"

When Howard hit the ball to right toward Tony C., Gibson knew it was in there, a clean base hit. The good thing was that there was no doubt about it. It was a solid, well-stroked hit, leaving Tony without any chance of making a play.

"It was sort of a letdown," Gibson said, "but what the hell, we're still in a 3-0 game and you can't let down too much because I've seen games turn around pretty damn fast. Once the no-hitter was gone, the idea was let's win the game and get out of here."

As for the young lefty for Boston, he hardly changed expressions as he watched Howard's single bounce into right field. If he was disappointed, he didn't show it. His attitude like Gibson's was matter-of-fact like, 'Hey, that's baseball. Next batter.'

While Gibson and Rohr stood silently with nonplussed expressions, the throng in Yankee Stadium howled in dismay at the loss of "their no-hitter." Hometown hero, Elston Howard, was the villain although he was only doing what he was paid to do -- hit the ball. The boos filled the huge expanse of the stadium. Later Howard would recall that "my job is to hit the ball and I've got three kids to feed and that's what I do. I looked over at Rohr when I got to first base and I could see that he was hurting, but I wasn't sorry a bit." After reflecting for a moment he said, "That's the only time I've ever been booed in Yankee Stadium for getting a base hit."

With Howard at first base, Charley Smith, New York's third baseman, came up to the plate. The fans' boos continued to wrack the air. Smith took his cuts and soon was retired for the final out. Rohr had a one-hitter.

Almost instantly, the roars of disapproval directed at Howard for getting a hit before his hometown crowd turned to cries of congratulations for Billy Rohr. The fans were baseball lovers first before partisan diehards and showed their appreciation for his great pitching effort with their sustained applause.

Rohr and his fellow players dashed toward their dugout only to run into their own teammates who rushed out to congratulate their pitcher. All were soon swept away into the dugout and the clubhouse by hordes of policemen, the media and fans who had broken through police lines. In the midst of all the excitement and whooping, Jackie Kennedy and her son came by to congratulate Rohr.

When things began to calm down and some sense of order was restored, Rohr told press people that he first "thought about a no-hitter about the fifth or sixth inning. Nobody on the bench talked about it and neither did any of the Yankees." In ironic acknowledgement of Howard's lone hit, he added, "Sure I'm a little disappointed that Howard got the hit. But he gets paid more to hit than I do to pitch, so how can you begrudge him one. When he was on first I looked over at him. Yeh, I was disappointed but I wasn't mad at all."

Howard disagreed with the Red Sox contention that he should have been struck out on the 2-2 pitch. "If the kid thought one of them curves was a strike up to the last one he wasn't right," said Howard. "Them other pitches were too low and Drummond can't call them strikes because they're balls." He was a far better hitter than a post-game quote-maker.

According to Gibson Red Sox manager, Williams, was "happy about the win. He congratulated us on a good game. His attitude was to win a game any way you can. No-hitter or one-hitter, it still went into the books as a win. And Dick was determined the team was going to win more than it lost in '67."

Rohr, of course, was "on top of the world", according to Gibson. "It was a great thrill for him. I'm sure he definitely wanted the no-hitter, but as a professional you do the best you can. And Bill certainly had on that day."

When Gibson was informed by Williams that he wouldn't be catching again until Sunday, he joined Yaz, Mike Andrews and the pumped up Billy Rohr on a trip downtown to a Wall Street pub.

"We were all on a high, coming off such a spectacular win over the Yankees in New York. We felt like we owned the town. A radio broadcast truck came by and we flagged it down."

They told the driver that they wanted a lift downtown to a Wall Street restaurant. When he demurred, Gibson said to the driver while pointing at Billy, "You know who you got here? Billy Rohr, the Red Sox pitcher who threw the one-hitter today at Yankee Stadium. Only tossed 122 pitches against your big guy, Whitey Ford. Billy here, it was his first major league outing. Your guy, Ford, was making his four hundred and thirty-second."

Once the truck crew realized the quality of their catch they insisted on taking the Red Sox players to their radio station for a live interview. Only then did they transport the Boston quartet to their eatery on Wall Street.

High on the list of congratulatory messages Rohr received was a telegram from Boston Mayor John Collins: "You gave Boston an unforgettable day. Red Sox fans everywhere salute you and congratulate you on a fine pitching performance. May today's victory be the first of hundreds in your major league career."

Sadly, it was not to be so for the lanky lefthander. For though Billy Rohr was swept victorious off the mound with his one-hitter that day in Yankee Stadium, he was to win only one other game in 1967, ironically against the Yankees again in Boston, and an additional game in 1968. Incredibly, Rohr's career began and peaked on that cold April day. Today, he is a successful lawyer in California.

In another ironic twist, Yankee catcher, Elston Howard, who got the lone hit off Rohr in the 3-0 Boston victory, was traded late in the season to Boston and made a successful contribution to their miracle finish. By the time he joined his Boston teammates in August, young Billy Rohr had been exiled to the minors.

This most improbable of starts on opening day in Yankee Stadium was the first clue that this was perhaps a team of destiny. Time and time again they would be counted out only to rise again from the canvas. It would take another 159 games, however, to determine how the drama would be played out.

Today, Russ Gibson lives in Swansea which is not far from his boyhood home in Fall River, and works as a regional salesman for the Massachusetts State Lottery.

"It's still incredible," he says, "when I think of the game that Billy pitched. To pitch a one-hitter and then win your second game again against the Yankees. And then not to win another game until 1968 and only one and then he disappears. He was traded to Cleveland the next year and couldn't perform on the mound."

Gibson surmises that "when you're a sinker ball pitcher like Billy, you lose your sinker ball if you don't throw hard. Billy didn't really throw that hard. He threw fairly hard, but he lost his sinker. When he lost that his ball stayed flat. They killed him because with his best pitch, the ball moved. When he stayed on top, the ball sank. Once he lost whatever he lost, the sinker went in straight. The same thing happens to a lot of pitchers in the majors. With Billy, bingo, he's gone! He's out of baseball two years later. How do you figure it?"

Gibson himself remained with the Red Sox through the "Impossible Dream" year and all of 1968 and 1969. "I was probably as close as anyone to being a regular catcher, playing in eighty to ninety games each of the last two years. My hitting was improving, .225 in 1968 and .251. in 1969."

Unfortunately for Russ, when Dick Williams was unceremoniously fired in late 1969, Gibson's days with the Red Sox were numbered. What price glory, heh? "When I heard that Dick got fired I knew I was gone. He, in effect, had been my mentor going back to Toronto, and it was just a matter of time."

Gibson's time came in at the end of spring training in 1970 when he was "leading the team in hitting in the Grapefruit League. I was the top catcher, headed for my best season ever. I remember that I was hitting something like over .400."

Despite his great spring, the Red Sox traded Gibson to the San Francisco Giants. To add insult to injury, he was traded for a player to be named later and that old Red Sox nemesis -- cash.

"Hell, they didn't even trade me for anybody. What a come-down."

What has it meant to Russ Gibson all the years since he was a member of that wonderful winning team of 1967? "I can only tell you that something like that changes your life as far as the way you live. Everybody knows you no matter where you go. People are always sending you cards, letters, whatever, asking for autographs. They want you to speak at banquets. People act like the 1967 season was just yesterday. Actually, most of the people hereabouts can recall better than I can just what I did that season. You play in so many games for so many years, including the minors and they all begin to blur. Still, I like to go and talk to the fans and tell fun stories. The ins and outs of the team. People though, they still remember things I have no recollection about."

Ultimately, Gibson said, "It's like a love affair because we shared so much together that season . . . a love affair not only with the fans but with the players who shared so many ups and downs with you and who became a close bunch of guys."

A final reflection about Russ Gibson: if the house next door to you is for sale, see if Gibby is interested. Russ Gibson is perhaps as nice a man as you will ever meet. He is everybody's ideal next door neighbor.

CHAPTER TWO

Boston Red Sox vs. Detroit Tigers

Doubleheader
Sunday, May 14, 1967

George Scott, the Red Sox twenty-three year old first baseman, was born and raised in Greenville, Mississippi. On this Sunday in Boston, he was a long way from home. He was a long way from home in miles and he was a long way from home culturally. The one thing Boston and Greenville had in common was a love for baseball and George Scott. Scott was beginning his second year with the Red Sox and the fans loved his enthusiasm for the game and his colorful quotes. George had hit twenty-seven home runs as a rookie in 1966 but he also led the league in strikeouts with 152. So far in 1967, he had shown signs of becoming a more disciplined hitter and he was playing like a potential golden glover as the everyday first baseman. There was every reason to believe that George had a very bright future to look ahead to.

The Red Sox began Mother's Day 1967 in eighth place with a record of eleven wins and fourteen losses. Dick Williams' spring training prediction that the Red Sox would win more than they would lose was beginning to look like a dubious proposition.

The Red Sox had followed Billy Rohr's near no-hitter in New York with a tough 1-0 loss and then a heart-breaking 3-2 defeat in eighteen innings to the Yankees. But they had shown some good pitching and they had demonstrated more determination than any Boston team in years.

Williams took out most of his frustration over the two losses to the Yankees on George Scott. George had gone one for eight in the third game of the series and left seven runners in scoring position. At this point in the season, he was hitting .185 and had produced no extra base hits and no RBIs.

Williams decided that Scott should sit down in favor of Tony Horton for their unusual one game trip to Chicago's Comisky Park. Williams fumed "the last three times up, he struck out with men on base." Then he uttered a quote that still lives with both men twenty-five years later, "Trying to talk to him is like talking to cement." Tony Horton was not the answer to the Red Sox' early season woes as they fell to Eddie Stanky's White Sox 5-2. Darrell Brandon took the loss for the Red Sox.

The Red Sox came home to play their annual Patriots Day doubleheader on April 19. Playing baseball in Boston in April is a dicey affair and the games were cancelled due to snow.

Williams temperament was as foul as the holiday weather. He took the occasion to lambast Scott and third baseman, Joe Foy, for being overweight. Scott, a large man with an enormous frame, had gotten up to 221 pounds. At 6' 2" this was probably fifteen pounds more than ideal for him. This theme of Williams' harping on Scott's weight would prevail all season long.

The next Red Sox game was scheduled for Friday night, April 21. Billy Rohr was the announced starter and 25,603 fans showed up to see if he could repeat his magic of a week earlier.

Rohr didn't have another miracle up his sleeve but he evoked memories of the Red Sox lefthanded star of the '40s and '50s: Mel Parnell. All Rohr did was pitch a complete game and shut the Yankees down for the second time in eight days with a 6-1 win. At that point, Rohr's lifetime stats read: two wins and no losses; nine hits in two games; ERA 0.50. Not a bad start.

The Red Sox split the next two games with the Yankees to take the series two games to one. One week and a half into the season the Red Sox were 4-5, tied for seventh place but only a game and one-half out of first place.

The Red Sox then journeyed to Washington where they won both games behind the relief pitching of John Wyatt and a complete game by Hank Fischer. From there they returned to Fenway Park where they took two out of three from the Kansas City A's including a fifteen-inning, 11-10 slugging contest.

As April came to a close, the Red Sox had edged up to third place, trailing the league-hitting Detroit Tigers by one game. Both Carl Yastrzemski and Rico Petrocelli were hitting .330 and Lonborg, Rohr, and Wyatt were all 2-0. It appeared that a lot of the pieces were fitting together.

The Red Sox began May with their first western road trip: always a test for a Boston team. Lefthander, Dennis Bennett, got things off on the right foot against the California Angels with a 4-0 win in which he also contributed a three-run homer. That high note was more than offset by two tough one run losses to the Angels. This brought the season's total of one-run losses to five. This was not a good sign if the team was to develop into a true contender.

The midwest proved no more hospitable to the Red Sox. Jim "Mudcat" Grant picked up his first win of the season in the series opener and Dean Chance five hit them in Saturday's 4-2 Tiger's victory. At this point the Red Sox had lost four in a row and five of their last six.

The Red Sox salvaged one game from the Twins as their bats came alive the following day in a 9-6 win. Williams raised a few eyebrows by not starting Yaz and then using him as a defensive replacement in the ninth. As the Red Sox boarded their plane to fly to Kansas City, they were 10-10 and three games off the pace.

The Red Sox split the doubleheader opener of the series to maintain their .500 record. They were actually in danger of being swept, trailing 2-0 going into the ninth inning of the night cap, but rallied for five runs as John Wyatt picked up another "W". These last inning heroics were quickly forgotten as the A's won the third game of the series, 7-4. The Red Sox staggered home with a 3-6 record for their trip and more than a few pieces to the puzzle still missing.

The Detroit Tigers came to town as clearly one of the American League's bona fide contenders. The Tigers were lead by future Hall-of-Famer, Al Kaline, who was recognized as the premier rightfielder in the league. Dick McAuliffe anchored a steady infield from his second base position and Bill Freehan gave the Tigers an All-Star behind the plate. The pitching staff featured former Red Soxer, Earl Wilson, who had won thirteen games in 1966, Mickey Lolich and Denny McLain, who was then best known to the Red Sox fans as Lou Boudreau's son-in-law.

The Tigers had won eighty-eight ball games in 1966 even though they endured three different managers. Given the stability of veteran manager, Mayo Smith, they were well-positioned to make a run for it in 1967. They were off to a great start and brought a 15-7 record into Fenway Park.

Detroit was soon to make it sixteen wins as the Red Sox fell 5-4 on Friday night. The low point of the evening occurred when Red Sox catcher, Bob Tillman, attempted to catch Kaline stealing in the eighth inning. Tillman was so intent that he managed to drill relief pitcher, John Wyatt, flush in the forehead. Wyatt was down for the count, and Kaline made it to third from where he eventually scored the game winner on a sacrifice fly. Tillman was buried so deeply in Dick Williams' doghouse that he never really escaped until he was sold to the Yankees in August.

Saturday afternoon was no better for the Red Sox nor for John Wyatt. He pitched well in the seventh inning, coming in for relief and held the fort in the eighth. Wyatt ran out of gas in the ninth, but Williams left him in to endure a six-run drubbing. The Red Sox lost again, 10-8, and Wyatt must have wondered what was going to happen to him next.

As George Scott got ready for the Sunday afternoon doubleheader, he knew he would be facing right hander, McLain, in game one. He hoped he would play the second game. Williams had been pencilling him in for every game for awhile, so he could face the left-handed Mickey Lolich. George loved to hit against left-handed pitchers.

While Scott had a serious communications problem with manager Williams, he had a wonderful relationship with third--base coach, Eddie "Pop" Popowski. Popowski had been in the Red Sox organization since the 1930s and he was universally beloved for his low key style and good nature. He and manager Williams played "good cop/bad cop" more than once in 1967.

Pop would talk to George before the games and counsel him on what to look for. He would tell him that Williams just wanted to see him reach his potential and not to take it personally. Scott was such a wonderful natural athlete that he wouldn't always concentrate and you can't get away with that at the major league level. Pop was on him constantly to stay alert.

The Red Sox starter in game one was their ace, Jim Lonborg; Jose Santiago would start game two. Given the pitching selections and the early season weather it looked like a long afternoon of defense with modest offense. What transpired was quite the opposite.

Both Lonborg and McLain were touched for a run in the first but this is fairly common. Power pitchers often need an inning to settle down and find their target. The baseball axiom is "get to them early and get them out of there, or forget it."

There were indications in the last of the second that McLain might not settle down and just might not have it this day. Rico Petrocelli took him into the left field net and the Red Sox were out to an early 3-1 lead.

McLain finally found his groove and shut the Red Sox down in innings three and four. Meanwhile, Lonborg had simply put it on cruise control and held the Bengals at bay during innings two, three and four. He came a little unglued in the fifth as the Tigers touched him for two more runs. As the game reached the halfway point, the score was knotted at three. Visions of a "pitchers day" were starting to become blurred.

When George Scott came to bat in the fifth, the score was still 3-1 but the bases were filled with Red Sox teammates. Two were gone but "Scotty" relished pressure situations. Recognition was important to him and he was delighted that he was batting clean-up in the opener.

McLain had been wild throughout the game and George disciplined himself to wait for a pitch he could drive. Pop had preached to him over and over that he could raise his average fifty points if he could learn to be patient. His learned patience had started to pay off for him and he wanted to show Dick Williams that he was a hitter. Dick Williams is nobody's fool.

Scott worked the count to 3-2 and he dug in knowing that McLain would have to come across the plate. The most exciting recurring moment in baseball may be the 3-2 pitch when the bases are loaded with two men out. Baseball is a game of waiting for action but at this point, everyone in the ballpark knows something must happen. Even if the tension is broken with a foul ball, the excitement is actually turned up a notch since the moment is prolonged. With the windup of pitcher, Denny McLain, all three runners were off knowing there was no reason to hold their base.

Scotty launched a tremendous blast in the direction of Kaline in right field. Kaline was perhaps the best defensive rightfielder in the history of the game (Dwight Evans fans would dispute that), but Scott's drive was a rocket and Kaline simply couldn't run it down. The third base runner was heading for home as the ball was retrieved and Scott was barreling for third. He moved well for a big man and when the dust cleared, he was safe with a rare Fenway triple.

The beleaguered McLain gave way to relief and the Tigers got out of the inning without further damage. But the horse was already out of the barn and Lonborg took the mound with a 6-3 lead.

This would not be Lonborg's finest day. He staggered through the sixth allowing the Tigers another run. Williams had gotten Hank Fischer, who the Red Sox had picked up at the end of the '66 season, warming up during the inning. When Williams sent Dalton Jones up to pinch hit for him, Lonborg left the game having given up nine hits and four runs, all of them earned. Not a bad day's work for most pitchers, but below the standard that he would set in 1967.

The Red Sox had scratched out another run in their half of the sixth and the right-handed Fischer was brought in with a 7-4 lead. Fischer was a twenty-seven year old native of Yonkers, New York, who was in his sixth major league season. He had pitched four plus years for the Braves and a part of the '66 season for the Cincinnati Reds who dealt him to the Red Sox.

Fischer shut down the Tigers in both the seventh and eighth innings and the Red Sox added an insurance run in the bottom of the eighth. He weakened in the ninth, giving up a homer to third baseman, Don Wert, but proved equal to his nickname of "Bulldog" to preserve the win.

Lonborg got credit for the win and Hank Fischer earned himself a save. Hank Fischer appeared in a total of nine games in '67 and picked up a win to go with his save. The Red Sox released him outright in mid-season and he never pitched in the big leagues again.

Scott was pleased with his performance in game one. His triple had proven to be the winning hit. He had also added a single which was more evidence that he was getting over his tendency to try to hit every pitch out of the ballpark.

Scott had been signed to a Red Sox contract by their scout and former second baseman Milt Bolling. Bolling had accompanied George's mother to the Greenville High School graduation. While they were walking home, Bolling, knowing that he was about to offer a five-figure bonus, asked George if there was anything he wanted. When Scott replied, "Yes. A basketball," Bolling stopped at the local sporting goods store and bought him one. George spent the rest of the walk home palming the ball with either hand.

George's journey to Boston began at the Red Sox minor league club in Olean, New York. From there he graduated to Wellsville where he hit fifteen home runs in only 106 games. His next stop was Winston-Salem, North Carolina in 1964. To this point, he had played second base, shortshop and third, but he hadn't spent any time at his ultimate position, first base. A .319 average and twenty-five home runs at Pittsfield in 1965 earned him a shot with the big club in 1966.

He had started his rookie year in 1966 on a home run tear that drew favorable comparison with old double x: Jimmy Foxx. Then the word went 'round the league. Don't give this kid a fastball that he can hit; he'll kill you! Give him slow breaking stuff until his tongue is hanging out for a "number one pitch". Then give him a fastball way outside and he'll chase it. The "book" on Scott had been perfect. He continued to chase pitches outside of the strike zone and his home run output diminished along with his batting average. He finished the year with twenty-seven home runs and a .246 batting average. Respectable numbers for a rookie, but a far cry from his torrid start.

Pop took him under his wing in spring training and urged him to become a smarter hitter. "Wait for your pitch. Don't swing at their pitch. Go where the ball is pitched. If it's outside, take it to right field. With your strength you can hit it out to the opposite field or drive it into the gap in right center. Don't try to pull every pitch."

All of Pop's advice on hitting was good advice. Scotty was starting to hear it and apply it. And the results showed as his average began to climb towards .300 from its low of .185 on April 17.

George looked longingly at the spread of food set out by the clubhouse boys between games. If there was anything he liked as much as his beloved "taters" -- a Scottism for his long home runs -- it was good food. He had a huge frame and an appetite to go with it. But George had already spent too much time arguing with Dick Williams over his weight and he wanted to be quick and agile for game two.

Scotty was delighted when he saw his name on the lineup card at first base against Lolich. He had been dropped to the fifth position in the batting order, but he told himself he was still in the heart of the order. A seemingly simple man, he is actually quite complex and sensitive. He took tremendous pride in his baseball skills and his ego was easily wounded by a Dick Williams' barb.

Scotty relished the thought of facing the left-handed Lolich. George was a pure fastball hitter who had trouble with breaking pitches. Naturally, he was fed a steady diet of curves, slurves and sliders, almost all of them off-speed deliveries. Although the breaking ball bothered him, thrown by a lefthander the pitch broke in towards him, and he found it easier to time his swing. George relished the thought of going up against a southpaw, particularly in Fenway Park with its attractive power alleys.

The big guy was known for his hitting and power. To the fans he was "Boomer", a nickname taken from his prodigious home runs. But George was a complete athlete and an outstanding fielder. For a big man, he moved with catlike grace.

George was a natural first baseman, as good a glove man as has ever been seen at that position for the Red Sox. But his athletic skills were such that he performed credibly at third base when the Red Sox had asked him to fill in there. Dick Williams had tried him in right field during spring training but after George collided with an outfield wall, the experiment was quickly abandoned. Scotty kept his fielder's glove, but his first love was his dependable first base mitt.

The Red Sox basically went with the same lineup in game two as they had in the opener. The big surprise was catcher Mike Ryan getting the call in both ends of the twin-bill. Manager Williams had been juggling Russ Gibson, Bob Tillman and Ryan at the position. Mike's three hits in game one caused "Riverboat" Williams to see if Ryan had been dealt the hot hand. The Red Sox lineup was packed with eight right-handed hitters to face southpaw Lolich.

After starter Jose Santiago disposed of the Tigers without incident in the top of the first, Red Sox hitters took dead aim on the portly Lolich. Joe Foy got things rolling with a double. Yaz moved Foy over to third with a single. George Scott came to the plate thinking, "Hit the ball where it is pitched. You can hit this guy if you wait for your pitch." And that is exactly what he did.

Scott lined sharply into center and Foy was home for the first run. Rico Petrocelli added a double off the wall and the Red Sox had jumped ahead 3-0. The fans had just begun to enjoy this cushion when Santiago found himself immersed in hot water. Norm Cash had touched Jose for a sole homer and before anyone realized what was happening, the Tigers loaded the bases with one out. The dangerous Don Wert was at the plate and the key play of the game was about to occur.

George Scott prided himself on his fielding instincts but the upcoming play was a unicorn for him. Wert hit a bouncing ball to Scott and you could almost see him start to turn towards second to go for the standard first-to-second-to-first double play. At the very last second, the ball took a weird hop, handcuffing him by bouncing towards the first base side, and high. Scotty immediately reacted and pegged a strong overhead throw to catcher Ryan for the force at the plate. Ryan's rifle return to George at first doubled up Wert. The Red Sox were out of the inning and a Tiger outburst had been squelched.

The first-to-home-to-first double play is not unheard of, but few first baseman in the game could have converted the double play on Wert's ball. Scott told Cliff Keane of the *Boston Globe*, "I never made that play before in my life."

Scott's defensive game seemed to energize the Red Sox bats. They drove Mickey Lolich to an early shower in the second with two more runs. Detroit manager, Mayo Smith, said after the game, "I will never start another lefty in Fenway Park. The last guy to win here was Mel Parnell." If that was a bit of hyperbole on Smith's part, it demonstrated his level of frustration with the beating that Lolich had experienced.

Meanwhile, Santiago was pitching just well enough to keep the Red Sox safely ahead. His effort was a mirror image of Lonborg's outing in game one. The day had truly turned into a hitter's paradise. The Red Sox came to bat in the last of the fifth with a 6-3 lead. Few present felt it was enough. Happily for Red Sox partisans, Detroit reliever, George Korince was about to unravel. George would only make nine appearances for the

Tigers in 1967 but two of them would be on May 14, 1967, reliving both McLain and Lolich.

"Moose" Korince was no mystery to Red Sox hitters and they tallied five runs in the fifth. Joe Foy sparked the uprising with a two-run homer. George Scott contributed another key single as the Red Sox made the most of Korince's wildness and five base hits.

Jose Santiago staggered into the eighth inning with a seemingly safe 12-4 lead. But Jose was perhaps worn out from watching all the balls fly around Fenway. He had given up homers to Cash, Willie Horton and Bill Freehan and got into the spirit of the day with one of his own in the second. Jose gave way to veteran Don McMahon in the eighth with two men on.

McMahon was a thirty-seven year oldster who was in his eleventh big league season. At this point, he had made over 600 appearances in the majors -- all but two of them in relief. While he would end a distinguished career in 1974 with 153 saves, this was just no day for pitchers. McMahon barely made it through the inning as the Tigers tallied five runs to move within striking distance.

The Red Sox added a final insurance run in the eighth. Only in Fenway could the thirteenth run of the game be an insurance run. Dick Williams took mercy on McMahon and brought in the fresh arm of Galen Cisco for the ninth. Cisco had started his career with the Red Sox in 1961, had been sentenced to four years with some dreadful New York Mets teams and had returned from exile in 1967. Perhaps the Tiger hurlers were simply exhausted, but Cisco set them down in order to preserve the Red Sox 13-9 win.

The official scorer needed a calculator to tally the offensive carnage for the day. Thirty-five runs had been scored, twelve home runs had been hit (six for each team), and fifty hits had been registered. Most significant of all, twenty-eight extra base hits had been struck. The 16,436 on hand witnessed American League history in the making. The 28 extra base hits was a new record for one day, eclipsing the mark of twenty-seven set by the

Red Sox-A's sixty-two years earlier in 1905. A pitcher's day indeed!

The day was a memorable one for the emerging Red Sox team as well. The doubleheader sweep of a strong Tigers team was important. It established the young Red Sox as a team to contend with. Not necessarily a contender, but one that would be heard from. The sweep also propelled them from eighth place to a tie for third place. While they were still six games out of first place, they would never fall more than seven games off the pace for the rest of the season.

The game was an important one to George Scott as well. He had performed well at the plate. His stats showed four hits and five key RBIs. More significantly, the doubleheader had showcased his newly discovered versatility. On this day of extra base hits, three of his hits were well-placed singles. He had run the bases well and he had executed the fielding play of the day. Yes, he thought, Dick Williams is going to have to recognize my contribution now.

Years later, Scott reflects on his relationship with Dick Williams. He told former Red Sox announcer Ken Coleman, "My relationship with Dick Williams in 1967 was often on, up and down because Dick thought I didn't respect him as a manager and I sometimes thought he didn't respect me as a player. But I honestly think it wasn't his thought to try to harm me or hurt me. It was his way of trying to get the maximum out of me. My thoughts were negative at the time, but later on I realized what he was doing."

The Boomer's fourteen-year career would prove to be distinguished, but it would be filled with ups and downs as well. In many ways, 1967, his second year, would be one of his best years. He continued to field flawlessly, he raised his average by fifty-eight points to finish at .303 and he still managed to hit nineteen homers and drive in eighty-two runs. George Scott truly did it all.

The following year, George's average plummeted an astounding 132 points to a dismal .171. This was no injury-riddled, shortened season. George came to bat 350 times and managed only sixty hits, three home runs and a paltry twenty-five RBIs. Keep in mind that George finished his career with a lifetime batting average of nearly .270, 271 homes runs and over 1,000 RBIs. With these figures in mind, his 1968 offensive output may represent the weakest single-year performance by any bona fide major league slugger ever.

George's incredible descent puzzled everyone and yet everyone had a suggestion. Probably too many suggestions. Some felt that his futility stemmed from personal confusion off the field. Others felt he was getting bad off-the-field advice to swing for the fences every pitch: the "sluggers drive cadillacs" theory. Whatever the cause, George was simply hopeless at the plate. Dick Williams was quickly running out of patience. The former Boomer spent most of the end of the season on the bench.

Scotty rebounded to .253 and sixteen home runs for the Red Sox in '69. It was no repeat of '67, but it was a big improvement over 1968. George continued at a steady clip for the Red Sox in '70 and '71. In 1970 he batted a commendable .296 and the following year he socked twenty-four home runs.

On October 11, 1971, almost exactly four years after the final game of the 1967 World Series, George learned that he had been traded to the Milwaukee Brewers in a massive trade. He, Jim Lonborg and four other players, including Tony Conigliaro's brother, Billy, and George Brett's brother, Ken Brett, had been traded for four Brewers. Most notable among the Brewers was Tommy Harper who performed admirably for the Red Sox over three seasons and Marty Pattin who did the best vocal imitation of Donald Duck in either league.

Scott was devastated by the trade. The Boston fans had always treated him well, even in the dark days of 1968. The Red Sox had been his only team and he had made a lot of friends in the city. But Scott came to realize that a change of scene might be good for him. The Brewers' fans recognized his boyish enthusiasm (even at age twenty-eight) and took him to their hearts.

George flourished in Milwaukee. There was less media coverage and fewer opportunities for misinterpreted "Scottisms".

Milwaukee is a blue-collar city and George Scott is a regular guy. His defensive prowess also began to achieve recognition around the league.

Scott had five good years with the Brewers. In 1973, he achieved his high water mark of a .306 batting average and in 1975 he led the league with thirty-six home runs and 109 RBIs. He played in more than 150 games for each year that he was there.

But George was thrilled when he was traded back to the Red Sox after the 1976 season. Ironically, he was traded by the Brewers along with Bernie Carbo. Never before have any two players been happier to be traded. The return of the prodigal sons to Boston.

Scott played extremely well for Boston in 1977. It was as if he was reborn. He bashed out thirty-three "taters" and scored 103 runs. But, in 1978, that heart-breaking of years, George's skills showed signs of erosion. He had lost a step in the field, his average fell to .233 and his home run output fell to twelve.

Scott started his last year in 1979 with the Red Sox but was traded to Kansas City and finished up with the hated Yankees. When the year came to an end, George Scott's affair with baseball was over at age thirty-five.

The years after baseball have not been kind to George. There is no great value in recounting his travails. One fact will suffice: George sold his 1967 World Series ring to meet living expenses.

George has tried over and over to find a job in baseball. Any job. He managed in the Mexican League for one year (no walk in the park) to demonstrate his seriousness of purpose. From all accounts, he managed well. No baseball doors have been opened for him.

When you think about the 1967 Red Sox try to visualize George Scott teaching a bunch of inner-city kids how to play baseball. Picture his enthusiasm of twenty-five years ago and imagine how the youngsters would respond to that. Perhaps the Boston Red Sox organization could find it in their hearts and wallets to share and fund that dream.

1967 BOSTON RED SOX

BACK ROW: Bill Landis, Russ Gibson, Dennis Bennett, Gary Bell, Dalton Jones, Bob Tillman, Jose Santiago, Darrell Brandon, Jim Lonborg, Gary Waslewski, John Wyatt

MIDDLE ROW: Equipment Managers Don Fitzpatrick and Vince Orlando, Jerry Adair, George Thomas, Hank Fischer, Lee Stange, Rico Petrocelli, Jose Tartabull, Dan Osinski, Galen Cisco, Mike Andrews, Bill Rohr, Mike Ryan

FRONT ROW: Carl Yastrzemski, Joe Foy, Tony Conigliaro, Coach Eddie Popowski, Coach Bobby Doerr, Manager Dick Williams, Coach Sal Maglie, Coach Al Lakeman, Reggie Smith, George Scott, Traveling Secretary Tom Dowd, Trainer Buddy LeRoux

BATBOYS: Keith Rosenfield, Jimmy Jackson

CHAPTER THREE

Boston Red Sox vs. New York Yankees

Wednesday, June 21, 1967

For Joe Foy, 1967 was a season of ironies. Foy had been the regular third baseman in 1966 for the Red Sox. He had appeared in 151 games as a rookie and batted a solid .262 with fifteen home runs. He had come to the Red Sox after being named MVP of the International League for Toronto in 1965. At age twenty-four, he was clearly the Red Sox third baseman of the future, but before 1967 came to a close, Foy would find himself sharing third base with both Dalton Jones and Jerry Adair. It was a further irony that Foy was originally signed by and played in the minors for the Minnesota Twins. As the season came down to the wire, the Red Sox and Twins would emerge as the prime pennant contenders. The Twins' biggest weakness? A lack of a regular third baseman. In the greatest irony of all, as the Red Sox arrived in New York for their series with the Yankees on June 19, Foy discovered his parents surrounded by flames in their Bronx home. Their home was a total loss. But for Foy's quick actions, his parents might have lost their lives as well.

As the Tigers left town with their tails between their legs following their doubleheader loss, the Red Sox prepared to establish their legitimacy. With better than a month of the season gone, they had gotten a chance to get used to their new skipper, Williams, and to one another. On more than one occasion, their starting nine had consisted of four rookies.

The struggling Baltimore Orioles followed the Tigers into Fenway for a two-game series. The reigning world champions were off to a terrible start and the Red Sox hoped to take advantage of the faltering Birds.

When the last Baltimore runner had touched home, it turned out that the Red Sox pitching staff was the one that took the pounding. The Orioles racked Red Sox pitching for twenty runs as they swept a pair. Reliever John Wyatt, who had been unhittable during the first month of the season, was hammered in game one's 8-5 loss. A variety of Red Sox pitchers, principally Galen Cisco and Bill Landis, were handled easily by the O's in a 12-8 loss in the second game.

Twenty-nine games into the season, one had to wonder about the Red Sox pitching. Any team that gives up fifty-six runs in six games has a suspect staff. The Red Sox hitters looked sharp but no amount of slugging could overcome that defect on a consistent basis.

Red Sox hopes were boosted when the home team took three games out of four from the visiting Cleveland Indians. Jim Lonborg gave the Red Sox bullpen a much needed rest in the series opener with a four hit, 3-2 victory. Gary Bell, who was to play a key role in the Red Sox pennant drive, took a tough loss for the Tribe. The Red Sox rebounded from a disheartening 4-3 loss on Saturday with a doubleheader sweep the following day. George Scott's two-run homer was the key hit in the 4-3 opening game win and Bucky Brandon pitched a complete game in the 6-2 nightcap win. At 16-17, the Red Sox were close to Dick Williams' spring training prediction.

The Red Sox moved one step closer to Williams' pledge by opening a three-game series in Tiger Stadium with a 5-2 win. Free-spirit Dennis Bennett pitched well enough to win and to avoid permanent banishment to Williams' doghouse. Bennett had earned Williams' enmity by missing a wakeup call during spring training and had been running uphill ever since. Besides, if anyone could spot a player who liked to stay up late, it had to be Dick Williams.

Lonborg carried the day in the second game of the series. All he did was go the distance, strike out eleven Tigers and earn his fifth win with a 1-0 shutout. His great effort was offset by a 9-3 shellacking handed the Red Sox the next day. Old friend Earl Wilson went the distance to add insult to injury. More than one player thought about how good Wilson would look in a Boston uniform again. Still, two out of three in Bengal territory wasn't shabby.

The next stop for the Red Sox was Baltimore's Memorial Stadium. After the Oriole's 20-run bombardment a week and a half earlier, their pitching staff must have been quaking. The Friday night opener wasn't a bomb shell, but it didn't make the 4-3 loss any easier to take. Billy (one-hit) Rohr had to be relieved in the fourth adding to Dick Williams' pitching concern. The O's bats really came to life on Saturday. Frank Robinson's two home runs set the tone of a 10-0 drubbing. In the Sunday wrap-up, Jim Lonborg put his finger in the dike once more. Jim served up the stopper and Reggie Smith, who was finally starting to hit, led the offense to a 4-3 win.

In spite of their erratic ways, the Red Sox drew 32,012 fans to Fenway for a Memorial Day doubleheader against the Angels. They hadn't found the key to consistency yet, but they had turned on Hub fans with their dynamic brand of ball. This near sellout was a dramatic change from 1966 when the Red Sox averaged only about 10,000 fans per game.

Doubleheaders seemed to be the Red Sox forte as they swept California 5-4 and 6-1. Dan Osinski took the win in game one. Nine different pitchers had shared in the first twenty Boston wins at that point. Pinch-hitter Tony Horton chipped in with a key double in the eighth to drive in the winning run. Dennis Bennett kept up his winning ways with a five-hit complete game in the night cap. The Red Sox used a variety of offensive tactics including a suicide squeeze bunt to seal the win.

First Quarter Report Card:
   Overall B+: The team had improved by five wins over '66 and was in third place only four and one half games off the pace of the league-leading Tigers.

Straight A's: Rico Petrocelli with a .325 average and infield leadership, and Jim Lonborg at 6-1, including several key wins, go to the head of the class.

A-: Tony Conigliaro, at .302 with ten home runs, Carl Yastrzemski, at .299 and renewed enthusiasm, and John Wyatt, as a tower of strength in the bullpen, all deserve recognition.

Solid B's: Mike Andrews at second, the catching combination of Gibson/Ryan, Tony Horton as a six for thirteen pinch-hitter, and Dennis Bennett with three wins and a 3.12 ERA are all contributing.

Needs Improvement: Reggie Smith must continue to improve his .210 average plus Lee Stange with one win and Jose Santiago with a 6.30 ERA must round into form if the Red Sox are going to have a run at it.

F for Weight: George Scott and Joe Foy continue to battle the scales and Dick Williams. The battle is tougher for Foy who is hitting twenty points under his weight at .190.

Next into Fenway were the heavy-weight Minnesota Twins for a two-game series. The Red Sox picked up their fourth straight win on Wednesday behind Yaz's two home runs and Bucky Brandon's good effort with relief from John Wyatt. The Twins earned a split as Dean Chance threw a second game four-hit shutout. Billy Rohr suffered his third straight loss.

The Red Sox then took their act on the road for six games. This midwestern swing brought them to Cleveland for three games and on to Chicago for three more. They were counting on Jim Lonborg to get them off on the right foot and the 6' 5" right-hander came through again. His three-hitter gave the Red Sox a 7-1 win in the opener at cavernous Municipal Stadium. Dennis Bennett was beginning to look like a potential number three starter as he improved his record to 4-1 on Saturday. The Red

Sox had tallied five runs in the first three innings and never looked back in their 6-2 win. Boston came up empty on Sunday as Steve Hargan blanked them 3-0.

The Red Sox made their first major player move that fateful Sunday on June 4th in Cleveland. General Manager Dick O'Connell announced the trade of Tony Horton and outfielder Don Demeter to the Indians for veteran starting pitcher Gary Bell. The big right-hander was thirty years old, and in his tenth big league season, all of them with the Indians. Bell was originally a starter for the tribe and averaged twelve wins a year for them in his first five years. Cleveland had used him in relief for a number of seasons and returned him to his starters role in 1966 with a resulting fourteen victories. The Red Sox projected him as a much needed number two starter. Ironically, Gary had taken the loss to the Red Sox on the day before he was traded.

Just three days earlier, O'Connell had dealt veteran reliever Don McMahon to the Chicago White Sox for the versatile utility infielder Jerry Adair. Clearly, the Red Sox front office was making their run for it. General Manager, O'Connell, told the *Boston Globe*, "This is one of those years when it looks like the pennant is up for grabs. I think we can win it."

The newly bolstered Red Sox set off from Cleveland to Chicago and venerable Comiskey Park. Except in 1967, it still wasn't old enough to be deified and fans stayed away in droves. If they had shown up for the opener on Tuesday, they would have seen an embarrassed Boston team. The Red Sox blew a 3-0 lead and watched their teammate of a week earlier, Don McMahon, contribute in relief to a 5-3 White Sox victory. Following a rainout on Wednesday, and a 5-2 loss in the opener of Thursday's doubleheader, the Red Sox came back to life. The first bright spot was the complete game victory by Gary Bell: just what they had picked him up to do. The second ray of hope was Carl Yastrzemski. Yaz went four for five in the nightcap, including a home run, to cap an eight-hit evening. His recent tear had brought his average up twenty-three points in a week to .322 and raised his home run output to twelve. The twenty-seven-year-old veteran was on fire.

The Red Sox had drawn a 3-3 split on their road trip, not bad for a Boston team. They were coming home still making Dick Williams a man of his word: they were 25-24.

The Red Sox were looking forward to their upcoming nine--game home stand and to the arrival of the Washington Senators for a four-game set. Washington had edged out the '66 Red Sox for eighth place by a game and a half. The Red Sox knew they had progressed tremendously but the Solons had done little to improve themselves.

The Red Sox jumped out to a good start with an 8-7 win in the Friday night opener. Joe Foy showed signs of coming to life with two key, late inning, home runs. Foy had been benched a few days earlier for newcomer Adair. His Friday night performance let Dick Williams know that his proud third baseman had gotten the message. The Senator's behemoth Frank Howard, 6' 7" with 260 pounds of muscle, did the Red Sox in 7-3 on Saturday with two towering four baggers.

The Red Sox had to settle for a doubleheader split on Sunday: a 4-3 win and a tough 8-7 loss. Rico Petrocelli had the winning hit in the opener and Foy continued hot with a key double. Tony Conigliaro's three-run homer was the Red Sox highlight in game two.

When the Senators left town, the Red Sox had played all nine of their opponents at least once at home and once away. Many of the veterans of the '67 Red Sox saw this as a turning point. Russ Gibson remembers, "We had seen them all a couple of times and we hadn't seen anyone who was noticeably better than us." Mike Andrews remembers it similarly, "Nobody scared us. We knew at that point that we had an even shot every time we took the field."

The arrival of the Yankees for a two-game stay lacked some of the lustre of visits of earlier years. The former Bronx Bombers had finished a desultory tenth in 1966 and showed no signs of improving markedly on that in 1967. But a Red Sox-Yankees contest was still an event and the almost 19,000 fans on hand for the first game weren't disappointed. Gary Bell came through for the second straight time and the home team had a 3-1 victory. Russ Gibson hit his first 1967 (and what turned out to be his only) home run. The Red Sox fell 5-3 on Wednesday night but Tony C. homered again and Joe Foy continued his torrid streak with a homer of his own.

The three-game series with the visiting White Sox proved to be another turning point in the year. After splitting a doubleheader on Wednesday, the Red Sox showed that they were a team that wouldn't quit in the "rubber" game.

Rookie Gary Waslewski and the White Sox' Bruce Howard hooked up in a classic pitcher's duel. Howard left for a pinch runner in the top of the eighth after putting seven shutout innings on the board, but Waslewski continued his string of zeroes through nine. The knuckleball specialist Hoyt Wilhelm kept Boston at bay through innings eight and nine. Dick Williams decided Waslewski had gone as far as he could at the end of nine. Red Sox ironman John Wyatt continued the scoreless streak in the tenth and crafty veteran John Buzhardt matched him in relief of Wilhelm in the Red Sox' half of the tenth.

The White Sox finally squeezed out a run against Wyatt in the top of the eleventh. In classic Go-Go-Chisox fashion, Walt "No Neck" Williams led off with a double, moved over to third on a Don Buford smash to Scott and scored the go-ahead run on a Ken Berry single. That one run loomed very large in this evening of pitching dominance.

The White Sox sole run looked even bigger when the first two Red Sox hitters went down meekly in the last of the eleventh. More than a few of the 16,775 fans started to the exits as Joe Foy stepped in against Buzhardt.

This was a rejuvenated Joe Foy and he refused to say die, sending a ground ball single into left field. Tony C., who Mike Andrews calls "the greatest clutch hitter I've ever seen", stood in against the right-handed Buzhardt who hailed from Prosperity, South Carolina. The count ran to 2-2. Then Tony sent a

Buzhardt fastball rocketing in the direction of the left field wall. Any fair weather fan who had made it to nearby Kenmore Square to catch the "T" must have thought a miracle had been performed judging from the roar of the remaining fans. Tony had snatched victory from the jaws of defeat with his game winning blast into the screen high above "the green monster".

If it failed to qualify as a miracle, the ensuing scene seemed to be a vision: every Red Sox player was gathered at home plate to welcome the conquering hero. Veteran press box observers were hard-pressed to remember the last time this had occurred. Historians may argue over the exact moment at which the Red Sox were dubbed, "the Cardiac Kids." But when most fans hear the term, the Tony C. homer of June 15 is the first memory to spring to mind.

The Red Sox left home on a natural high. The win over the White Sox was one of the more dramatic comebacks in Boston history. They were in third place, only four games behind the just vanquished White Sox. And they were heading for Washington with new stopper Gary Bell slated for game one.

The '67 Red Sox had something of a schizophrenic side and it showed in the series opening twinight doubleheader in Washington. Gary Bell did everything that could be asked of him going all the way and holding the Senators to but one run. Unfortunately, his teammates came up with nine hits but could not score one runner. In game two, the Red Sox blew a three-run lead giving up four runs in the last of the ninth. Kids, Cardiac or otherwise, will have their ups and downs.

Jim Lonborg proved to be a legitimate stopper on Saturday as he pitched the Red Sox to a 5-1 victory. His win brought his record to 8-2 and his win total represented more than twenty-five percent of their wins to date. Unfortunately, the Red Sox dropped another tough one on Sunday to the Senators. Washington prevailed 4-3 in ten innings. Their record was back to .500: 31-31. Boston fans wondered if the real Red Sox were the team that performed wonders on Thursday night in Fenway or the group that dropped three out of four in Washington over the weekend.

Joe Foy symbolized the Red Sox erratic performance more than any single player. Coming off of an excellent rookie year with the Red Sox, Foy expected to really shine in 1967. Playing for the ninth place '66 Red Sox, he had still managed to score ninety-seven runs and put together a slugging average of .413. With old teammates Reggie Smith, Mike Andrews and Russ Gibson coming up from Toronto, he expected to play the role of the seasoned veteran and show them how the game was played in "the Bigs". Instead some of the rookies were outperforming him.

Joe also hadn't anticipated any problems with rookie manager Dick Williams. Foy had been Williams' star in his managing debut in Toronto in 1965. He had burned up the International League and led his team to the Calder Cup. His starry season was highlighted by designation as the MVP of the highest minor league. Then Foy became the first ballplayer that Dick Williams sent to the major leagues when he became the Red Sox regular third baseman.

Foy didn't have any illusions about Williams -- he certainly didn't expect any special treatment. But he didn't expect to end up in Williams' doghouse within the first month of the season. Nor did he expect to be treated like another George Scott. Scott and Foy had been rookies together in 1966. Both were young black infielders with enormous potential. But that was where the similarities ended. Joe was street-smart having grown up in the Bronx. George was from rural Greenville, Mississippi, and the twenty-three year old was naive in the ways of dealing with the city. Foy had learned to use his mind and rapier wit to cope with his mostly white teammates and an all-white press corps. George had a tendency to say whatever was on his mind to whomever he was speaking. Scott's presence actually helped Foy as a rookie. The Boomer was such a lightning rod for attention that Foy was able to quietly establish himself.

In any event, Foy was glad to be heading to New York for the scheduled three-game series with the Yankees. New York was home and it would give him a chance to visit with his parents and friends. It would also give him a chance to put his season into perspective. His season of high hopes had threatened to turn into a nightmare as he struggled to bring his batting average to .200. He had really bottomed out when Williams benched him in favor of veteran utility man Jerry Adair. But in the last week or so, he had started to come around and his home run swing had returned. There was still plenty of time to turn this season around.

Foy's parents lived within a mile or so of Yankee Stadium. He always looked forward to staying with them when the Red Sox came to New York. It was a big thrill for a kid growing up in the Bronx to journey from "home" to the ballpark he had only dreamed about playing in as a kid.

When Foy's cab pulled up in front of his parent's home, he almost went into shock: their house was in flames. He had the presence of mind to rush into the building, locate his parents and lead them to the safety of the street. There, they watched with neighbors as the three-story structure burned to the ground.

Foy had lost all of his boyhood memorabilia. His trophies and clippings heralding his starry New York schoolboy athletic career were all in the ashes. But his parents were fine and he knew they would start over.

Joe was relieved when the Monday night game with the Yankees was rained out. It gave him some time to help his parents to relocate and come to grips with the near tragedy. He was glad for the time but he was also anxious to get back to baseball to get his mind off the shock of the fire.

Foy was ready for the Tuesday night game against Yankee veteran Mel Stottlemyre. His parents had settled into temporary living quarters and he always looked forward to playing before his old home town crowd. Besides, he had raised his average almost fifty points since his benching and he was on a long-ball streak.

Just how ready he was would become apparent when he came to bat against the Yankees with the bases loaded in the fourth inning. Foy got all of a Stottlemyre fastball and rode it into the distant left field bleachers for a grand slam home run. Joe felt as if he was all of the way back. A Carl Yastrzemski homer was the frosting on the cake as the Red Sox eased into a 7-1 victory. Gary Bell showed once more why the Red Sox had wanted him so badly as he picked up his third victory in two weeks.

The Red Sox were skyhigh as they took the field for the second game with the Yankees on Wednesday night. Their ace Jim Lonborg was on the mound and the prospect of facing twenty-six year old rookie pitcher Thad Tillotson didn't fill them with fear either.

The Red Sox jumped out ahead quickly. Tony C. did most of the damage with a three-run homer and Boston led 4-0 when they took the field in the bottom of the first. Lonborg handled the Yankees with ease in their at bat and the Red Sox were sailing.

The Red Sox were back after it in the top of the second. Reggie Smith singled but was thrown out trying for second. After Lonborg struck out, Andrews walked bringing Joe Foy to the plate. Conscious of the previous night's grand slam, Tillotson worked Foy high and tight. His third pitch was so high and tight that it struck Joe flush on his left temple. Foy stood his ground -- his batting helmet had taken the force of the pitch -- and stared intently out at the mound. After registering his feelings, he trotted down to take his place at first. Yaz then singled in Andrews to put the Red Sox up 5-0.

When Thad Tillotson came to the plate in the last of the second, the whole ballpark was waiting to see what would happen. They didn't have to wait long as Lonborg nailed him between the shoulder blades with his first pitch. As Tillotson trotted to first, everyone watched for the spark that would ignite the blaze. Tillotson struck it by mentioning to Lonborg that he would get even.

Joe Foy didn't need a formal invitation to the festivities. He had plenty of pent-up emotion and Tillotson's body language brought him from third base to first base in record time. His words to Tillotson? "If you want to fight, fight me."

What happened next was a classic baseball brawl out of "This Week in Baseball", or in some ways, a re-run of "The Keystone

Cops." Joe Pepitone, one of the most colorful Yankees of all time, led his teammates' charge from the dugout. Rico Petrocelli, anxious to renew acquaintances with his old Brooklyn neighbor Pepitone, rushed to the scene from his position at short. Rico's brother, a special policeman at Yankee Stadium, anticipating a neighborhood reunion, raced on to the field brandishing his night stick.

Both bullpens emptied. It's a long way from the pens in cavernous Yankee Stadium but they were all at first base within moments of the start of the altercation. Tony Conigliaro was racing in from right field when one of the Yankees tackled him from behind. He told the late Ray Fitzgerald of the *Boston Globe*, "It definitely was an illegal block and a fifteen-yard penalty."

Reggie Smith finally got into it with Tillotson. Reggie was a student of karate and apparently saw this as an ideal opportunity to try out his skills. In Fitzgerald's words, Reggie "...gave it the old Crusher Casey treatment by picking Tillotson up, spinning him around and throwing him to the ground like an old candy wrapper."

But the real show was Pepitone and Petrocelli or the Petrocellis. After the game, they both claimed they were kidding. George Scott responded, "They said they was only kidding, but that was a helluva time to be kidding around, with everybody on the field."

Pepitone told the *Globe's* Cliff Keane, "I was having this session with Rico Petrocelli. I know Rico. We were kidding. All of a sudden somebody said something I didn't like. Maybe it was Rico. Pretty soon I was on the ground. I don't know who got me, but he was mussing up my hair and I don't like that. All I know is I grabbed some dirt and half tossed it at Rico to joke and the whole place was in a jam."

Yankee John Kennedy was angriest at Rico's brother. He told Keane, "I know the guy. He was out on the field. He's a special cop and he's out on the field yelling, 'I'll kill all you guys,' and that's a hell of a thing for anyone to be saying."

One player stood apart and alone as the battle was pitched. Gentleman Jim Lonborg stood on the mound with his arms folded as the melee took place. "I didn't want to get hurt," is the way Jim remembers it. Would that Bill Lee had used the same good judgement in Yankee Stadium about ten years later. The flakey left-hander emerged from a similar brawl with his "money" arm twisted and was never the same pitcher again.

Lonborg recalls, "Tillotson knew I was going to hit him. I didn't have any choice. I'm out to protect my teammates and to win the game." Jim had come a long way in overcoming his image as too nice to win.

A semblance of order was finally restored and the game was resumed. Actually the game was somewhat anticlimactic as most of the fireworks had already taken place. Scott homered in the third to put the Red Sox up 6-0 and now everyone waited for Lonborg's at bat in the fourth. That proved somewhat anticlimactic as well. Tillotson came in tight to Lonborg but did not hit him. Whether his control wasn't good enough to nail him is unknown, but Lonborg eventually went down on strikes.

Joe Foy contributed a key single after Andrews had followed Lonborg's strike out with a walk. Yaz brought in Andrews with a single to extend the lead. When the top of the fourth came to an end, Yankee manager Ralph Houk had been ejected for arguing a Bill Haller call at first as the Red Sox were up 8-0.

The balance of the game was largely uneventful. Lonborg did bean Dick Howser in the bottom of the fifth but the umpires said "enough is enough" and there were no further incidents. Lonborg recorded his ninth win of the year and the Red Sox prevailed 8-1.

A baseball season consists of 162 games and a few critical incidents. These critical incidents indicate a team's character and its make up. One such critical incident had occurred a week earlier when the Red Sox had come from behind to beat the White Sox 2-1 in eleven innings. The make up of the team had been indicated when every Red Sox uniform had crowded around home plate to acknowledge Tony C.'s game-winning homer.

Another critical incident had occurred that evening in Yankee Stadium when Lonborg put the league on notice that Red Sox pitchers would protect their hitters. And the team had backed that up by showing they were ready to do battle. Dueling with fastballs would come back to haunt them on August 18 at Fenway Park, but this was not a Red Sox team of "twenty-five players and twenty-five taxi cabs."

Joe Foy would continue to play well for the next six or seven weeks. By the end of July he was hitting a solid .240 with sixteen home runs. But he would fail to hit one home run in the final two months. On August 8, Foy was benched for Jerry Adair again and Adair got hot once more. For the rest of the season, Foy shared his third base spot with Adair and Dalton Jones. Foy ended the season with a batting average of .251, eleven points off his rookie mark of .262 and only forty-nine RBIs after bringing in sixty-three in 1966.

Although Foy's performance tailed off, he remained one of the best-liked players on the team. His company was prized for his quick wit and unfailing good nature. Later in the year, when the Red Sox were mobbed by a crowd of more than 10,000 on a triumphant return to Logan Airport, the players were warned to stay in their seats on the plane until a proper escort was arranged. Undaunted, Foy arose from his seat and commanded, "Take me to my people."

Dick Williams gave him a shot to redeem himself in the World Series against St. Louis. He started him at third in three games and used him as a pinch hitter in the others, but the best he could manage was one single and one double in fifteen at bats. Foy's series batting average of .133 symbolized the personal disappointment that 1967 had turned out to be for Joe.

Foy was returned to his regular role at third for the Red Sox in 1968. After all, he was still only twenty-five years old and had a world of potential. But like many of his '67 teammates, he couldn't seem to get untracked. His average deteriorated further to .225 and his home run output declined to ten. A much-publicized off the field incident with itinerant Red Sox pitcher Juan

Pizarro apparently exhausted the Red Sox' patience. During the off season, he was plucked from the Red Sox by the newly created Kansas City Royals.

Kansas City represented a fresh start for the free-spirit Foy. He was one of the more talented players on an expansion team and he brought his average back up to the .262 mark he had achieved as rookie. He led the team in at bats and RBIs with seventy-one. Demonstrating his athleticism, he appeared at every infield position and even played sixteen games in the outfield.

The New York Mets were so impressed that they traded Amis Otis and Bob Johnson to get Foy. Otis went on to star for Kansas City in their outfield for fourteen seasons. The trade appeared to be just the second chance that Foy needed.

The 1969 Mets had been the amazing Mets who had defeated the Baltimore Orioles four games to one for the World Championship. They appeared to be a dynasty in the making with only one weakness: a solid third baseman. At age twenty-seven, Foy seemed made to order to fill that role. Best of all, Joe was coming back to his native New York.

Things just didn't work out for the Mets or for Foy in 1970. Their pitching collapsed and they finished in third place, six games behind the Pittsburg Pirates in the National League East. Foy's average fell off to .236 and he managed only six home runs. Even worse, he committed eighteen errors in only ninety-seven games at third base. To round it all out, the ebullient Foy and taciturn Mets manager Gill Hodges never saw eye to eye.

Joe's next stop was with a terrible Washington team under manager Ted Williams. This Williams knew that Foy still had some talent left and he was willing to give him a shot. But Foy's skills were largely dissipated and he managed only thirty hits in limited action and produced no home runs in 128 at bats.

Washington turned out to be his last stop. At age twenty-eight, Foy left baseball never to return. The promising career which had begun only five years earlier was over.

Foy was not only out of baseball, but generally out of the public eye. While he stayed in touch with some of his '67 teammates, he was little more than an answer to a trivia question for the Boston Red Sox fans. In 1989, at the age of forty-six, Foy died of a heart attack. Like teammates Tony Conigliaro, Jerry Adair, Elston Howard and Don McMahon, Joe was gone too soon.

Foy's son, Joe, Jr., was the starting guard on the Holy Cross football team at the time of his father's death. He played for the Purple on the very next day. After the game, he said "My father played on the day right after a tragedy, and I wanted to play too."

Before his death, Joe, Sr., was extremely proud of his son. The first thing he said to former Red Sox' public relations director, Bill Crowley, at the twentieth reunion of the '67 Red Sox was, "Will you tell all these guys that my son is at Holy Cross on an **academic** scholarship!"

Joe Foy had to deal with a fair amount of adversity in his life after baseball. And deal with it he did. At the time of his death he was a substance abuse counsellor in New York City.

It is often said that an abundance of talent is the greatest curse of all. In Joe Foy's case, there was a lot of truth in this quotation. Requiescat en pacem, Joe Foy. Rest in peace.

CHAPTER FOUR

Boston Red Sox vs. Cleveland Indians

Sunday, July 23, 1967

When Gary Bell took the mound for game two of the double-header in Cleveland, he had been a member of the Boston Red Sox for seven weeks. Before then he had spent nine and a half years wearing the uniform of his opponents, the Cleveland Indians. The thirty-year-old veteran pitcher was determined to show the raucous home crowd that he was still in his prime and could keep the Red Sox winning streak alive. Bell had started strong upon joining the Red Sox but he had faltered of late. Gary Bell was arguably the funniest man on the Red Sox. When Bell and manager Williams attended a function where Gary was the featured speaker, a questioner asked Bell what kind of hitter Williams was when the two played against one another. Without missing a beat, Bell replied, "Without a doubt, the toughest hitter I ever faced."

After their "main event" in Yankee Stadium, the Red Sox returned home for a three-game series against the Cleveland Indians. Home cooking seemed to agree with them as they took two out of three from the Tribe. In the opener, Lee Stange won his second game with an 8-4 complete outing and Joe Foy continued hot with four hits and four RBIs. On Saturday, the Red Sox dropped another one-run game, a disturbing trend. Carl Yastrzemski and Joe Foy homered on Sunday to set the tone for an 8-3 win. Gary Bell prevailed over his former club achieving his 100th career victory.

As the Red Sox packed for a long thirteen-game road trip, they were in third place, five games back and three games over .500. Most Red Sox teams have been tailored for Fenway and the road has often been their downfall. Experts felt that the next two weeks would tell a lot about the Red Sox' prospects.

Their first stop was St. Paul-Minneapolis and veteran Jim Kaat brought them down to earth immediately. Kaat outdueled Jim Lonborg 2-1 and the Red Sox had another frustrating one-run loss. The following evening the Red Sox proved they could win a close one, as Tony C.'s two-run homer sparked them to a 3-2 win. Rookie Gary Waslewski from Kensington, Connecticut, was the surprise starter and the even more unlikely winner. It was the twenty-five-year old hurler's first major league victory.

Kansas City proved particularly hospitable to the Red Sox as they swept a three-game series. Gary Bell advanced his Boston record to 5-1 as Tony C.'s three-run homer powered the Red Sox 5-3. Saturday was a "laugher" as Jim Lonborg coasted to his tenth win, 10-2. Conigliaro continued to set the offensive pace with three hits including his eleventh home run. Rookie Waslewski continued his initiation of Christy Mathewson as he three-hit the A's on Sunday. Joe Foy's mammoth homer in the eighth proved to be the winner as reliever John Wyatt preserved a 2-1 win.

It was a happy band of players who enplaned to Los Angeles from Kansas City. The calendar had flipped to July and they were very much in the hunt. Best of all, they were 4-2 on this road trip.

Game one against the Angels continued on a positive note. Starter Lee "Stinger" Stange pitched well to pick up the 9-3 win. Three players under the age of twenty-five: Mike Andrews, Reggie Smith and Tony C. all homered in the game. The Red Sox juggernaut finally ran out of gas as they dropped game two by a score of 4-3. Things deteriorated the next day as they lost by the identical score. This rubber game loss was even tougher as supersub, George Thomas, had put them up 3-2 in the top of the ninth with a two-run homer only to be outdone by Don

Mincher's two-run game winner in the bottom of the ninth. The Red Sox were now 5-4 on their road trip.

The Red Sox moved into Detroit recognizing that the Tigers were a formidable foe but remembering their own doubleheader sweep in the last meeting of the two teams. This time the Tigers were anything but toothless as they bested the Red Sox 5-4 in eleven innings. The Red Sox wasted a three-run ninth inning comeback and John Wyatt took the "L". On Saturday, Denny McLain did a complete reversal of his Mother's Day form as he shut the Red Sox down 2-0. The Red Sox needed a doubleheader win on Sunday to resurrect their winning record for the road trip.

Things looked grim in game one as the Tigers hammered starter Gary Bell. Old friend, Earl Wilson, who would go on to win twenty-two for the year, took the 10-4 decision. Enter Jim Lonborg in game two. Lonborg fought off oppressive heat and humidity as the Red Sox earned a split with a 3-0 victory. Reggie Smith's two-run homer and Carl Yastrzemski's single provided the margin of victory. Once more, Lonborg had come through with an important win and the Red Sox concluded their road trip with a respectable 6-7 record.

All Star Break Report Card:

Straight A's: Conigliaro, Yastrzemski, Petrocelli and Lonborg. Go directly to California for the mid-season classic.

B's: Scott, Andrews, Foy, Wyatt and Bell. Go directly to some well-earned rest (watch the calories, George and Joe).

C's: Smith, Tillman, Santiago and Brandon. Go and concentrate on a second-half improvement.

The All-Star game is an important benchmark in the baseball season. It marks the approximate halfway point and patterns have begun to be formed. At this point, the Red Sox were in the middle of the pack. They were in fifth place, within striking distance at six games out of first. The offense looked solid, but the pitching was definitely suspect. Dick Williams continued to be bothered by those one-run game defeats.

The Second Half:

The Boston Red Sox returned from the All-Star break with renewed enthusiasm. They recognized that they had as good a shot at the pennant as any of the contenders. When asked right after the break if the Red Sox would finish in the first division, Joe Foy replied, "First division? That's fifth place. Forget that. Why not go all the way?"

The Red Sox drew the slumping Baltimore Orioles in the first series of baseball's "second season". The Birds had swept the Dodgers four games to none in the previous years' World Series, but their pitching staff had collapsed en masse in 1967. They were not a factor in the race.

The Red Sox got off on the right foot as they won the opener of a Thursday doubleheader. Lee Stange appeared to be rounding into form as he picked up another win in a 4-2 victory. The Red Sox showed their schizophrenic side in game two, however. Gary Bell had absolutely nothing for the second start in a row and the home team was embarrassed by a score of 10-0.

The Red Sox shook that one off quickly as they came back Friday night with a resounding 11-5 win. Yaz and Tony C. powered the offense with long home runs and Jim Lonborg picked up another win immediately following a Red Sox loss. On Saturday, Jose Santiago earned the win in long relief as the Red Sox had the edge, 5-1, in a game highlighted by a rare Red Sox triple play.

Next into town were the Tigers for an unusual Sunday-Monday, two-game series. The visitors quickly discovered that they preferred the confines of Tiger Stadium to friendly Fenway, as the home team tallied nine runs in the series opener. Once again, homers by Yaz and Tony C. set the tone. On Monday, Boston moved into third place with an easy 7-1 win. Lee Stange showed strong once more and Joe Foy joined Yaz in the homer parade.

Their brief home stand was over but the Hose were off to a great start. They were 5-1 since the break and Stange looked like he could really help in the pennant drive. Their thirty-six runs in six games showed that the offense hadn't missed a beat.

The Red Sox feasted on the Birds once more the following night in Baltimore. Jim Lonborg earned his thirteenth win in a 6-2 triumph and Boston moved within two and one half games of the league-leading Chisox. Six was the magic number again on Wednesday at Memorial Stadium. The Red Sox came out ahead 6-4 as Mike Andrews clouted a three-run homer to join "the hero of the day" brigade. Jose Santiago picked up his second win since the All-Star game in relief.

The Red Sox jumped out ahead of the Orioles 2-0 on Thursday night when the heavens opened. The game was eventually rained out, but that was about the only thing that had gone wrong in the past week or so. The Red Sox headed to Cleveland having won eight of their last nine and on the crest of a six game winning streak.

Ballplayers usually dread a four-game weekend series in Cleveland in late July. Cavernous Municipal Stadium usually features 60,000 empty seats and the heat can be oppressive. But on this occasion, the red hot Red Sox couldn't wait for the Friday night game to begin.

As it turned out, their anticipation was for good reason. Bucky Brandon added his name to the list of rejuvenated Boston pitchers, going all the way to pick up a 6-2 win. Make it seven in a row! Almost everybody got into the act on Saturday. Carl Yastrzemski poled his twenty-third home run. Mike Andrews contributed three hits and Joe Foy pitched in with a pair. Best of all, the Boston bullpen got another much needed day of rest. Lee Stange was never in trouble as he pitched his way to a 4-0 decision. Eight in a row and counting!

Sunday was get away day. Immediately after the second game of the doubleheader, the team would head to the airport for a return flight to Boston. Then they had a twelve-game home stand running into early August to look forward to. But all twenty-five ballplayers were totally focused on that afternoon's twin bill with the Tribe. They were hot and they wanted to stay hot. They were one half game out of the lead and they wanted to move up.

The team's intensity was heightened by the fact that their ace, Jim Lonborg, would be on the mound in game one. Lonborg had been there when they needed him all year. With lanky number sixteen on the mound, the team felt almost unbeatable.

The Indians countered with 6' 4" portsider, John O'Donoghue, in the opener. O'Donoghue was only a journeyman hurler, but he was the best the Tribe had available that day.

The Red Sox touched up the Cleveland southpaw for two runs in the opening frame on a Tony C. fourbagger. They really opened up on them in the second. The bases were filled with players in the Boston visiting grey flannels as Joe Foy stepped to the plate. Foy promptly unloaded on O'Donoghue and deposited a fastball deep within the left field bleachers. Jim Lonborg, who could nurse a one-run lead with the best of them, had been staked to a six-run cushion.

The outcome was generally predictable: Lonborg pitched as well as he had to for the win. Yaz added some frosting on the cake with his twenty-fourth home run and the Red Sox eased into an 8-5 win. The Red Sox had won their ninth straight and Tony Conigliaro had become the youngest player in major league history to total 100 career home runs. Sixth months shy of his twenty-third birthday, he was on a track to take his place with the immortals of baseball.

The Red Sox clubhouse was a frenzy of excitement between games. In a season of 162 games, momentum can be a great uplifter and the Red Sox were on a roll. Momentum breeds enthusiasm and emotion follows. The Red Sox couldn't wait to get on the field for the second game.

The sparse crowd of 13,787 fans couldn't wait for Gary Bell to get to the pitchers mound. During his almost ten seasons in Cleveland, the Indians had never won a pennant. The previous year Bell had lost fifteen games in a Tribe uniform. The Cleveland faithful were a frustrated lot that day and Gary Bell made a handy scapegoat.

Bell also made a handy target for the Cleveland brass that weekend. Stung by his comeback after getting off to a 1-5 start in Cleveland, "unnamed sources" were taking a shot at Gary at every opportunity. Their theme was "Gary pitches just well enough to lose ball games."

Ironically, Bell would be opposed in the nightcap by a future Boston legend, Luis Tiant. El Tiante had been shelled by the Red Sox on Friday night but manager Joe Adcock decided to have another go with him on Sunday.

This was Bell's first appearance in Cleveland in a visiting team's uniform. The fans' "welcome home" made it appear that Bell had single-handedly started the fire on Lake Erie. The cries of "Ding Dong" -- Bell's nickname -- didn't exactly resound with a thank you note.

Gary had some mixed emotions about facing his former teammates. After all, he had spent more than twelve years in the Indians' system and he had dressed in the clubhouse across the way for almost ten years. Just seven weeks earlier, he had been sharing beers and laughs with the batters he was about to face. But Bell was the consummate professional and he wanted more than anything to extend the Boston win streak to ten.

El Tiante held the Red Sox at bay in the top of the first. Bell prepared himself for the jeers that were about to rain down upon him. Bell remembered going to spring training with the Indians as a twenty-year old in 1957 and the going over he received from Tribe pitchers Bob Lemon, Mike Garcia and Early Wynn. Anything the fans could dish out would seem tame compared to the barbs he endured from the grizzled veterans who saw Bell as a threat to their jobs. Then he thought about Cleveland general manager, Gabe Paul, and his parsimony when it came to negotiating players' contracts. This memory really made Bell want to concentrate and shut his old teammates down.

Gary had not been that strong in his last several outings and he was determined to get off to a good start. Unfortunately, lead-off hitter Lee Maye got hold of a fastball and drove it sharply into right. By the time Tony Conigliaro tracked it down and got to it, Maye was safely encamped on second base. Bell looked in to second baseman, Vern Fuller, and forced himself to concentrate. He might have been putting too much intensity into it as his next effort was a wild pitch, advancing Maye to third. The Cleveland crowd finally had something to get excited about and they were really enjoying Bell's misfortune. Bell got a serious scare when Fuller launched a long fly ball to left but Yaz gathered it in and the only damage was Lee Maye's tally after tagging at third. Gary breathed a sigh of relief when he got out of the inning without further damage.

For his part, Luis Tiant was proving as tough to hit on Sunday as he had been easy to hit on Friday. The Red Sox were retired meekly in the top of the second.

Bell felt himself finding his rhythm in the second. Primarily, a fastball pitcher, it often took him a few batters to get into synch. He set the Cleveland batters down without incident in the second.

Tiant continued to twirl and whirl and generally confuse the Red Sox hitters in the third. Luis frequently had the reverse experience from Bell. It often took at least one turn through the batting order for hitters to adjust to his corkscrew motion. When Luis shut the Red Sox down in the third without a run, Boston had gone seven straight innings (since the fifth inning of the first game) without scoring.

The Gary Bell who took the mound in the third inning could have spent his entire career in the Red Sox system if things had turned out differently. A superb all around athlete in high school, Bell was actually better known around San Antonio, Texas, as a football and basketball star. But Bell had attracted the attention of the scouts in American Legion baseball and the scout who did the most to ingratiate himself with Bell was the Red Sox' scout, Hank Severeid. Severeid had spent fifteen years in the majors as a catcher and he dogged Bell persistently. Gary was leaning in the direction of his friend Hank, but was persuaded that the great Indians pitching staff was aging and this offered a quick path to the majors. As it turned out, he probably would have made it to "the bigs" by age twenty-one as well with the pitching-poor Red Sox. Bell handled the Indians with ease in the bottom of the third frame and the game was beginning to take the look of a pitcher's duel.

The Indians came a little bit apart at the seams in the top of the fourth. Third baseman Max Alvis started things off by throwing high to former Red Sox first baseman Tony Horton, giving George Scott safe passage to first. After Jerry Adair singled, Reggie Smith lined one safely into right. Scott scored and Smith took second when Lee Maye's outfield throw was high to third. Next Luis Tiant threw one in the dirt, but Adair was too aggressive on the play. While Adair was being tagged out at the plate, Reggie Smith managed to advance to third. Mike Ryan drew a walk and proceeded to surprise his team, and more importantly, the Indians, with his baserunning skills. Ryan took off for second to the astonishment of catcher Joe Azcue, who authored a weak toss to shortstop Chico Salmon. Reggie Smith was off for the plate as soon as Azcue drew back to throw and he easily outran Salmon's return throw to put the Red Sox up 2-1. The Red Sox had done more running in one inning than many previous Red Sox teams had done in a week.

Gary Bell was really feeling confident now. He was in his groove and he had a one run lead to work on. He also knew the strengths and weaknesses of the Cleveland hitters better than any other team and he set about exploiting his knowledge. Bell added another "0" to the total in the bottom of the third.

Now the Red Sox really felt that they had momentum on their side. Yaz got things going again in the top of the fifth with a single. Then Tony Conigliaro stepped to the plate. Bell remembers Tony C. as the most aggressive hitter he ever saw. Conig stood so close to the plate that "you could hit him with a strike," is the way Gary remembers it. The only hitting going on in this at bat was Tony's smash that easily cleared the left field wall. The Red Sox dugout was ecstatic.

Gary Bell sailed through the Indians in the last of the fifth: he was in total control at this point. After Mike Ryan chipped in with an insurance run RBI in the top of the sixth, the Red Sox were up 5-1. If the Indians were to make a counter-strike, it would have to come soon.

Bill Crowley, the Red Sox public relations director, was watching the game on T.V. at his Needham home. When the customary announcement of the team's travel plans was made as a courtesy to the player's families, Crowley began to worry about a mob scene at the airport. He called the State Police at Logan Airport to apprise them of his concern. Crowley was told by the State Police that they had handled Presidents and The Beatles and that he was probably overreacting anyway. Still, Crowley continued to worry.

The Indians opened the last of the sixth by sending the left-handed Vic Davalillo up to pinch hit for Tiant. At 5' 7" and 150 pounds, Vic was no power threat, but he was a pesky little singles hitter who usually hit around .280. Actually, the Indians used to kid Davalillo that he was a giant compared to his brother Yo-Yo, who played briefly for the old Washington Senators. Yo-Yo Davalillo played nineteen games for Washington in 1953 at 5' 3" and 140 pounds soaking wet. When he successfully retired Victor, brother of Yo-Yo, Davalillo, Bell knew he had the game in hand. He walked off the mound at the end of six with a solid 5-1 lead.

At this point, the Red Sox bats went silent. It was almost as if they had complete confidence in Bell and they were anxious to celebrate in the clubhouse and start heading home. George Culver, in for relief of Luis Tiant, dispatched them easily in the seventh and the eighth innings. Anxious to please his new mates, Gary matched Culver's scoreless frames in both innings. Bob Allen came in for Cleveland in the ninth after Fred Whitfield successfully pinch hit for Culver in the last of the ninth. Allen breezed through the Red Sox in the top of the ninth and now it was all up to Gary Bell.

It was a confident Bell who headed for the mound with Red Sox win streak resting on his shoulders. Today, when he looks back, Gary marvels at just how strong this young team was. "You think about Yaz as the oldest guy on the field other than me and then you realize that he went on to play another sixteen years. Reggie Smith played another fifteen years and Tony might have played longer than either of them if he hadn't got hurt. Scott and Rico were two more great players. They all were really. It was far and away the strongest team I ever played for."

Gary Bell really wanted this one. He had been a serious baseball fan as a youngster and the thought of finally playing on a pennant winner really excited him. He had grown up a short distance from the home park of the San Antonio Missions, the St. Louis Browns' double-A affiliate, and he had spent every minute he could either inside the park or outside shagging foul balls. Not all ballplayers grow up as fans, but the ones who do have a special passion for the game.

Rocky Colavito and Max Alvis touched him for hits in the ninth, but Bell was determined to finish the game. He had played for serf's wages in Cleveland, but he knew of the Red Sox generosity and he knew that complete games translated into contract dollars. After almost 100 career wins, Cleveland had rewarded him with a contract of $26,000 in his last year. Bell was determined to upgrade his pay.

Old friend Tony Horton stepped to the plate with two men on and two men out. Tony was a very dangerous hitter. When Horton turned on a Bell fastball, Gary had a momentary sinking feeling in his stomach, but that feeling quickly receded as he watched Reggie Smith settle under the long fly for the final out. The next thing he knew, Gary was engulfed by his onrushing teammates. Ten straight!

The Red Sox clubhouse was awash in celebration following the second game. While few, if any, of the Red Sox players realized it, the ten-game winning streak was Boston's longest since 1951.

In addition, they had won all ten games by at least two runs and their average winning margin was four runs. Another plus was that the over-worked bullpen finally got some rest as the starting pitchers flourished.

The plane ride home provided a chance for relaxation and celebration. The players were mildly amused and pleased by the announcement en route that there was a large group of fans waiting at Boston's Logan Airport. The announcement put the Red Sox entourage on notice, but hardly prepared them for the scene to follow.

Spontaneous crowds are always difficult to estimate. This crowd was very spontaneous. No media personality had urged the Red Sox faithful to turn out at Logan for Red Sox pride. There had only been the brief mention of their itinerary on the T.V. during the second game, but nothing more. Fans had been starved for a pennant contender for so long that it seemed like the thing to do. The spontaneous turnout was variously estimated at from 5,000 to 15,000 people. State Police were certain of one fact: it was a bigger crowd than had turned out to greet the Beatles one year earlier. Bill Crowley had been right!

The players were generally overwhelmed by the turnout. Team members like Yaz and Tony C. who had been flying into Logan for many years were used to welcoming parties of fifty to sixty family members and friends. Sometimes the players worried that even this group would boo their arrival. They couldn't believe their eyes.

Ten years or so earlier, another Red Sox team had landed at Logan after a particularly disastrous road trip. Resident team comedian and .500 pitcher, 6' 6" Frank Sullivan had set the tone for all future Red Sox landings. Sullivan took to the center aisle and waited until he had the attention of all. "Men, if we all spread out, they won't be able to take us with one, single round." That would not be a problem on Sunday night, July 23.

There would be another safety problem, however. The fans were so eager to get a look at their conquering heroes, that they spilled out of the terminal and on to the actual landing area.

Airport officials diverted the Red Sox plane to the far western extreme of Logan, the general aviation area. Players were escorted to a waiting bus that took them to the American Airlines terminal. Fans still managed to surround the bus and Tony Conigliaro was heard to utter, "How can you lose with people like this behind us?"

The American Airlines reception area was bedlam. Mike Andrews and Rico Petrocelli remember being a little bit frightened by the mob scene but mostly excited by the outpouring of support. Dick Williams told Kevin Walsh of the *Boston Globe*, "They told us on the plane that there'd be fans at the airport. But I never expected anything like this. It's really something."

For one brief moment at least, every long-term Red Sox fan's dream had come true.

Gary Bell felt like he was a long way from Cleveland at that moment. It was great to be with a contender at last and it was even better to have this kind of fan support.

It is fair to say that if the Red Sox hadn't picked up Bell, they would never have won the pennant in 1967. Gary would gather six more wins over the next two months and he gave Boston a solid number two starter. His overall record after being obtained by the Red Sox on June 4 was 12-8 and he appeared in twenty-nine games, mostly in a starting role. Gary wasn't much of a factor in the World Series but 1967 still represents his fondest memory of a twelve-year big league career.

Gary parlayed his great 1967 season into a $40,000 contract in 1968. He figured that it would have taken seven more good seasons for the Indians to get that amount from Cleveland general manager, Gabe Paul. Gary got off to a great start in 1968 and was named to the All-Star game in Houston, Texas. He tailed off in the second half but still managed a 3.12 ERA to go with his 11-11 record.

Red Sox general manager Dick O'Connell had originally offered Bell a 1968 contract at $35,000. Bell figured, "Why not go for it?" He asked for $40,000. O'Connell agreed saying, "As long as you'll go out and win twenty games." Although Gary only got about halfway to that total, there is no record of his having returned any of the Red Sox' money.

Bell's lacklustre second half caused Red Sox officials to re-evaluate his future with the team. The combination of his age and the earlier acquisition of Ray Culp and Dick Ellsworth, led them to leave Gary unprotected in the expansion draft. The new franchise in Seattle was delighted to pluck a proven major league starter.

Bell's honeymoon with manager, Joe Schultz, was short-lived. Gary was traded to the Chicago White Sox on June 8, 1969, for Bob Locker after compiling a 2-6 record and an ERA of 4.70. His most significant accomplishment in Seattle was rooming with former Yankee pitcher Jim Bouton of *Ball Four* fame. Bouton was sufficiently impressed with Gary's nocturnal activities that Bell was featured prominently in Bouton's writing.

Asked about Bouton, Bell says, "I'm one of the one and one half friends Jim has in baseball. Mike Marshall is half a friend of his and I'm his one whole friend. I've always gotten along with everyone."

Gary appeared in twenty-three games for the White Sox, mostly in relief. Gary's record for his last major league team was 0-0. At age thirty-two, a little over a year since his All Star designation, Bell's big league days were over.

Bell spent the first six months after his release in Hawaii. His next stop was Arizona, first in Tucson then in Phoenix. Gary recalls, "Most of us weren't trained to do anything except play baseball. Back in the 1950s, very few baseball players went to college at all. I had to figure out a way to make a living."

Given his affable nature and ability to get along with people, Gary gravitated naturally to sales. Eventually he headed back to his boyhood home of San Antonio, Texas, where he presently resides. Gary operates a sporting goods business which keeps him involved in the game and gets him around to the schools and teams in the area.

When asked what the 1967 season meant to him, Bell responds, "It was the most exciting season of my major league career. It seemed like we had a different hero every day. Joining the team after the season started and being accepted right away meant a great deal. They were a great bunch of guys."

Nice guys can finish first.

Russ Gibson rode the buses in the minor leagues for ten years before making his major league debut in 1967. (Photo courtesy of the Boston Red Sox).

Billy Rohr flirted with immortality for 8⅔ innings before Yankee Elston Howard broke up his bid for a no-hitter. (Photo courtesy of the Boston Red Sox).

George "Boomer" Scott raised his average 58 points over his rookie level to finish fourth in the American League batting average race at .303. (Photo courtesy of the Boston Red Sox).

Joe Foy had hammered out 17 home runs by July 31, 1967 but tailed off and ended up sharing third base with Dalton Jones and Jerry Adair. (Photo courtesy of the Boston Red Sox).

Gary Bell contributed 12 wins to the Red Sox after his acquisition from the Cleveland Indians on June 4, 1967. (Photo courtesy of the Boston Red Sox).

Mike Andrews became the tallest starting second baseman in major league history and was a steady contributor throughout the 1967 season. (Photo courtesy of the Boston Red Sox).

George Scott, facing the Twins Jim Kaat, displays the swing that produced 19 home runs and 82 r.b.i.s. (Photo courtesy of the Boston Red Sox).

Joe Foy welcomed home by teammates Mike Andrews, Carl Yastrzemski and Mike Ryan. The batboy is Rick Williams, Manager Dick William's son. (Photo courtesy of the Boston Red Sox).

Jim Lonborg shows the determination that earned him 22 victories and the Cy Young award. (Photo courtesy of the Boston Red Sox).

Tony Conigliaro became the youngest player in major league history to hit 100 home runs, in Cleveland on July 23, 1967. (Photo courtesy of the Boston Red Sox).

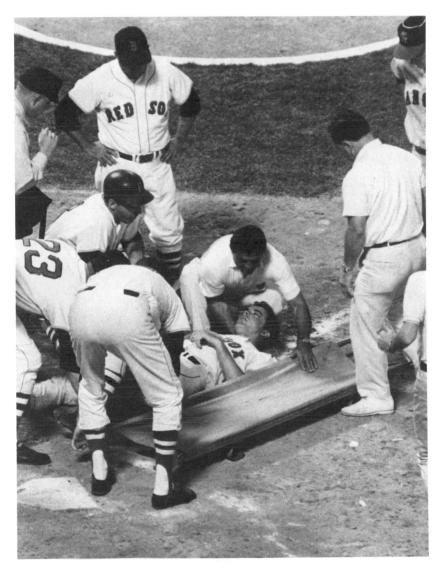

A stretcher is readied for Tony Conigliaro moments after being struck by a Jack Hamilton fastball; manager Dick Williams (23) is shown at far left, Rico Petrocelli is leaning in towards his pal, and trainer Buddy LeRoux is directly to the right of the stretcher. (UPI photo courtesy of the New England Museum of Sports).

CHAPTER FIVE

Boston Red Sox vs. Kansas City A's

Thursday, August 3, 1967

Mike Andrews took his familiar position at second base as the Red Sox began their 104th game of the season against the last-place A's. Two and a half weeks earlier during the celebrated sweep over Cleveland, the Indian's general manager, Al Rosen, had said of the twenty-four year old southern California native, "Without that guy (Andrews) you Red Sox would be nothing." Pretty heady praise for a rookie surrounded by stars like Yaz, Lonborg, and Tony C. Andrews appeared to be a likely candidate to give the Red Sox a steady all-around second baseman for the first time since Bobby Doerr had retired in 1951. Having the future Hall-of-Famer, Doerr, around as a coach that season was a real plus for Mike. Doerr was calm and positive in contrast to Dick Williams' volcanic and acerbic style. Andrews looked at the afternoon's game against the A's as just one more contest in a very long season. The previous day the native of Torrance, California, and former football star, had hit his first Fenway homer. But Andrews was the consummate team player and the home run had been in a losing cause as the A's won 6-4. His game was giving himself up to advance a runner to second and taking the hard slide while turning the double play at second. That's what he was prepared for on August 3.

When the Red Sox won game two of the doubleheader in Cleveland to extend their winning streak to ten, the Impossible Dream began to take shape. The season was more than half over, first place was within shouting distance and the club had momentum. Pennant fever was abroad and alive in the Hub.

Mike Andrews remembers this as the first time he really thought concretely about winning the pennant. Mike had been brought up to the Red Sox in the waning weeks of September of 1966, and in his words, "I didn't like what I saw. I didn't like losing, I didn't like the atmosphere of losing, and I didn't want to be any part of it. I had always been in a winning environment and I wanted to do everything I could to make the Red Sox a winning team."

There was every reason to be optimistic about the two weeks following the Red Sox' triumphant return from Cleveland. The Red Sox had thirteen games scheduled in their cozy bandbox and some home cooking was likely to help their position in the standings.

The fans felt that the Red Sox were about to make a serious move. The demand for tickets was the highest it had been since the contending teams of 1946-49. After years of frustration, Bostonians were finally willing to wear their hearts on their sleeves.

The home stand began on an upbeat note. The contending California Angels came in for a three-game series that could determine who was a contender and who was a pretender. The teams split the first two games, setting the stage for a crucial "rubber game".

The A's held the upper hand as all-star pitcher, Jim McGlothlin, brought them into the last of the ninth with a 5-2 lead. At this point, the Red Sox mounted a comeback which was typical of the style which earned them the title: "Cardiac Kids."

Andrews led off with a single. Joe Foy followed with a blast into the screen which brought them within one run. One batter later, Tony Conigliaro matched Foy's feat and the game was tied at five and on its way to extra innings.

Yaz made two outstanding defensive plays in the top of the tenth to preserve the tie. Reggie Smith tripled to open the inning and all 34,193 fans knew he would score. They were not disappointed. Jerry Adair bounced a ground ball by A's third baseman, Paul Schaal, and the Red Sox had come from behind once again.

Andrews recalls that this was a team that really believed in itself. "The first time around the league, some of the newer guys, Reggie Smith, Gibby, myself, might have been a little bit in awe. Seeing ballparks you had only read about before. But after we had gotten a look at everybody, we felt we were as good as anybody."

The Red Sox won the series but it would be almost two months before California would prove to be pretenders. Nineteen sixty-seven was not a year of knockout punches.

The Minnesota Twins were next to step into the Fenway ring with the local heroes. The Twins were truly heavyweights led by the burly Harmon Killebrew and the equally burly, Bob Allison.

After four games in three days, the Boston pitching staff knew just how formidable this opponent was. In these four games, the Twins had pushed twenty nine runs across the plate against the beleaguered Red Sox hurlers. Only Dalton Jones' clutch hitting and strong relief from iron man John Wyatt had allowed the Red Sox a 6-3 win in the first game of a Saturday doubleheader.

Lee Stange came through with a shutout in an unusual Monday wrapup to the five game series. This coupled with a Yaz three-run homer allowed the Red Sox to salvage two games from the series. As the calendar turned into August, the Red Sox were in second place two games behind the league-leading Chicago White Sox. With last-place Kansas City heading into town for a three-game series, the Red Sox appeared poised to make up some ground.

Someone forgot to tell the lowly A's that the home team was about to make its move. The best the Red Sox could manage in an August 1 doubleheader was a split. They lost to a Chuck Dobson five hitter in the opener and rallied to an 8-3 victory in the nightcap.

To make matters worse, the Red Sox dropped the third game of the series by a score of 8-6. About the only bright spot of the game was Mike Andrews' sixth home run which also represented his first at Fenway.

The home stand which had opened with such optimism was slipping away. The momentum which had been gained was slowly receding.

August 3 is awfully early to call one single game a crucial one. After all, there were still fifty-nine games to play. And, as it would turn out, the standings would have more ups and downs than a see-saw on a kindergarten playground.

If the game wasn't critical to the Red Sox, it was certainly important. They had come home from Cleveland only one-half game out of first place. They had had hopes of using the home stand to vault into the lead. Now they were in danger of leaving town with a losing record for the stay and falling three games out of first. A win in this wrapup was very important psychologically.

Mike Andrews was a player who took games one at a time. He was a distance runner, not a sprinter. He recalls of his school days, "Lots of guys had better numbers than I had. I might hit a couple of home runs while someone else had 15-17. But I was consistent and I always did what it took to win." Thursday's game was important to Mike Andrews. Every game was important to the rangy second-sacker.

The pitching-poor Red Sox started twenty-four year old lefthander Bill Landis on this Thursday afternoon. Landis was to win only one game all year for Boston and August 3 would not be the one. The A's climbed all over Dick Williams' latest starter candidate, tallying three runs before they were retired in the first. The biggest damage was a two-run homer from Ken "Hawk" Harrelson. It is impossible that anyone in the ballpark could have foreseen that Hawk would end up playing right field for the Red Sox before the year came to a close. There was very little about 1967 that anyone could have foreseen.

Mike Andrews was the leadoff hitter as his team set about to work their way out of a three-run hole. Throughout his career, he was always one to make things happen. "I was always ready to throw my body at a ground ball or drop down a surprise bunt. I concentrated as hard as I could on every play," recalls Mike.

Make things happen he did as he sent a Jim "Catfish" Hunter fastball in the direction of the Green Monster in left. Andrews thought double as soon as he took off down the first base line. To this day, he can't remember if first base coach Bobby Doerr waved him on to second or not. Green light or not, Mike was going to get things going. The weak-armed Danny Cater in left field for the A's threw the sliding Andrews out by ten feet at second base.

It can be a long way from second base to the home team dugout if you've just run your team out of a rally and Dick Williams is there waiting for you. When asked if Williams had a nice sense of humor about base running blunders, Andrews responds, "Dick didn't have a sense of humor about anything that went on around the ballpark. He had a great sense of humor away from the park but he was deadly serious about everything to do with the game. You didn't want to make him mad."

If Andrews was a little bit down as he headed out to his second base position, it certainly wasn't the low spot of his professional baseball career. That might have come in Olean, New York, in his rookie year when he made seventy errors. Sometimes he even wondered why they kept him. Or it might have been the following year when he was demoted in mid-season from the Winston-Salem ballclub. The front office told him that Winston--Salem was a bad ballclub and they didn't want him in that environment. The nineteen-year-old Andrews wasn't too sure he believed that.

The home team squeaked in a run against Hunter in the bottom of the second and Dick Williams summoned Dave Morehead in from the bullpen with instructions to keep it close. Morehead was another in a long-line of high potential, low achievement Red Sox pitchers. For some reason, the franchise has always produced hitters but has failed to develop pitchers. The left field wall contributes to the problem but to single that out as **the** reason is a cop-out. The Mel Parnells and the '67 Lonborg were the exceptions and the Tommy Brewers, Willard Nixons, Frank Baumanns and Mickey McDermotts were the rule.

And Dave Morehead. Morehead was a southern Californian like Mike Andrews and he was gifted with a great right arm. Two months younger than Andrews, he had actually broken in with the Red Sox four years earlier as a nineteen-year old. Morehead won ten games as a rookie and displayed great promise. He fell off to eight wins in 1964 but he was still young and he was pitching for a poor ball club. Then in 1965 it all came together for him on one day. Pitching against the Cleveland Indians on September 16 -- just eleven days following his twenty-second birthday -- Morehead pitched a no-hitter. His was the first no-hitter pitched in the American League in over three years. The last American League no-hitter had been pitched on August 26, 1962, by Jack Kralick of the Minnesota Twins.

Although he had only matched his rookie output of ten wins, the no-hitter seemed to signify the beginning of a great career. It was not to be. Plagued by arm trouble and the sizeable burden of a "can't miss" label, Dave won only one game in 1966 and began to shuttle back and forth between the parent club and their Triple-A affiliate in Toronto.

Dick Williams believed in Morehead and he had recently recalled him from exile in Toronto. He had started the first game of the Kansas City doubleheader on August 1 and he had been horrible. But Williams had a hunch that Morehead would hold the A's this time and Dick always went with his hunches.

Looking in from second base, Andrews saw a more confident Dave Morehead this time out. Mike was able to make a nice running catch of a Danny Cater fly into right field to help the cause. Andrews had played with Morehead in Toronto in 1966 and he wanted to see him come back.

Andrews worked Hunter for a walk in the third inning. Perhaps the A's were beginning to see him as a long ball threat? Andrews didn't come around to score but the Red Sox managed to put another run on the board. The A's lead had been cut to 3-2.

In many ways, it was a surprise that Andrews was out there at second base at all. He had grown up a mile from the Pacific Ocean and had spent as much time at the beach as he could. In his formative baseball years -- ages sixteen and seventeen -- surfing had just become the rage and the Beach Boys were singing their song. While Andrews toiled on the diamond, most of his buddies were "hanging ten".

Even more to the point, Mike was more highly touted as a football player than for his baseball prowess. A sure-handed pass catcher, he was headed for UCLA on a football scholarship. He played football at El Camino Junior College as a kind of warmup for his big time debut. Actually, he almost took a detour. He was spotted by Paul Brown, the legendary coach of the Cleveland Browns, who urged him to go to Arizona State since their style was more attuned to the pros.

From time to time, as he toiled in the Red Sox farm system, Andrews would ponder the road not taken. Red Sox scout Joe Stephenson -- father of Red Sox teammate Jerry Stephenson -- had convinced him to sign a pro contract at age eighteen holding out the lure of being the Red Sox shortstop of the future. Each year, as he looked at the depth chart with Rico Petrocelli slotted one level above him, Andrews would grow discouraged. Since Rico was only twelve days his senior it didn't seem likely that Mike would outlast him.

Morehead continued to pitch well, holding the A's in check during the fourth inning. Catfish Hunter seemed to be settling down as well. The future Hall-of-Famer was still a few years away from being the toughest pitcher in baseball, but he was good enough to hold the Red Sox scoreless in the last of the fourth inning. Morehead matched his zero in the top of the fifth and as the game reached its halfway point it had evolved into a tight, one-run ball game.

Switching positions was probably the best option for Andrews as he tried to climb the ladder to "the show". But third base was not a natural position for him and if he made it as a 6' 3" big league second baseman, it would be as the tallest regular second baseman in major league history. It seemed like kind of a long shot. The traditional second baseman was a 5' 10" Nellie Fox or 5' 9" Bobby Richardson and baseball decision makers are traditionalists of the highest order.

If the Red Sox were to salvage the home stand they had to make their move and fast. Hunter was the ace of the A's staff and Jack Aker was no slouch coming out of their bullpen. The previous year Aker had made sixty-six appearances and compiled a sparkling ERA of 1.99. If Hunter could hold the foes at bay for two or three more innings, the Red Sox could be in real trouble.

Hunter continued his mastery over the Red Sox in the last of the fifth. When Petrocelli was retired to end the inning, Hunter had to feel good knowing that the seventh, eighth and ninth hitters would be coming up in the last of the sixth inning.

Morehead had held the A's hitless during his first three innings but he faded a little as the hitters got their second look at him. Mike Hershberger got to him first with a double to right that gave Tony Conigliaro a lot of trouble. Third baseman Dick Green sent a groan through the crowd when he singled sharply into left field. The third base coach waved him on and it looked as if the Red Sox were to go down by two.

But this was the year of the Yaz and he rose to one more occasion. Hershberger had good speed but Carl charged the ball and let it fly. It was another perfect strike from Yastrzemski and when catcher Mike Ryan put on the tag, the Red Sox were out of the inning unharmed.

The Red Sox were down to twelve outs and they had the bottom third of the order coming up. Time for more magic.

Center fielder George Thomas, playing in place of Reggie Smith, who had jammed his thumb up against the center field wall the day before, led off the sixth. Thomas was one of the genuinely funny men in baseball. Andrews remembers that he was a good man to have around to offset Dick Williams' stern demeanor. George was also versatile: he could handle almost any position including catcher. In spring training when pressed to name the starters on opening day, Williams had replied, "George Thomas" for all nine positions.

Thomas could also run some and he got things going by beating out a grounder down the third base line. Catcher Mike Ryan was up next. Ryan was a local boy from Haverhill, Massachusetts. Mike was good with the glove but weak with the bat. In 1967, he finished up with a .199 batting average.

Ryan did the sensible thing and dropped a bunt down the third base line. Hunter pounced on the ball and threw down to second to keep the tying run out of scoring position. Unfortunately for the A's, but fortunately for the Red Sox, his throw pulled shortstop Bert Campaneris off the bag and both runners were safe.

Now Dick Williams had to make a decision that American League managers don't have to make any more in these days of the designated hitter. Should he let Morehead hit for himself or send a pinch hitter up to the plate? Sparky Lyle and John Wyatt were warm in the bullpen. The situation screamed for a bunt and Williams elected to have Morehead execute it. This also showed Dave that his manager thought he had some more innings left in him.

Morehead did his job perfectly, laying a soft bunt down the third base line. The Red Sox had the tying run on third and the lead run on second.

Now A's manager, Alvin Dark had a decision to make. The former star of the Braves and New York Giants could walk Andrews and set up a force at any base. Or he could take his chances against the .268 hitter. Dark elected to take his chances.

Dark had his reasons for the choice but it was a little bit insulting to Andrews. He dug in a little deeper, determined to make things happen.

Catfish got a one strike edge on his first pitch, a nasty slider. He came back with the same pitch and Mike was in an 0-2 hole: a bad place for a hitter to be. Andrews shortened up on the bat as Bobby Doerr had taught him, to protect the plate.

Catfish got a little too cute with his next pitch and Andrews leaped on it. He lined it cleanly into left field setting both runners in motion. Thomas scored easily to tie it and Ryan steamed around third to put the Red Sox into the lead. Ryan was no speedster but Cater's throw was off the mark and the Red Sox were up 4-3.

Standing happily on first, Andrews must have felt a long way from Waterloo, Iowa. Playing there for the Red Sox farm team, he had broken his ankle landing on first base in the next to the last game of the season. Andrews can still remember the sight of the bone sticking through his sanitary hose. The fans felt so badly they took up a collection and gave him $130. The nasty bump on his left ankle is a lasting reminder of Waterloo, Iowa.

Alvin Dark had seen enough of Hunter and brought Aker in to relieve him. He put out the fire and the inning ended with the Red Sox ahead by one run.

Morehead continued to hold the A's at bay. When he retired the side in the seventh, he had given up only three hits and had shut out the A's in his five inning stint. The fans gave him a nice hand as they rose for the traditional seventh inning stretch.

The "lucky seventh" was of no help to the Red Sox and they took their position in the field nursing a one-run lead. The big questions was: how much longer could Morehead continue his mastery?

That question was answered quickly as Campaneris opened the inning with a double off the left field wall. The ball was still in the air when Williams left the dugout to summon the left-handed Al "Sparky" Lyle from the bullpen. Morehead had given everything that could be expected of him and he had earned the standing ovation from the 18,920 patrons gathered at Fenway.

Sparky, who would go on to fame and some fortune with the hated Yankees, had been brought in specifically to retire the left-handed Ted Kubiak. Kubiak showed bunt all the way and Lyle gave him heat inside. Down two strikes to Lyle he finally grounded to Rico at short and Lyle's day at the office was over.

Williams semaphored to the bullpen for his right-handed relief ace, John Wyatt, to take the mound and face the right-handed Cater. Wyatt may well be the unsung hero of the '67 Red Sox. They had picked him up during the '66 season after spending almost six years with the noncontending A's. Not only did the Red Sox rescue Wyatt from oblivion, they probably saved him from having his arm blown out. Kansas City had used him in eighty-one games in 1964.

In 1967 Wyatt had a direct impact on thirty of the Red Sox ninety-two victories: ten wins and twenty saves. Of course, the Red Sox starting rotation consisted of Jim Lonborg and whichever three starters were currently hot and not in Dick Williams' dog house. That insured Wyatt of a lot of work. He appeared in a total of sixty games that year for Boston, all of them in relief. Wyatt's victory total placed him fourth on the Red Sox staff in that category, an unusual distinction for a reliever.

Wyatt was not on the mound for very long before Campaneris had easily stolen third base. The Red Sox infield edged toward the inner grass of the diamond to position themselves to cut off the tying run at the plate. Cater hit a ground ball to Rico's right and Petrocelli was up and firing to Mike Ryan covering the plate. Rico's hurried throw sailed towards the first base line but Ryan gloved it and applied a sweep tag to Campaneris all in one motion. Campaneris was out by an eyelash and the Red Sox' one-run lead was preserved.

A one-run lead is never safe in Fenway. The eccentric dimensions invite offensive mischief and in August, the prevailing winds are towards the inviting left field wall. To a man, the Red Sox dugout was hoping for a cushion to hold their lead.

John Wyatt made the first out of the eighth inning. Dick Williams was going to go all the way with his bullpen stopper. Mike Andrews stepped to the plate with the bases empty to face A's starter/reliever, Lew Krausse. Krausse was a solid journeyman pitcher who was to spend twelve years in the major leagues with five teams. He was also from solid baseball stock: his father had pitched for the **Philadelphia** Athletics in the early '30s.

Andrews was anxious to make something happen, to get something going. He turned on a Krausse pitch and drove it strongly towards left. Mike went down the line with the same all out intensity as he had on his ball that struck the wall in the first inning. This time he could relax; the ball had landed in the left field net to open the Red Sox' lead to two.

Wags in the pressbox calculated that Andrews, with his home-run-a-day pace started the previous day, would tie Roger Maris' season home run record on September 23 and pass him on September 24 against Baltimore. Andrews wasn't thinking about his home run pace. His focus was always on winning and doing whatever it took to achieve that end.

Andrews felt comfortable at his position as he set himself near second base. It had taken him some time after years of playing shortstop. He had worked hard at his new position in Toronto and Bobby Doerr had been a great help in Boston. His one disappointment at the position had come in spring training in 1966 when he had been promised a shot that never materialized. He confronted then manager, Billy Herman, who replied, "I pushed for the trade (with Detroit) to get George Smith to play second and I'm going to make sure it works."

Wyatt retired the first two Kansas City batters without a problem but gave the crowd a little excitement by giving up a double to ex-Red Soxer, Jim Gosger. When Wyatt bore down to force a groundout the Red Sox had salvaged the home stand 7-6 and kept their winning attitude alive. When they arrived in Minnesota the next day to start their road trip, they would be in second place, only two games behind the Chicago White Sox.

Andrews had put together quite a day: three hits, one home run and three RBIs, including the game winner. But Andrews was never the lead in the game story. Although he rated the headline ("Red Sox Come From Behind Again, Topple A's, 5-3, on Andrew Hit", *Boston Globe*, August 4, 1967), his only quote was on his base running blunder in the first inning. His words to Cliff Keane of the *Boston Globe*? "That was awful."

It was truly an outstanding day for Andrews but he was the type to look ahead to the next series with Minnesota. Twenty-five years later he is hard-pressed to remember even one detail about August 3, 1967.

Andrews went on to provide the Red Sox with leadership for the balance of 1967. He is still slightly distressed that he didn't start the first two World Series games at Fenway Park after doing the job all year. But in typical, generous fashion, he counters, "I'm glad that Jerry Adair got his chance to see if he could make a contribution."

Andrews returned to his native California after that season. His objective was to get a job to make some money and to stay in shape. When his teammates who had remained in the Boston area convinced him that New Englanders couldn't get enough of the 1967 Boston Red Sox, he packed his young family in their car and headed back east. Peabody, Massachusetts, has been home ever since.

Mike played a total of four full seasons for the Boston Red Sox. His best year was probably 1969 when he batted .293, swatted fifteen home runs and made the American League All Star team. But the highest the Red Sox finished over the next three years was third place.

Andrews would have been very content to play his entire career in Boston. It was his home, his family loved the area, and he had a great rapport with the fans. Baseball generally doesn't cooperate in these matters, however.

After the 1970 season came to an end, a hot rumor circulated in Boston and in Chicago that Andrews was going to be traded for the White Sox' outstanding short stop, Luis Aparicio. When the rumor reached its height, Red Sox General Manager, Dick O'Connell, denied it saying Mike wasn't going anywhere. Andrews should have known that was the kiss of death. Days later, a few weeks before Christmas, Andrews was playing cards with a buddy when a bulletin came over the radio station they were listening to. He friend asked, "Did you hear what I just heard?" Mike would get new Sox for Christmas and they would be White.

Andrews put together a couple of good seasons in Chicago. He found easy-going Chuck Tanner to be a welcome antidote to the hard-nosed Dick Williams. He still wondered, though, if Williams didn't get a tad bit more out of him with his constant needling.

Andrews hit .282 for the White Sox in 1971 as the club finished third in the Western Division. Mike had a tough year in 1972, personally batting only .220 and being troubled all year by the wrist he had broken at the end of the '71 season. Always the team man though, Andrews remembers '72 as the year the White Sox, with the help of a rejuvenated Dick Allen's thirty-seven homers and 113 RBIs, gave the Oakland A's a run for their money.

Andrews began the 1973 season in Chicago but the front office was in chaos. More than halfway through the season, Andrews still hadn't been signed to a new contract for the season. He went to Rollie Hemondd in the front office and told him that he couldn't continue to play under those conditions. The White Sox obliged him with his outright release.

Free to sign with any major league team as the pennant races took shape, Mike contacted Dick Williams to get his advice. Williams allowed as how the division-leading A's could use him as a utility infielder and Andrews began a brief but eventful career in Oakland.

Oakland was on their way to their third straight division title and they were the defending World Champions having defeated the Cincinnati Reds four games to three the previous year. Andrews didn't play much -- only eighteen games -- but he enjoyed the winning environment and he was pleased to find himself in the World Series against the New York Mets.

Quite unexpectedly, Andrews found himself in the national spotlight in game two. Mike was playing second base in the top of the twelfth inning with the score tied at six all. The Mets' John Melner hit a ball right at him. Unfortunately, the ball hit something, skidded through his legs, and two Mets runners came on to score. Jerry Grote, the Mets catcher, was next up and he also hit a ball directly at him. Mike fielded it cleanly but the replay shows clearly that first baseman, Gene Tenace, better known as a catcher, got his feet tangled and mishandled Andrew's throw. Unfortunately, the scorer gave Andrews his second error and the Mets were four runs up.

A's owner, Charlie Finley, went into one of his classic tantrums. He insisted that Andrews be placed on the disabled list and replaced by second baseman, Manny Trillo. Finley browbeat Andrews into signing a form saying that he was hurt and according to Dick Williams in his book, *No More Mr. Nice Guy*, both Andrews and Williams ended up in tears.

Ultimately, Commissioner Bowie Kuhn intervened to have Andrews reinstated.

He was vindicated, when, pinch-hitting in game four at Shea Stadium, 55,000 Mets fans rose to give him a standing ovation. A partial winner's share in the World Series split didn't hurt either as Oakland defeated the Mets four games to three. But Mike Andrews would never play major league baseball again.

Andrews attempted to get a "look see" from some major league team in 1974 but there were no takers. Even the San Diego Padres who had finished forty-two games off of the pace declined to give him a shot.

He was convinced that he had some more baseball left in him even if it meant packing up his young family and moving to Japan. Move to Japan for nine months they did and Andrews finished his career not being able to read about his team in the sports pages. His strongest memory of his time in Japan is what an adventure it was for his family.

Back in the U.S., Mike thought briefly of returning to Japan for one more season. His wife, Marilyn, his teenage sweetheart, replied, "If you go back, you'll go back without me." That was the end of that idea and the end of baseball for Andrews.

At that point, Andrews did what, in his words, all former ballplayers are duty-bound to do. "I tried my hand at broadcasting and I sold life insurance." Mike did well enough selling life insurance that he ended up working for five years for Mass Mutual.

In 1979 Ken Coleman, one of the great sports announcers of his generation, was part-time executive director of the Jimmy Fund. The Jimmy Fund has raised many millions of dollars to help find a cure for cancer in children and has enjoyed a long--standing relationship with the Red Sox. Ken asked Andrews to work part-time for the Jimmy Fund and Mike agreed. Shortly afterwards, Coleman accepted an offer to broadcast the Red Sox games and Andrews succeeded him as Executive Director.

In this capacity, Mike is charged with raising the money needed to continue this critically important fight. The results to date in the treatment of cancer in children have been tremendous and the need to continue the battle is essential. The good works achieved by his efforts are readily identifiable and a source of great satisfaction to Andrews.

Mike says it best, "I had a great career in baseball. I'm proud of making the All Star team and I treasure my memories of the '67 season. But the sense of accomplishment I get from this job far exceeds anything I got from baseball."

Would that all former ballplayers could say the same thing about their current positions.

CHAPTER SIX

Boston Red Sox vs. California Angels

Friday, August 18, 1967

Anthony Richard "Tony" Conigliaro. Born in Boston. Lived in Boston. Died in Boston. In many ways, Tony was the ultimate extension of all Red Sox fans. For nearly his entire life he lived within ten miles of Fenway Park. He grew up a Red Sox fan. Two years after graduating from St. Mary's High School in nearby Lynn, Massachusetts, he was starting in center field for his home team. He had his glory years in a Red Sox uniform. For the last eight years of his life, he was always referred to as "the former Red Sox star." Tony Conigliaro had everything going for him when he stepped to the plate that Friday night before a full house at Fenway Park to face Angels' pitcher Jack Hamilton. Only twenty-two years old. Tall, dark and handsome. Sparkling brown eyes brought the girls running. And he could even sing to them in a fine baritone voice. In his fourth successful season with the Red Sox and clearly on a career track to baseball stardom and the Hall of Fame, Tony C. already had a single off the fastball hurler and was looking for another hit when he came up in the fourth inning behind George Scott and Reggie Smith. Within moments, Hamilton's first pitched ball had rocketed like a spherical missile into Tony's left cheek, shattering it and sending shock waves reverberating within his skull. The Red Sox' rightfielder whirled about and went down on his face like he had been poleaxed. "It was a fastball that got away," Hamilton said later. Many wondered whether the Angel pitcher deliberately tried to hit the Boston slugger. Dick Williams had complained to the umpires early in the game about Hamilton's spitballs. As for Tony, who would never play again for the "Impossible Dream"

team, he graciously concluded that Hamilton didn't "have any good reason to go after me."

After their 5-3 win over the Kansas City A's on August 3, the Red Sox headed immediately to St. Paul-Minneapolis for a three-game series with the Twins. Although they were disappointed with their 7-6 homestand which had begun with such promise, they were still well positioned in second place, only two games back.

The upcoming nine-game road trip represented another important test. They would cover a lot of miles -- Minnesota to Kansas to California and then back home to face Detroit -- and two of the three of the opponents would be contenders. They hoped to bag five wins and felt they needed at least three to even stay close.

The three-game series against Minnesota was a rude awakening. By the time they left town, they knew just how strong the Twins were.

About the only thing that went right in the opener was the arrival of veteran catcher Elston Howard who had been picked up from the Yankees. Left-hander Jim Merritt shut them out limiting them to just five hits in the 3-0 loss.

The Red Sox got excellent pitching from Lee Stange in game two, but Dave Boswell was even tougher for the Twins. Tony Conigliaro lost a ball in the sun in the first inning resulting in a Twin double and subsequent run. Zoilo Versalles' home run in the third proved to be the margin of victory as the Twins came out on top 2-1.

The Red Sox offense hit a new low on Sunday as Dean Chance shut them down with five innings of perfection. Lonborg pitched well, but not perfectly. When the rains came, Chance's name went into the record books with an asterisk and a 2-0 perfect game.

The Red Sox bats had nowhere to go but up, but they still couldn't come up with a win. In the first game of a doubleheader against Kansas City on Tuesday, Dave Morehead lasted only four and one third innings and Boston lost their fourth straight, 5-3.

By game two of the doubleheader, Dick Williams felt that he had seen enough. Joe Foy was pulled at third in favor of Jerry Adair, Reggie Smith was sat down, Yastrzemski moved over to center and Norm Siebern was inserted in left field. For six innings, it looked as if all of this activity was for naught. Gary Bell had been shelled and the Red Sox were down 4-1 at this point.

In the seventh, the Red Sox bats came to life. They finally caught up with Kansas City pitcher Johnny Lee "Blue Moon" Odom and pushed across three runs. This uprising was led by Tony C.'s double which tied the game 4-4.

The Red Sox put it away in the ninth. The key hit was delivered by Norm Siebern with the bases loaded; another Williams' hunch had paid off. Bucky Brandon got the 7-5 win in relief.

The Red Sox showed signs of returning to life in the rubber game of the three game series with Kansas City. Jim Lonborg interrupted two weeks of active duty with the Army Reserves to fly in from Atlanta to pitch a 5-1 victory. Jerry Adair paced the offense with three hits and the Boston pennant express appeared to be back on track.

Another derailing took place in Anaheim, California, over the next weekend. The Red Sox got excellent pitching on Friday night from Lee Stange, but just could not mount any run production. Boston managed only three hits and George Scott was benched by Williams for being over his weight limit.

On Saturday, Scott was still in the steambath and the Red Sox bats were still in the deep freeze. Gary Bell pitched well and managed to hold California to two runs. But Boston produced only one run and dropped their sixth game out of eight on the road. Now the Angels were nipping at their heels, trailing the slumping Red Sox by one percentage point.

Sunday was more of the same. Even Lonborg couldn't save the day. California prevailed 3-2 as the Red Sox saved their only runs until their last at bat.

The Red Sox had a 3,000-mile airplane ride to ponder their fate. As they returned to Boston, there was some evidence that they had "peaked". Two out of nine on a road trip was not pennant contending ball. To make matters worse, they had managed only a total of seven runs in the seven losses.

Detroit came into Fenway to kick off a twelve-game home stand with a three game series. Dave Morehead carried the evening for Boston in the series opener. Pitching his first complete game since his September 16, 1965, no-hitter, Morehead shut out the Tigers 4-0. George Scott celebrated his return to the lineup by launching a first inning "tater" while Yaz and Smith added four baggers of their own.

The Wednesday night game against the Tigers attracted 32,501 to Fenway. George Scott used his newly-svelte body to power two home runs and Boston never looked back in an 8-3 trouncing of the Tigers. Bucky Brandon pitched seven shutout innings in relief and picked up the win.

A crowd of 28,653 was thinking "sweep" on Thursday as the game moved into the tenth, tied at four. But Sparky Lyle gave up three runs in the tenth and the Red Sox fell, 7-4. Still, two out of three from the Tigers wasn't bad, and with nine games remaining in the home stand, the Red Sox were only three and a half games behind the league-leading White Sox.

Tony Conigliaro laughed a bit to himself as he watched his close pal George Scott try to stretch a single into a double as the first man up in the fourth inning. George could stroke the ball but he was no track star when it came to running the bases. It was inevitable that George was nailed at second.

Tony knew that George liked to talk to his bats before he decided which one to take up to the plate. Sometimes he'd do it for an hour or more, endlessly asking, "You got any hits in you? You got a hit? You got a big hit for me tonight?" Obviously, George's bat in the fourth had a hit for him but not the double he had hoped for. He figured Dick Williams undoubtedly would get all over George for not holding up at first. If there were any two players on the club that Williams disliked, Tony knew he and Scotty were numbers one and two.

He put George and the manager out of his mind and swung several of his own bats as centerfielder Reggie Smith started for the plate. He shouted his encouragement. It was a sell-out crowd that night. Be great to get another hit or two in front of them, especially where his parents and two brothers, Billy and Richie, were among them.

The Red Sox were going for the pennant. And everybody knew it now in the middle of August. Tony reflected on the fact that he had been only one year old back in 1946 when Boston had won its last league pennant. As a lifelong fan himself, he knew personally the frustrations that the Red Sox loyalists felt. The fans were coming out in droves. Only the day before, the Red Sox had a crowd of 28,653 to put them over the one million mark in attendance for the first time in seven years. Not since Teddy Ballgame had hung 'em up in 1960 had they gone over the magic million mark.

Reggie hadn't even gotten to the plate when an idiot fan tossed a smoke bomb into left field. Reggie and Tony looked at each other and shook their heads while the crowd shouted in a mixture of irritation and good humor. Even though Tony himself had been sitting up in those very same stands just five short years earlier, he was constantly amazed by the antics of the Fenway crowds.

Still, it was ten minutes before the black smoke -- which turned slowly to white as it hovered above the ground -- completely dissipated. As he waited, Tony didn't consider it an evil omen, a sign of impending tragedy. Like he said, he wasn't superstitious then, but afterwards he began to wonder whether it had been some kind of spectral message for him.

Finally, all traces of the smoke had blown away and the game was resumed with Reggie at the plate to face the battery of pitcher Jack Hamilton and catcher Bob Rodgers. Rodgers gave

Hamilton the sign and the pitcher hurled the ball. Reggie came around quickly and whacked the ball deep into far center where it was caught easily by Jose Cardenal.

There were two outs when Tony came to the plate. Since he had singled off a curve ball his first time up, he took his stance in the right-handed batter's box expecting a fastball. Ever the scrapper, who determined in his early childhood that he would never back off from anyone or anything, he dug in to try and smash the first pitch out into center field.

If Tony had a trademark, it was his aggressiveness. He stood in the batter's box crowding the plate as if he owned it. He seemed to almost dare the pitcher to throw it inside knowing that if the pitch was off by even a fraction of an inch, he could turn on it and drive it into the inviting left field screen.

Later Tony would note that "Hamilton was a hard thrower who was frequently accused of throwing spitballs, or greaseballs, or whatever you want to call them. The point is his ball broke in a funny way like no breaking pitch is supposed to break. He has been known to throw at hitters."

As he set himself in the batter's box, Tony was very much aware that the visiting Angels were a serious contender in the hunt for the pennant. In a five-team race anything can happen. He knew that California needed a good showing in this series in order to keep their own hopes alive and that they would look for every edge.

Tony, alert as a rousted rabbit, wondered whether the ten minute delay had caused Hamilton's arm to stiffen up. He'd find out in a moment. Hamilton reared up and whipped a fastball toward the plate. It zoomed across the intervening space right toward Tony's head.

The youthful batter had always figured with his lion's heart that he would always instinctively know when to pull back and duck any ball by a fraction, no matter how hard it was thrown -- even if directly at him.

Tony did duck as he saw the ball headed for his chin. Still the ball as though radio-directed and fixed on his head came right at him. "It seemed to follow me in," he'd say later. "I know I didn't freeze, I made a move to get out of the way." As he threw up his hands to protect himself and began to turn away to his right, his helmet flew off.

Tony never went to the plate thinking he was going to get hit or beaned. But he realized then that there was no way he was going to escape the impact of Hamilton's pitched ball. The ball was only four feet from his head when he knew it was going to get him. Simultaneously, he knew it was going to hurt like hell because Hamilton had tossed it with enormous force.

Thousands of the fans to this day and all the players on both teams can recall the wicked cracking sound the ball made when it crashed full force into Tony's left cheekbone and ricocheted directly downward to bounce off home plate. A huge audible groan, mingled with female shrieks of dismay and disbelief, echoed about the park. This was followed by the eerie silence that can only be produced by the sound of 33,000 people standing totally still in shock.

Tony admitted later that he was "frightened. I threw my hands up in front of my face and saw the ball follow me back . . ." The ball crunched into his cheek just below the left eye socket.

When the ball struck him, Tony's legs collapsed and he continued to twist to his right as he hurtled toward the ground. "It felt as if the ball would go into my head and come out the other side . . . I went down like a sack of potatoes. Just before everything went dark I saw the ball bounce straight down on home plate."

Prostrate on the playing field but still conscious, Tony had lost sight temporarily in both eyes. As his teammates rushed toward him, led by Williams, Rico Petrocelli and Mike Ryan, his best friend and roommate on the road, the rightfielder laid without moving. The idea crossed many minds that he was dead.

Rico knelt and gently shook his shoulders. "Tony, Tony, are you all right? It's okay. You're gonna be okay." More Red Sox gathered. The club trainer, Buddy LeRoux, rolled Tony over.

When he didn't move, they all began to fear the worst. Rico almost got sick looking at his crushed cheek and swollen shut eye.

A call went out for a stretcher. Just then Tony stirred and kicked his feet in the dirt. Out on the mound, Jack Hamilton, his arms folded, stood motionlessly as he was roundly booed by the hometown fans. He was convinced that he hadn't thrown at Tony. He also knew that according to baseball etiquette, he would not be welcome at home plate. That is the unwritten code.

Tony would contend that he "was never knocked out by the impact of the Angel pitcher's fastball." He admitted though that he wished he had been because of the pain. The blow from the baseball within minutes had sealed both eyes shut and turned them a reddish blue color. Blood streamed from his nose.

Tony began to roll around on the ground to try to stop the pain. He also had a huge swelling in his mouth that was fast filling up with fluids. Besides thinking he was blind and never going to see, he was convinced that the mass in his mouth was going to close up and keep him from breathing.

"I won't be able to breathe," he thought. "If this thing closes up on me, I'm gone." He said that it was at that point that he began to pray to God to keep him alive. In his mind, God could have taken him right then and there, if He wanted to. It was like a showdown between them: God would make the choice. Hopefully it would be in his favor although he never had been much of a true believer. He had mostly gone to his Roman Catholic Church out of a habit drilled into him as a boy growing up in Revere and Swampscott, Massachusetts.

Tony was rushed on the stretcher into the clubhouse where LeRoux placed an ice pack against his head. Dr. Thomas M. Tierney, the team's physician, was in the stands when Tony went down and hurried to his side in the clubhouse. The physician was an old friend of the Conigliaro family but had no time then for small talk. He ordered an ambulance to be called and began testing Tony's blood pressure and reflexes.

The clubhouse was full of people, including Tony's father and two brothers, but to the young player "the room was deathly still."

He remembered that several players came by to squeeze his arm and whisper encouragement. Coaches popped in and out. All were very reassuring. Strangely, Dick Williams "never came back," Tony would recall later, "and that's always bothered me. Maybe he was too busy at the time . . ." in managing the team to a 3-2 win over the Angels.

Tony was rushed by ambulance to Sancta Maria Hospital in Cambridge where he was examined by Dr. Joseph Dorsey, a neurosurgeon. The doctor would say later that Tony had suffered a fractured cheekbone, a scalp contusion and that it was too soon to determine the extent of the injury to his left eye. He acknowledged that Tony might have been killed if the ball had hit him an inch higher.

The Angels' battery stuck to their position that Hamilton had not thrown at Tony. "I've not struck anyone all year, " the pitcher noted. "I certainly wasn't throwing at him. I was just trying to get the ball over the plate. Tony tends to hang over the plate as much as anyone in the league."

Similarly, Angel catcher Rodgers contended that the pitch "was about eight inches inside. It took off when it got near Tony. It was a fastball and it just sailed." When a fastball is thrown at a velocity approaching 100 miles per hour, it can develop a mind of its own.

Bobby Doerr, a one-time Red Sox second baseman, Hall-of-Famer and then a coach under Williams, wrote in his diary then, "There was a real ironic, almost strange thing about the game tonight, especially in the light of Tony's injury, which looks like it's serious. Jack Hamilton has been accused all during the season by a lot of people of throwing spitters. Well, in the first part of the game tonight, Dick Williams complained to the umpires of this. Dick also voiced a protest early on (maybe the second inning) that we all thought Hamilton was throwing spitters. The ball was acting strangely. Dick said that he was afraid someone would get hurt. Unfortunately, he was right."

Part of the beauty and appeal of baseball is its continuity. Even if one team is trailing 14-2 in the ninth inning, each hitter strives for success and the opposing pitcher works diligently to frustrate the hitter's efforts. On the last day of the season when two opponents have long since been eliminated from the race, they both show up and go about the business of securing victory.

In the case of the August 18 Red Sox-Angels contest, the continuity was almost too much to bear. Every person in the park had a part of his mind on the game and a part remembering the sight of Tony sprawled lifelessly at home plate. Somehow Tony's close friend, Rico Petrocelli, who had been on deck at the time of the dreadful beaning, found the concentration to drill a base hit off the rattled Hamilton. Somehow the Red Sox were able to dig down deep and put together two runs in that fateful fourth inning. The close of that inning will be forever recorded as 2-0 Boston. Jose Tartabull took Tony's place at first base and scored what proved to be a very important run.

The game lasted for nearly an hour and one-half after Tony's tragedy. Almost incredibly it featured near flawless baseball and intense pressure. If anyone ever doubted the professionalism of major league ballplayers, this game was the proof. The Red Sox got up 3-0 after six innings and hung tough for a 3-2 victory. Gary Bell pitched a gutsy four-hitter and helped his own cause with two hits and an RBI. Such is the continuity of baseball.

Gary Bell recalls how difficult it was to focus on the game that evening. "All I could think of was the terrible sound of the ball when it hit Tony. We weren't really sure how he was doing and it was difficult to put the incident out of our minds. But we were in the middle of a pennant race and concentrating on the game was our only way to cope with Tony's misfortune."

Jack Hamilton was taken out for a pinch hitter after five innings and took the loss. The official scorebook shows that he gave up four hits, two runs -- both of them earned -- struck out five batters, walked one man and hit one batter.

No matter what some people might think about his pitch, Jack Hamilton demonstrated his class by being among the first arrivals at the hospital in the morning to try and visit Tony. Except for his family, Tom Yawkey and Mike Ryan who sneaked in, Tony was forbidden visitors but was apprised that Hamilton had attempted to see him.

Tony was a big fan of Yawkey and was surprised when he was awoken the next morning by a voice saying, "Wake up, Tony. It's me, Tom Yawkey." The Red Sox owner had always been kind and patient with his young outfielder and often listened to his personal problems. "Now as busy as he was, he was sitting in my room, holding my hand, and telling me not to worry about anything."

After a few days in the hospital, Tony's head pain began to subside and he began to see out of his right eye. Still he was confined mostly to his bed and could do little but think about his situation. Once he realized that he wasn't going to die and that he was out of danger, he began to think about how he was hit.

Tony kept asking himself whether Jack Hamilton had intended to hit him. It didn't figure. "I had been in a slump going into the series with the Angels. Pitchers usually don't stir up guys who are in a hitting slump. If I had been hot at the bat, I could see where he might."

Tony decided to give Hamilton the benefit of the doubt even though he knew the pitcher had a tendency to hit players occasionally. "I figured he had no good reason to go after me." Ultimately, he figured, only one person in the world knew whether Hamilton was trying to hit him that night and that person was Jack Hamilton.

One of the things that bothered Tony the most during his weeks in the hospital was the fact that he never heard from Dick Williams at any time. "He never came up to the hospital and he never dropped me a line or anything." This particularly upset Tony because he felt he had made a contribution to the team's "Impossible Dream" drive to the pennant and had given Williams everything he had. "I had been hit in the face by a baseball and nearly lost my life. I felt the least Dick could do was show he knew I existed."

In his heart, Tony acknowledged that he and Williams had never hit it off from the time they first met in 1964. Tony was a rookie then, only nineteen, trying to make the Red Sox club after one year in the minors at Wellsville, New York, and Williams was a thirty-four-year-old utility player trying to save his pro career. Williams called Tony "Bush" in the condescending manner of the veteran.

Quick to fly off the handle and ready to fight anyone, Tony never forgot the ball that Williams threw at him as he came out of the dugout during his first spring training with the Red Sox in Scottsdale, Arizona. The very next day, Tony retaliated by brushing off Williams with a thrown ball as he came up from the dugout. When he picked himself up and wiped away the dust, the enraged Williams came after Tony, but was warned off by Dick Stuart. "We just never hit it off after that incident," Tony recalled afterwards.

Neither Tony nor Williams realized it but they had a lot of personality traits in common. Both had a confidence level that was on the cusp of arrogance. Neither of them would back down from anyone. Tony was once shown a video of himself being interviewed after hitting a homer as a new rookie in Yankee Stadium. When asked what pitch he had hit for the homer, he had replied with supreme confidence, "Oh, a spitter." When asked to critique his performance on the video, he responded, "pretty cocky."

This game against the Angels on August 18 was the last one for Tony Conigliaro in 1967. Vision problems with his left eye ruled out any possibility of his returning to the Red Sox. The blind spot in the eye just wouldn't get any better. Moreover, he still had a lot of swelling in and around the eye and he was told that "your distant vision is so bad that it might be dangerous for you to play anymore this year. You just can't be ready to play in the World Series if the Red Sox make it."

Tony, of course, was crushed by the news. He was always hopeful that the eye would improve and he'd get back with the team to make a bigger contribution to the race for the pennant. He went back to his apartment near Fenway and cried. "For the first time I realized how much I loved it all . . . I missed the games, the competition, especially now with the ball club fighting for the pennant. There was nothing else I wanted to do except play baseball."

Although he was to be out of baseball until 1969, Tony had already chalked up a commendable record in the game, beginning with 1963 when he hit .363 with Wellsville and was named MVP of the New York-Penn League.

Tony moved up to the Red Sox in 1964 at the call of manager Johnny Pesky and as a nineteen-year-old rookie, hit .290 with twenty-four home runs -- the most by a teenager in baseball history. On June 3 of that year, he hit a bases-loaded homer off Dan Osinski of the Angels to earn the distinction of being the youngest player in he majors ever to hit a grand slam.

In 1965, Tony led the American League in home runs with thirty-two; at twenty years of age, he was the youngest player ever to lead the league in four-baggers. All told, he was at bat 521 times and got 140 hits for eighty-two RBIs.

Johnny Pesky was fired as manager that year and replaced by Billy Herman, a man that Tony claimed was on "different wavelengths" than him. Tony was to say that 1965 was the year that "a lot of things happened to me that pretty much established my baseball image: I proved myself as a home-run hitter. I got myself into a lot of hot water with the baseball writers. I couldn't get along with Billy Herman."

Tony came to discover that his candid and outspoken views did not play well in the papers or in the front office. For the most part, he was a guileless local boy who spoke his mind. He never claimed that he was a rocket scientist and it took him a while to realize he was living in a fish bowl. Before he caught on he had made as many trips to general manager Dick O'Connell's office as he had made to the principal's office at St. Mary's of Lynn.

Tony managed, however, to achieve another exemplary year in 1966 by hitting .265 and rapping out twenty-eight homers. He was at bat 558 times and got 148 hits for ninety-three RBIs.

Tony's string of injuries, big and small, continued during spring training in 1967 when teammate John Wyatt, pitching batting practice, struck Tony on the arm with a fastball. The blow caused a hairline fracture and put Wyatt in the doghouse with Dick Williams who had so many players on short leashes that he needed a kennel.

While Tony seldom had a good word for Williams, he did note after the "Impossible Dream" year that the manager "did an incredible job, taking a ball club that finished ninth two years straight and managing it to a pennant. If Williams ever was likable, it was in 1967 because he was up there fighting all the time and personalities never were a factor. We were a happy club and showed up every day knowing we were going to win."

Curiously, Tony was told by his business manager, Ed Penney, that he had bumped into Ted Williams who told him to tell Tony "to stop crowding the plate. Ted said you should back up before one of those guys hits you."

Tony recalled that his only reaction was to ask Penney, "The way I'm hitting, who'd want to hit me?" Later he would remember that he had this conversation on August 18, 1967.

Until he was hit by Jack Hamilton's pitch, Tony was enjoying a twenty-homer season and batting .287. He had been up to the plate 349 times and collected an even 100 hits and sixty-seven RBIs. He was obviously a young man on his way to induction into baseball's Hall of Fame in Cooperstown, New York.

After missing the entire 1968 season, Tony was back with his beloved Red Sox for opening day 1969 against the Orioles in Baltimore. Everybody thought that Jack Hamilton's pitch had finished him, but he was determined to prove them wrong. He did it by hitting a tenth inning homer that tied up the game which the Red Sox finally won 5-4.

All in all, he came back big in 1969, slamming out twenty homers and winning the Hutch Award for being the player "who best exemplified the fighting spirit and burning desire of the late (pitcher and manager) Fred Hutchinson." He was also voted Comeback Player of the Year.

The next year, 1970, was even more of a banner year for Tony as he batted a career-high thirty-six homers and hammered out

116 RBIs. Incredibly, the Red Sox traded him in October to the California Angels, ostensibly because the Red Sox didn't want Tony and his younger brother, Billy, who had joined the Red Sox, to be playing on the same team. Red Sox general manager Dick O'Connell, perhaps Tony's best friend on the ball club over the years, said, "Frankly, we considered Billy a better ballplayer under the circumstances." For serious Red Sox fans the move was akin to trading the U.S.S. Constitution to Baltimore in return for the U.S.S. Constellation. Pure unadulterated blasphemy!

Billy Conigliaro had three decent years with the Red Sox, debuting in 1969. Two years younger than his brother, Billy was three inches smaller than Tony and lacked his power-hitting prowess. Billy was basically a .270 hitter with the Red Sox and was traded to the Milwaukee Brewers after the 1971 season. Two years later, Billy was out of baseball.

The Red Sox apparently made the right decision because Tony's eyesight began to fail when he went to the Angels and he only played seventy-four games total for them in 1971 before calling a middle-of-the-night news conference in June to announce his retirement.

Four years later in 1975 he asked the Red Sox to invite him to spring training where he made the varsity as a designated hitter. He played in twenty-one games that season but hit only two homers and .123 and finally decided to call it quits. It should be remembered, however, that Tony had burned up the Grapefruit League and astounded everyone with his hitting prowess. This may have been one of the most amazing feats in the history of baseball. The man had been out of baseball for nearly three and one-half years and there is some evidence to suggest that he was hitting literally from memory.

The years passed and Tony got into sports broadcasting as an announcer and a color man. After being interviewed by the Red Sox for a broadcasting job, Tony was being driven to Boston's Logan International Airport on January 9, 1982, by his brother Billy when he suffered a massive heart attack. The vicious blow disabled him completely, requiring his mother, Teresa, and his brothers, Billy and Richie, as well as nurses, to provide constant care.

During the week of February 19, 1990, Tony C., the local boy who shone as a star outfielder for the Red Sox in the 1960s, was admitted to a hospital in Salem, Massachusetts. He developed a lung infection and kidney failure and died peacefully in his sleep at 4:30 p.m., Saturday, February 24, 1990. He was forty-five years old.

Tony Conigliaro was born in Revere, Massachusetts, on January 7, 1945. He played his first baseball on North Shore sandlots and was a three-letter athlete at St. Mary's in Lynn. After only a year in the minors, he was called up to the Red Sox.

He made his debut with the Bostonians at the age of nineteen. The date was April 17, 1964, and the site was Fenway Park. He hit a home run in his first major league game.

Johnny Pesky, the special assistant to the Red Sox general manager, called the death of Tony Conigliaro "so sad and a damn shame. He was the best young hitter I ever saw. He was six foot, three inches tall, and weighed about 190 pounds. A good-looking player with a lot of ability. A great hustler who could do a lot of things -- run, hit and throw. Ted Williams always thought he could be another Joe DiMaggio. Remember, he was the youngest guy to hit 100 home runs."

On a cold, crisp winter morning in Revere, Tony's funeral mass was celebrated at St. Anthony's Church, a big and truly beautiful edifice, the Yankee Stadiums of churches. He had been baptized, taken his first Communion and confirmed in the same church.

Bishop John Mulcahy told the nearly 1,000 mourners, "Tony did what God wanted him to do. God gives special talents to many people, and it's obvious that He gave Tony a singular, unique talent of being able to hit a baseball. God gives those talents to people so they can make other people happy."

When fans think of Red Sox players, they think first of Ted Williams and then of Carl Yastrzemski. Neither of them ever gave an iota more to the Red Sox and to their fans than Anthony Richard "Tony" Conigliaro.

In the end, though, *Boston Globe* columnist Dan Shaughnessy probably said it best of all for most baseball fans, "Now he is gone and will be frozen in time -- forever tall, dark and handsome, a slugger for the ages. He will not grow old before our eyes. He will not get flabby and slow, and stumble around Fenway Park on old-timers' day."

CHAPTER SEVEN

Boston Red Sox vs. Chicago White Sox

Saturday, August 26, 1967

Rico Petrocelli, a Yankee fan as a youngster growing up in the Sheepshead Bay section of Brooklyn, was the anchor of the Red Sox infield when the Red Sox moved into Chicago for a crucial series against the White Sox. There was a certain irony in Rico's de facto position as the Red Sox "captain". In 1966, Manager Billy Herman had fined him $1,000 for leaving a game without permission and he had a reputation as a sensitive sort for a ballplayer. But baseball was extremely important to Rico and he had matured rapidly. He had long been singled out as the Red Sox short stop of the future, but on finally gaining the position, he had suffered with the Red Sox through almost 200 losses in his first two seasons, 1965-66. When Williams came to Rico on March 1, 1967, and told him that he was looking to him for leadership, it was the vote of confidence he needed. Rico felt that he had been empowered to pass on his baseball knowledge to the others, and more importantly, he felt accepted as a big leaguer for the first time. As the Red Sox got ready for the third game of the five game series, they were in a flatfooted tie for second with Chicago, one-half game behind the league-leading Twins. Rico knew that his teammates were counting on him and it was leadership that he would provide.

The Red Sox followed Tony Conigliaro's tragic beaning on August 18 with some of their best baseball of the season. They were shocked by the near-fatal accident of their star hitter and friend. But they reacted to this adversity by increasing their intensity. Jose Tartabull, a veteran of six major league seasons, filled in for Tony in right field and performed credibly.

The day after Tony's injury, the Red Sox bats answered back to the California Angels and their pitchers. Carl Yastrzemski and George Scott paced the hitting attack. Yaz had four hits, Scotty had three and they each had a home run. In all, the home team pounded out seventeen hits and entered the ninth inning with a comfortable 12-7 lead. The Angels made it interesting by tallying four runs, but reliever Jerry Stephenson held on desperately and the Red Sox squeezed by 12-11.

The next day featured a Sunday doubleheader between the two teams. The Red Sox bats still had plenty of zip in the first game as they coasted to a 12-2 win behind a masterful performance by pitcher Lee Stange. Reggie Smith set the tone by making Red Sox history. All the switch-hitting rookie did was to homer swinging right-handed **and** left-handed. A first for the Red Sox and for Fenway Park. It seemed as if the Red Sox hitters just couldn't be stopped.

They were halted, but only temporarily in game two. The Angels devastated Dave Morehead and jumped out to an 8-0 lead in the fourth inning. An 8-0 lead should always be safe but no lead is ever big enough in the friendly confines of Fenway.

The Red Sox chipped away with a Reggie Smith sole homer in the fourth, followed by a Yaz three-dinger in the fifth. All of a sudden things were getting a little more interesting. They got very interesting in the last of the sixth. The villain of Friday night, Jack Hamilton, had been brought on to protect the Angels' lead. The negative reaction of the capacity crowd was quite predictable and the stage was set for drama.

Joe Foy lead off the Red Sox sixth with a double. Hamilton appeared to come unglued as he walked the next two hitters. Manager Bill Rigney removed the beleaguered Hamilton who left with the cat calls of the crowd raining down on him. Dalton Jones drove a Minnie Rojas fastball off the center field wall and two more runs were in. Jose Tartabull chipped in with a sacrifice fly to bring the Red Sox within one. When utility player par excellence, Jerry Adair, singled in the tying run, the crowd went nuts. The Cardiac Kids had struck again.

Things settled down for a few innings as neither team could push ahead. Then Adair stepped to the plate again. Jerry had come over from the White Sox in a trade in June and had filled in admirably in the infield. He had been the regular second baseman for the Orioles earlier in his career but he had become the classic utility player for the Red Sox.

Role players like Adair seldom get their moment in the sun. But in the summer of '67 every Red Sox fan thought of Jerry as a hero. Adair would contribute to his legend by depositing a Rojas pitch into the left field net to provide their margin of victory. At that moment it seemed as if the Red Sox would not be denied.

If the Angels were thankful to get out of town, the Washington Senators must have wished for almost any other destination. The Red Sox had won four straight and their red hot hitters had rung up thirty-three runs in just three games. The Washington pitching staff must have shuddered at the prospect of five games in Fenway over four days. The Senators had only a remote shot at the .500 mark and the Red Sox were on a tear.

The Monday opener against the Senators was a see-saw affair. The teams traded runs and the lead. The Red Sox came up to bat in the last of the ninth with the score knotted at five. Jerry Adair, "Mr. Clutch" as he was starting to be known, opened up with a double. After Yaz grounded out and two were walked, Elston Howard became the hero of the day with a single to score Adair with the winning run.

Things got even better the next day as the Red Sox swept a twin-bill from the Senators. In the first game, Dalton Jones was the man of the moment. His triple in the seventh brought in two runners and that was all John Wyatt would need to save the win for starter Jerry Stephenson. Gary Bell and Darrell Brandon teamed up to give the Red Sox a 5-3 win in game two. Reggie Smith continued his home run heroics and Yaz, Scott, Adair and

Rico Petrocelli all contributed key hits. The Red Sox had moved within percentage points of the first place White Sox.

Boston fans' obsession with a pennant reached a fever pitch on August 23 as 33,680 fans crammed into Fenway hoping to be there as the Red Sox finally climbed into first. Washington starter, Bob Priddy, had other ideas however, and he pitched a masterful complete game as the Red Sox fell 3-2. First place would have to wait.

On the final day of the home stand, Dave Morehead pitched well into the seventh inning and three Red Sox home runs -- Jerry Adair (of course), newcomer, Jim Landis and a three-run job by Elston Howard -- gave the Red Sox a 7-2 lead going into the ninth. The Red Sox faltered in the ninth -- nothing would be easy that year -- but held on for a 7-5 win. The win moved the team into a virtual tie for first place with the White Sox.

The twelve game home stand had been an eventful one for the Red Sox. They had come in with a 4-9 record for August and a three-game losing streak. They had turned it around with a 10-2 mark including several amazing comeback wins. Most importantly, they had won when they had to.

Tony Conigliaro's tragic accident was the low point of the home stand and the season. It had shaken his teammates, but it hadn't slowed them down. Jose Tartabull and veteran utility man, George Thomas, had both filled in acceptably in right field. They would miss Tony -- he was clearly gone for the season -- but his absence from the lineup would not defeat them.

The scene was set for a classic late August crucial series as the Red Sox flew to Chicago for a five-game showdown with Eddie Stanky and the White Sox. There was no love lost between the Red Sox and Stanky. Eddie had referred to Yaz as "an all-star from the neck down" earlier in the season. While everyone realized that he was just playing head games, they still wanted to beat the diminutive manager who was known as "the Brat".

The pennant race in the American League was as tight as it had been in years; no one could open up a lead of any significance. The Sox, Red and White, were in a virtual tie for first place. The Minnesota Twins and Detroit Tigers were hanging within a game of the two leaders. The California Angels refused "to say die" and made it a five-team race. The season had only a little over a month to go and the contenders were running out of room to maneuver. The leaders only had about thirty-five games remaining to make their move.

For Rico Petrocelli, 1967 was the year he finally felt like a legitimate major leaguer. Even though he was in his third big league season, he was just starting to feel like he belonged. Baseball had been the most important thing in his life for as long as he could remember but he still had to battle insecurity. Many observers thought he was just too serious, that he just needed to relax.

Rico was the youngest of five brothers from a close-knit Italian family in Brooklyn, New York. His brothers were all fine ballplayers and big fans, but a job to provide some income for the family was a higher priority. It wasn't until Rico came along, that a Petrocelli could afford the luxury of concentrating on baseball. He was an outstanding young ballplayer on the Brooklyn sandlots and his brothers tutored him and cheered at his games. Throughout his career, they fulfilled their missed opportunities through his exploits.

The birddogs first took note of his potential as a fifteen-year old performing for the Cadets at nearby Prospect Park. He continued to improve and earned the tagline "can't miss". As high school graduation loomed closer, veteran Red Sox scout, Bots Nekola, who had also signed Carl Yastrzemski, took over the pursuit of the young phenom personally. While it was heresy in his neighborhood, and blasphemy to his brothers the Yankee fans, Rico signed with the Red Sox before his eighteenth birthday.

Rico's first stop was Winston-Salem, North Carolina, in the Carolina league. It was a long way from Sheepshead Bay in Brooklyn. Rico recalls, "It was there that I saw my first cow!" It was also his first taste of professional pitching and it caught him a little off guard. "When you're playing sandlot, you hit .400

something, but all of a sudden you're struggling to hit .280. It was a real adjustment. Sometimes it was discouraging."

While it might have been discouraging to Rico, the Red Sox had identified him as their shortstop of the future. No one has a good explanation for why it is so, but the major league parent typically has little to say to prospects about their futures. They pass on some basic advice, "come to spring training in shape" and some platitudes, "keep up the good work and you'll continue to move up", but little else is said. Perhaps it is baseball tradition. Perhaps it is almost an initiation rite. Regardless, if Rico was on the fast track to Fenway, like all minor leaguers, he would have to read about it in the newspapers.

Rico moved up the ladder to Reading, Pennsylvania, in the fast Eastern league. Rico continued to improve as a hitter as he moved through the system. There never was any doubt about his fielding. After his third minor league season, in 1963, the twenty-year old Rico was brought up to "the Bigs" to spend the last two weeks of the season. For a minor leaguer, this was as close to becoming "anointed" as you could get. He even got to play short for one game and banged out his first big league hit: a single.

Rico started the 1964 season with great optimism. At training camp in Scottsdale, Arizona, he felt that he was being singled out as a prospect. For the first time, he felt as if he belonged with the Red Sox. Then Red Sox manager, Johnny Pesky, understood shortstops and that helped.

Rico was only twenty-years old but he was assigned to the Red Sox top farm team in Seattle, Washington. He was in Triple-A ball, the last stop before the majors. He was in good company at Seattle. Jim Lonborg was honing his pitching craft and Russ Gibson was demonstrating to the brass on Jersey Street that he was ready for "the Show".

Rico's roommate was thirty-six year old journeyman, Billy Gardner. Billy was coming off a ten-year major league career which encompassed six teams and experience at second, short and third base. Gardner had finished up his career in the majors with the Red Sox and he was determined to hold on for one more shot. Baseball was his life and he was just the mentor Rico needed.

Things got off to a good start for Rico but then he pulled a hamstring and his batting average began to fall. Rico kept playing hurt, afraid he would lose his big opportunity if he sat down, and his average continued to deteriorate. Billy Gardner recognized the syndrome and told him to go to manager Edo Vanni and ask for some time to heal before he put his career in jeopardy.

Rico went to Vanni and explained the situation as best he could. Edo told him that he didn't want to hear about it and implied in baseball terms that Rico was "jaking it" i.e. malingering. Where Rico grew up, that was akin to questioning your manhood. In the tradition of his Brooklyn neighborhood, Rico responded by questioning Vanni's parentage. Things deteriorated from there.

This began a period of time when Rico developed a reputation as a moody ballplayer, in some eyes a prima donna. These labels came easily in baseball -- a macho culture -- but die hard. The Red Sox ended up bringing him to Fenway for ten days to have their medical staff examine him. When Rico returned to the minors he was still so hampered by his injury that the Red Sox decided to try to convert him into a switch-hitter. Overnight, it seemed he had gone from a future superstar to a weak-hitting, good-fielding shortstop with a questionable disposition.

In spite of a dreadful '64 season, shortstop had his name on it at Fenway Park. He played ninety-three games at the position in 1965 but the grand experiment of Rico as a switch hitter was abandoned early in the season. As a rookie, he banged out thirteen home runs in only 323 at bats and it didn't make sense to have a guy with that power slapping 125-foot line drives from the left side. When asked when he felt like a genuine big leaguer, Rico replied, "Not in 1965, I didn't."

The following year, Rico was installed as the regular shortstop right from Opening Day. While he batted only .238, he increased his home run output to eighteen and he fielded his position brilliantly. But his relationship with Red Sox manager, Billy Herman, left something to be desired. The players respected Herman's baseball knowledge but he was not a great communicator or motivator. By his own admission the twenty-three year old Petrocelli was still coming of age and he and Herman had their differences. It all came to a head when Rico was fined $1,000 by the Red Sox for leaving a game early in 1966. He was starting to develop a reputation as a temperamental ballplayer.

Dick Williams recognized Rico's full potential. He knew the seriousness could be converted into leadership. He knew the emotionalism could be channeled into an intensity to win. He knew the histrionics were just a manifestation of Rico's frustration at losing. He was the right manager for Rico at the right time.

Williams' demonstration of confidence got Rico off to a great start in 1967. By the end of June, he was batting .296 with eight home runs and thirty-two RBIs. He was playing at a level which would earn him a position on the '67 All Star team. But injury struck again when the Indian's George Culver nailed him on the left wrist with a fastball.

Williams gave Rico the rest he needed. When Rico returned to the lineup, his average fell -- he had dropped to .267 by the end of July -- but he still fielded his position flawlessly, anchored the young infield and got the job done. Rico's average stabilized in the .260s during August and he continued to do the small things that don't show up in the box score. He advanced the runner from second with a groundout to the right side. He took the extra base on a throwing mistake and he picked up an extra step by moving the Red Sox fielders around depending on the upcoming pitch. He was Dick Williams' kind of ballplayer.

Eddie Stanky was all over the Red Sox before Friday night's series opening double header. His most outrageous quote was " . . . the City of Culture is crying about Conigliaro's injury. Big deal. We've had injuries all season, but we aren't crying." The Red Sox players resolved to ignore him.

Jim Lonborg did their talking for them in the opener with a seven-hit complete game. Once again, Gentleman Jim had been the stopper: winning a key game when it really counted. The Red Sox pounded out sixteen hits to give Lonborg his seventeenth victory: 7-1. Rico contributed a key RBI single. White Sox ace, Gary Peters, took the loss for Chicago. Take that, Brat!

The nightcap turned out to be a nightmare for the Red Sox and for Rico Petrocelli. Boston starter, Lee Stange, pitched masterfully but White Sox rookie Cisco Carlos pitched even better. Incredibly, Carlos was pitching in his very first major league game. Perhaps he didn't feel the pressure of the pennant race as much. Ken Berry's home run had given Carlos a 1-0 lead when Rico found himself on second with the potential tying run in the top of the seventh. He had a good shot at scoring on a Dalton Jones looper, but Rico played it too cautiously and was stuck on third with Norm Siebern coming to bat with only one away. Siebern took a big swing that produced only a nubber in the direction of the pitcher's mound. This time Rico elected to take a risk but he made the wrong decision. He was a dead duck at the plate. Dick Williams wouldn't even look at him when he returned to the dugout. The White Sox ultimately prevailed 2-1 and Rico was as low as you can feel.

After the game, Rico joined his pal, Carl Yastrzemski, and clubhouse major domo, Donnie Fitzpatrick for a steak. Under his *Boston Globe* byline in the next day's edition, Yaz wrote, "I spend a lot of time with Rico. We talk. We try to improve each other. We talk about pitchers and situations. We just talk, talk, talk."

Rico much preferred being at home to the long, lonely road trips. He was, and is, a family man. He had come from a close family and in 1967 he was married and the father of three children, including a set of twins. He missed them a lot when he was traveling with the team.

Saturday, August 26 was a new day for the Red Sox. In a season of 162 games, you can't get too high after a win or too low after a loss. When you split a doubleheader, you just forget it and concentrate on the next game. The Sox -- White and Red --

remained tied and they were both one-half game off of the pace following the Twins' victory Friday night. It was going to be that kind of year.

Boston nominated Gerry Stephenson as their starter for the afternoon game. He had pitched well since his recall from Toronto, but he appeared overmatched in comparison to Chicago's starter, Joel Horlen. Horlen was 13-5 going into the game and would end up the season with an ERA of 2.06 to top American League pitchers. But funny things happen in a long season. Gerry Stephenson pitched like the reincarnation of Cy Young -- or at least Billy Rohr -- for the first five innings. Meanwhile, Red Sox batters were drilling out timely hits off Horlen. In the third inning, Jose Tartabull started things going with a triple that totally befuddled White Sox rightfielder, Rocky Colavito. Adair, Yaz and Scotty all followed with singles and the Red Sox had jumped out to a 2-0 lead.

In the top of the fourth, with Mike Andrews at first after a walk, catcher Mike Ryan sent another triple in Colavito's direction to score Andrews. To some observers, Colavito appeared to be playing right field on skates. After Stephenson had set the White Sox down in the bottom half of the fourth and fifth, the Red Sox had a semi-comfortable 3-0 lead. More amazingly, Gerry Stephenson had a no-hitter going!

The Boston dugout was upbeat but they knew they had to get some more runs. Stephenson was likely to run out of gas any time now. Five great innings was a god-send but nobody expected any more. And Horlen looked like he was up for grabs. Not even the greatest pitcher is outstanding in every start and Joel wasn't quite as sharp as usual. "Let's put him away," was the chatter of the dugout.

Super-sub, Jerry Adair, got it rolling with a single. George Scott followed suit and Reggie Smith brought Adair home with a single of his own. Eddie Stanky had seen enough of Horlen and wig-wagged knuckle-baller Wilbur Wood in from the bullpen. In the on-deck circle, Rico Petrocelli tried to recall everything he knew about Wood. Wilbur was a Boston guy. He had made his mark as a schoolboy athlete growing up in nearby Belmont, Massachusetts. He had been signed originally by the Red Sox and spent parts of four seasons with them in the early '60s. But Wilbur had never put it together with the Red Sox and he ended up in the Pirates' organization where he learned the knuckle ball. The White Sox had picked him up for Juan Pizarro and he would go on to a sparkling twelve-year career with Chicago. Why can't the Red Sox ever find pitchers like that?

There was a certain irony as Rico dug in against the left-handed Wood. Wilbur had grown up dreaming of playing for the Red Sox and here he was trying to pitch them out of the pennant. Rico had grown up as a die-hard Yankees fan and here he was trying to propel their most-hated rivals to the pennant. And both of them playing for serious money a thousand or so miles from their boyhood homes.

Rico thought, "knuckle ball", "contact", "patience" as he waited for Wood's delivery. His patience was rewarded as he lined a knuckle ball into left center and he lit out in the direction of first. Scott was home easily as Rico picked up the sign from first base coach, Bobby Doerr, to leg it for second. Rico went in to second standing up since the White Sox were more interested in holding Reggie Smith at third. Rico's RBI had given Boston a five-run cushion and the Red Sox dugout relaxed a little.

In the last of the sixth, Stanky outmanaged himself just a bit. Stephenson was, predictably, losing it and he walked Don Buford and Pete Ward. Down by five runs, with a tiring pitcher on the mound, the genius Stanky put on a double-steal. Mike Ryan's snap throw caught Buford at third base. While the White Sox went on to drive Stephenson from the mound with two runs, an opportunity for a "jumbo" inning had been missed. Darrell Brandon came in to relieve Stephenson and pitched shutout ball the rest of the way. A Red Sox run in the seventh was icing on the cake as they went on to a 6-2 victory.

For Rico Petrocelli, it was just another day at the ballpark. He had fielded flawlessly and kept the hyperactive Stephenson settled down. He felt that he had redeemed himself for the base running gaffe on the night before with his key double. He was pleased with his day's work but it was just one more game in a 162-game season.

For Red Sox fans, this game was a lot more important. The Red Sox win, coupled with a Minnesota loss to Cleveland, gave Boston undisputed possession of first place. **This represented the latest point in the season that Boston had been in first place since 1949.** It was just another game for Rico but it was a landmark for Boston fans.

The Red Sox-White Sox series was far from over, however. Their doubleheader the next day will long be remembered by Red Sox fans. And the outcome would set the tone for the balance of the '67 season.

Gary Bell squared off against the White Sox Fred Klages in game one. Everyone remembers the Chicago White Sox for their pitching. Few remember that Eddie Stanky started Cisco Carlos and Fred Klages in this crucial series. Between the two of them they were to total sixteen lifetime major league wins!

Bell had his good stuff on Sunday and he went into the ninth inning with a 4-3 lead. His one run lead was courtesy of two Carl Yastrzemski home runs. Bell gave off a lead off double to Red Sox nemesis, Ken Berry. After Berry was sacrificed to third, Dick Williams decided it was time for relief ace John Wyatt to face pinch-hitter, Duane Josephson.

Wyatt would throw one pitch to Josephson. That one pitch would produce one of the more memorable plays in Red Sox history. Josephson lofted an average fly ball to Jose Tartabull in right field. Tartabull was known for his weak arm. Berry, tagging at third, was known for his base-running. Jose got off the best throw he could, a rainbow in the air, to catcher Ellie Howard. Howard had to leap to catch the throw one-handed while Berry was barreling in on top of him. Howard somehow came down with his left foot blocking Berry's access to the plate and made the tag in one sweeping motion. A Red Sox fan can see that replay 100 times and still get excited every time. Berry was out, the ball game was over, and the Red Sox were still in first place. For perhaps the first time it seemed that they really could do it.

The second game was almost as exciting, but it ended with a whimper, not with a bang. Jose Santiago pitched his heart out for nine and two-thirds innings. He didn't give up one single run, but the Red Sox had even more trouble with the crafty Gary Peters. Darrel "Bucky" Brandon was on the mound in the eleventh inning of this 0-0 game. With the bases loaded and a three and two count, "Bucky" walked in the winning run and went immediately into Dick Williams' doghouse. Williams was heard to utter, "I'd rather lose on a grand slam home run than a __-__ bases-loaded walk." The pennant race would be like an elevator for the rest of the year. Rico's distinguished Red Sox career covered thirteen years, including his brief stint as a twenty-year old at the end of the 1963 season. The year 1967 will always stand out as the year he came of age, the year he became a stable veteran.

Rico's peak years were probably 1969-1971. During those three years, he played in almost every game, averaged over thirty home runs and knocked in nearly an average of 100 runs each year. In 1969, he socked forty home runs and batted .297. Not bad for a hitter who was considered so marginal that he tried switch-hitting.

In 1971, Rico was moved over to third base to make room for the newly acquired All Star shortstop, Luis Aparicio. Petrocelli had been the regular shortstop for six years, but he made the move without a word and without missing a beat. If anything, he was an even better fielder at third than at short since the "hot corner" suited his range.

The year 1972 was a disappointing one for the Red Sox and for Rico. The Red Sox finished one half game behind the Detroit Tigers in this strike-abbreviated year. Rico saw his home run output cut in half to fifteen and his batting average fell to .240. Still, he was solid in the field and he lead American League third basemen in double plays with thirty-eight.

Rico had become a role-player as he entered his thirties. He would start at third in 100 or so games each year, hit around .250 and serve as a good role model for the rookies.

When lightning struck again in 1975, Rico was the starting third baseman in 112 games. While his home run total declined to seven, he still managed to knock in fifty-nine runs in only 402 at bats. He was also a stabilizing force for twenty-four-year old Rick Burleson who had been installed as the regular Boston shortstop.

Rico had a great World Series against Cincinnati. He started all seven games and fielded magnificently at third. He rapped out eight hits and finished with a batting average of .308 as the Red Sox went down to a heart-breaking defeat at the hands of the Reds. He and Carl Yastrzemski go into the record books as the only Red Sox players to appear in the 1967 and 1975 World Series.

During his career with Boston, Rico rapped out 210 homers, knocked in 773 runs, and finished up with a batting average of .251. But statistics don't tell the Rico Petrocelli story. He went from the "itinerant short stop" to a leader. He developed from a moody young player into a leader.

One story from 1967 may tell you all you need to know about Rico Petrocelli. It was a hectic year and Rico had a young family. But community and church are important to Rico. When a parish priest prevailed on Rico, he gave up an afternoon to visit an inner city parochial school. Rico was a big hit with the kids and the nuns at St. Kevin's in Dorchester. When reminded of the visit twenty-five years later, Rico recalls, "I had a great time. The kids reminded me of my roots in Brooklyn and I always felt that I should give something back to the community." Then he takes a few moments to send his personal greeting to Sister Ann Cecelia Roberts, a nun at St. Kevin's at the time, on the occasion of her fiftieth jubilee. Rico's values are firmly grounded.

After his release from the Red Sox during spring training in 1977, Rico tried his hand at a number of things. He worked as a baseball correspondent for the *Boston Herald* for a while and did some broadcasting. He has done his share of sales and promotional work and he managed in the minor leagues for the White Sox (Rico with the White Sox? Bobby Doerr with the Toronto Blue Jays organization? What's wrong with this picture?). Rico enjoyed managing, but he just didn't fit in with Chicago's long-term plans.

Rico is presently director of Sports Programs for the Jimmy Fund. He oversees about seventy golf tournaments, runs basketball and little league tournaments and contributes to public relations. Rico is ideally suited for his job, performs admirably, and likes it a lot. But Rico's first love, after his family, is baseball. He ran a batting school in Lexington this past winter and he will always remain connected to the game.

When asked what the 1967 season meant to him, Rico replies, "It really affected me. It has influenced where I live, what I do, who I am. When people think of me they say, 'You're the guy who played for the 1967 Red Sox. And I am."

Yes you are, Rico. Yes you are.

CHAPTER EIGHT

Boston Red Sox vs. Detroit Tigers

Tuesday, September 19, 1967

At age twenty-two, Carl "Reggie" Smith was the finest all-around athlete on the 1967 Boston Red Sox squad. He was strong, he was gifted with natural speed and he was an outstanding hitter from either side of the plate. Like Joe Foy, he was originally signed by the Twins and was picked up by the Red Sox when Minnesota failed to protect him on their forty-man roster. Smith advanced swiftly through the Red Sox system with outstanding seasons at Pittsfield and for Toronto in 1966. Dick Williams knew that he was ready for the big leagues and he probably exhibited more patience with Reggie than any other single Red Sox player in 1967. At the end of June, Reggie was still only hitting .204, but Williams stuck with him. In part, this reflected Smith's defensive contribution in center field and the dimension that his speed provided offensively. Mostly it reflected the manager's conviction that Reggie would be a star. This faith was rewarded throughout the second half of the season as Reggie Smith finally came into his own.

The Red Sox left Chicago downcast over their tough loss in the second game of the doubleheader and one percentage point out of first place. They flew to New York for a four game series at Yankee Stadium. With thirty-two games remaining in the season, every series was critical and every game was important.

The Red Sox got off to a good start on Monday night with a 3-0 victory. Dave Morehead pitched well for five innings and Sparky Lyle, who was emerging as a positive factor coming out of the bullpen, earned another save. Reggie Smith had the key hit as he deposited his thirteenth homer into the right field bleachers. In another important development, Ken "Hawk" Harrelson, who had been "fired" from the A's by Charlie Finley, reported to the team to provide some much needed help in right field.

General Manager Dick O'Connell had been making player moves the way a great symphony conductor orchestrates his musicians. His only peer with a better record that year was Arthur Fiedler who was leading the Boston Pops to an undefeated season at the Esplanade on the banks of Boston's Charles River.

O'Connell had added Adair and Bell in June to provide infield depth and a number two starter. Ellie Howard's acquisition had shored up the catching and provided veteran leadership with a winning attitude. Harrelson was the "coup de grace".

Neil Mahonney and Ed Kenney, Sr. of the minor league system deserved a lot of credit as well. There were many games when every player who took a starting position had come up through the Red Sox system. Not many teams could say that, not even in 1967.

In Tuesday's doubleheader, Jim Lonborg came through once more pitching brilliantly and driving in the winning run with a single. Reggie Smith's speed was the other offensive key to the first game 2-1 victory.

Game two went on for twenty innings and took over six hours to play. The game was tied 2-2 after nine innings and the Red Sox looked good when they took a 3-2 lead in the top of the eleventh. But Steve Whitaker homered in the bottom of the frame to knot it up for the Yankees. Horace Clarke, of all people, won it for the Yanks in the twentieth with a single and hard-luck Bucky Brandon took the 4-3 loss.

The Red Sox showed a lot of character the day following their exhausting defeat. Gerry Stephenson and Yankee southpaw, Al Downing, went toe to toe and matched pitch for pitch. At the end of regulation, the game was tied at one. Yaz had begun the game on the bench. The combination of the previous evening's marathon session and an 0-17 hitting drought had convinced Yaz and Dick Williams that a rest was in order. Yaz was inserted in left in the eighth and in the tenth propelled a Downing serve into the right center bleachers for a key 2-1 victory.

The Red Sox were heading home for Boston in first place by one game and a half. The Chicago White Sox were coming to town for a four game series, trailing the Red Sox by two and a half games. The stage was set for the **knock-out-punch**.

August 31 Report Card:
  *A's:*Yaz (.308, 35 homers)
  Scott (.304, 17 homers)
  Lonborg (18-6, 3.26 ERA)
  Wyatt (8-6, 2.39 ERA)
  B's: Petrocelli (infield leader)
  Adair (super-sub)
  Smith (from .204 to .262 in two months)
  Andrews (solid at second)
  Foy (17 homers)
  Stange (8 wins, 2.64 ERA)
  Disabled: Tony C.

Unfortunately, Eddie Stanky and his White Sox temporarily derailed Boston's pennant express again. With 35,138 of the faithful on hand to bear witness, the home team went down to defeat, 4-2. As if to rub salt in the wounds, former teammate Don McMahon picked up the win in relief.

On Friday night, the Red Sox redeemed themselves before 34,054 loyalists. Hawk Harrelson finally earned some of the $80,000 that Tom Yawkey had ponied up in the bidding war for Hawk's services with a double, triple and a home run. Boston won going away as Jose Santiago picked up his eighth win. Their hold on first place was down to one-half game over the second place Twins.

Jim Lonborg failed to rise to the occasion for one of the few times all season in game three on Saturday. The White Sox got to him for three runs in the opening frame and Joel Horlen pitched them to a 4-1 win. The defeat dropped Boston to second place, one-half game behind the Twins.

The White Sox pitching carried the day in the Sunday finale as well. Twenty-four-year-old stylish southpaw Tommy John, who would go on to pitch for over twenty distinguished seasons in the majors, shut them down, 4-0. As Labor Day, 1967 dawned, the American League standings looked like this:

Team	Games Behind
Minnesota	--
Boston	1/2
Chicago	1
Detroit	1 1/2

The four contenders were strung together like beads on a pearl necklace. Nothing would come easy in 1967.

The Red Sox headed down to Washington for a three-game series against the Senators who were twelve and one half games off the pace and going nowhere. The Red Sox knew they had to take at least two out of three to stay in the hunt.

Labor Day is another benchmark in the six-month season. With only two dozen games remaining, every single game is important. Unfortunately, the Red Sox continued to struggle in game one of the doubleheader. Red Sox jinx, Camilio Pascual, tantalized them with slow curves and the lowly Senators prevailed by a score of 5-2.

If there was one single victory that Dick Williams could take credit for, it was probably the second game of this Labor Day doubleheader. His first move was to bench regulars Foy, Harrelson and Scott. After dropping four of five crucial games, drastic measures were in order. Besides, the Boomer hadn't had an extra base hit in over fifteen games. His next move was to "jury-rig" a pitching corp which produced five decent innings from Gerry Stephenson, three good innings from Sparky Lyle, and featured John Wyatt in his role as closer in the ninth. Every move worked including George Scott, appearing in a cameo pinch-hitting role as the Boomer, driving a key double in the eighth. The Red Sox held steady with the Twins, who also split, with a much needed 6-4 win.

Carl Yastrzemski assumed the leadership mantle in the deciding game of the series. Yaz rocketed home runs numbers thirty-seven and thirty-eight and the Red Sox coasted to an 8-2 decision. Gary Bell picked up his tenth win in a Boston uniform.

Wednesday was the Red Sox' first day off in almost a month and it was a good time to reflect on the remainder of the season. There were only twenty-one games remaining and thirteen of them were scheduled in friendly Fenway. The Red Sox were positioned to control their own destiny, but they would have to "make hay" in the upcoming nine game home stand against New York, Kansas City and Baltimore. These were three teams they had handled easily all year. There were only two brief series left with any of the contending teams: a two game series against the Tigers after the home stand and a two-game set at home against the Twins on the last two days of the season. The season wrap up against Minnesota was beginning to loom awfully large.

The Red Sox needed a big home stand and the logical choice to get them off on the right foot was Gentleman Jim Lonborg. Once more Lonborg didn't disappoint as he three-hit the Yankees for his nineteenth win. Rico Petrocelli spear-headed the batting brigade with three hits and two RBIs in the 3-1 opener of a four-game series. Former Red Sox pitching stalwart, Bill Monboquette, turned the tables on his old mates on Friday night. Monboquette bested Lee Stange 5-2 as the Yankees tied the series at one game apiece.

Spot starter Dave Morehead saved the day on Saturday as he gave the Red Sox seven quality innings. Carl Yastrzemski's thirty-ninth homer and Rico Petrocelli's fifteenth set the tone for the 7-1 decision. The Red Sox needed a victory on Sunday to stay within a half game of the Twins and they won in a "laugher" by a score of 9-1. Gary Bell came through with a four-hit complete game for his eleventh triumph for Boston. Mike Ryan put the game out of the Yankees' reach in the sixth. Ryan drilled a bases loaded triple to increase the margin to 7-1 and the game was effectively over.

With last-place Kansas City coming to town for two games, the Red Sox knew they had to demonstrate some killer instinct. Jim Lonborg went to the mound on Tuesday night determined to do whatever it took to secure his twentieth victory. Lonborg didn't have his best stuff -- he had to work himself out of trouble in the second through the fifth innings -- but he hung tough against the A's Catfish Hunter. He came to bat in the last of the eighth with pinch-runner, Jose Tartabull, on first, locked in a 1-1 battle. Jim "showed" bunt and swung away to produce a towering drive to the right center triangle. Lonborg's long legs propelled him to third from where he tagged up on a long Mike Andrews fly to ice a 3-1 win.

On the following Wednesday afternoon, Rico Petrocelli provided all the fireworks the Red Sox needed as he drove in three runs. Lee Stange (seven innings) and John Wyatt (contest.two innings and credit for the win) teamed up in the 4-2 decision. The Red Sox looked forward to a day off on Thursday and the arrival of their "cousins", the Baltimore Orioles on Friday for a three-game series.

The O's appeared to be the ideal candidates for the Red Sox to improve their position in the standings. Although the teams hadn't met in almost two months, Boston had handled them easily in their two July series. Unfortunately, a poor effort by starter Dave Morehead -- three wild pitches -- and a number of fielding gaffes resulted in a 6-2 loss in Friday's opener. To make matters worse, the Red Sox bats went silent on Saturday night. Red Sox hitters could only manage one run off Baltimore rookie, Jim Hardin, as Lonborg proved human by dropping a 4-1 decision. The Red Sox were fortunate to be holding in second at one game out of first.

With only twelve games remaining after Sunday, it seemed that the Red Sox had to have a win against the O's. Gary Bell had emerged as their number two starter and he drew the nod for this all-important game. But once again, the Red Sox bats were somnolent and Bell was mediocre. O's starter, Gene Brabender, picked up his fifth win of the season as the Red Sox were limited to only two runs. Baltimore's tally of five was more than enough as Bell absorbed the loss.

The only salvation in the Red Sox three game "swoon" to the Orioles was that neither the Tigers, the White Sox, nor the Twins could open up any daylight either. The four contenders were all within one game of one another. Detroit was in first holding a half-game lead over the White Sox. The Red Sox had gone only 5-4 in their homestand, but incredibly, they were still very much in the running.

Boston was heading off for a two-game series with the front-running Tigers and they recognized that they were flat out of reprieves. Dick Williams pledged to shake the team out of its lethargy. Williams inserted Jose Tartabull, Russ Gibson and Dalton Jones into the starting lineup. Jones was a calculated gamble since he hit like Ted Williams in Tiger Stadium. Dick Williams cracked, "Wouldn't it be something if I put Jose Tartabull up there in the cleanup spot? I just might."

The opening game on Monday night included everything that a game between two contenders in a tight pennant race should contain. The ten inning contest featured suspense, drama, disappointment, and heroics. If the game contained more offense than defense it was as it should be in this ballpark between these two teams.

The game unfolded like a classic heavyweight championship fight. Starter Jerry Stephenson, struggling with his control throughout, labored gallantly through seven to keep Boston in the game. The Red Sox threatened as they came to bat in the eighth with the contest knotted at four, but Dick McAuliffe's heads-up, unassisted double play killed that rally. Tiger-killer Dalton Jones' three hits were the Red Sox highlight at this point.

Stephenson gave way to John Wyatt as the game moved in to the last of the eighth. Wyatt had been the Red Sox' most dependable reliever all year, but this was not to be his night. Jim

Northrup doubled home Al Kaline and the Red Sox would enter the ninth trailing 5-4. More than one Red Sox fan wondered if the team was finally running out of gas.

Carl Yastrzemski wasn't out of gas by any means. In fact, beginning in the top of the ninth, Yaz would put it on high-test and he would keep it there for the next two weeks. He kicked off the best two-week stretch by any hitter in major league history with a game tying home run deep into the right field bleachers. The Red Sox' hopes were still very much alive.

Yaz's clutch blast seemed to be just the catalyst his teammates needed. They held the Tigers in the bottom of the ninth to set up an opportunity for Dalton Jones to seize the hero's mantle. The crown was a perfect fit as Jones drove rookie Mike Marshall's fastball into the upper deck in right. Jones also made a nice defensive play on a Bill Freehan bullet to end the game and prove what a genius Dick Williams really was. The Red Sox had finally won a big one, and what a big one it was!

The morning of September 19 found three American League teams in a dead-heat for first place: the Red Sox, the Twins and the Tigers. Following a loss to the California Angels, Chicago was in fourth place, one-half game behind.

The story in the National League was very different. The morning papers recounted the St. Louis Cardinals' victory over Philadelphia by a score of 4-1 behind Bob Gibson. This victory clinched the National League pennant for the Cards. While they had no idea of who their opponents would be, they did know that games three, four and five would be played in Busch Stadium.

Reggie Smith went about his pre-game rituals in Detroit representing another in a starry history of Red Sox centerfielders. Much has been made of the Red Sox royalty in left field and rightfully so. The unbroken string of stars from Ted Williams, to Yaz, through Jim Rice, and on to Mike Greenwell today is unprecedented in baseball history. This group includes two Hall-of-Famers, one legitimate Hall-of-Fame candidate and a potential super star.

While the continuity is lacking, center field in Boston has been manned by some outstanding players as well. The first great star center fielder was Tris Speaker who patrolled the ground for the Red Sox from 1909 to 1915. Speaker hit .383 in 1912 and never hit less than .309 in his seven full years with the Red Sox. In 1967, Speaker still held the Red Sox record for stolen bases with his fifty-two steals recorded in 1912. Dom DiMaggio held down center field with great distinction for the Red Sox from 1940 to 1952. While he always suffered from the long shadow cast by his big brother, Joe, Dom's lifetime average of .298 is testimony to his skills. Jimmy Piersall also played a number of spectacular seasons in center field for Boston in the mid-50s. Piersall overcame a nervous breakdown to achieve stardom and some of his great catches are still relived by long-time Sox fans.

While he couldn't have known it then, Smith would ultimately be succeeded by Fred Lynn and the legacy would eventually be picked up by Ellis Burks. Not quite as spectacular as the left field tradition, but a formidable group nonetheless.

The Tigers felt they had to have a win on Tuesday night. To be swept in their own home park would be devastating to their morale. Manager Mayo Smith went with veteran lefthander, Mickey Lolich, to combat Yaz and the lefthanded hitting, Dalton Jones. Manager Williams countered by lifting Jones in favor of the righthanded hitting, Jerry Adair.

The Red Sox started righthander Lee Stange who had a record of 8-10. The "Stinger" had pitched well of late and Williams was looking for six or seven good innings from him.

Both pitchers got through the first inning without damage. Lolich put an exclamation point on his effort by striking out Adair, Yaz and Scott. In the top of the second, the Red Sox started a mild uprising.

Reggie Smith opened the second with a single to center. The one unique dimension Reggie brought to the Red Sox was his speed afoot. The Red Sox have always featured power hitters and Smith was one of their few players who could manufacture runs with this base running. With Ken Harrelson at bat, Micky

Lolich uncorked a wild pitch and Reggie was on second in a flash. After Harrelson struck out, Reggie tagged and moved to third on a long fly ball by Rico Petrocelli. When Russ Gibson singled into center, Smith scampered home with the first Red Sox run and the first tally of the game.

A native of Shreveport, Louisiana, Reggie had been an all-around athlete as a youngster. He was All League in football and basketball at Centennial High and the MVP in baseball. The Minnesota Twins signed him directly out of high school and shipped him to Wytheville, North Carolina, in their lower minors. He showed speed and power in his debut, but his forty-one errors in sixty-six games gave the Twins pause. When they left him unprotected in November of 1963, the Red Sox drafted him. After four years in their farm system, he was pronounced major-league ready in 1967.

Stange breezed through the last of the second and Lolich did the same in the top of the third. The Tigers came to bat in the last of the third trailing 1-0.

Stange got into a bit of a jam in the Tigers' third. After one runner was retired, Don Wert, Lolich and McAuliffe all singled. This brought the weak-hitting second baseman, Jerry Lumpe, to the plate with the bases loaded. Mike Andrews then made a nice play on a Lumpe grounder by tagging McAuliffe and firing to Scott to turn the inning-ending double play.

Lolich retired the Red Sox in 1-2-3 order in the Boston half of the inning. Stange ran into a little more hot water in the Tigers' fourth. After walking Al Kaline to open the inning, a Willie Horton single and Ken Harrelson overthrow put runners at the corners. Stange bore down and induced a popout, struck out the dangerous Norm Cash and finally got out of the inning unscathed when a Bill Freehan grounder forced Horton at second.

Lolich was cruising but the Red Sox mounted a mild threat in the top of the fifth. With one out, Russ Gibson came through with his second hit, a single to center. Lee Stange moved him along nicely with a sacrifice bunt, but Lolich made Mike Andrews his tenth strike out victim to end the inning. Stange handled the

Tigers with ease in their half of the inning and after five, it was Boston 1, Detroit 0.

The best the Red Sox could muster in the sixth was a Carl Yastrzemski liner which went off Jerry Lumpe's glove for an error. The Tigers sent Kaline, Horton and Jim Northrup to the plate looking to stir things up in the sixth.

Kaline got things going by sending a liner left to center which placed him on second. After Horton grounded out, Northrup picked on a Stange slider and put it into the third deck in right field. With one swing of the bat, the Tigers had obtained a very large 2-1 lead.

The Red Sox had no luck against Lolich in the top of seventh and the Tigers appeared poised for their knockout punch. Don Wert singled to open the seventh. When Lolich followed with a single of his own, Williams knew it was time to get Stange out of there. His choice was young reliever Al "Sparky" Lyle and he was the right choice. The first batter he faced, McAuliffe, forced Lolich at second as Wert moved to third. Ray Oyler then pinch hit for Lumpe and lined a hard shot towards third. Jerry Adair snagged it smartly and stepped on third to trap Wert. The Red Sox had wiggled out of another jam.

The Red Sox were down to six outs and they needed a rally fast. Lolich struck out Gibson to start the eighth. Joe Foy was sent up as a pinch hitter for Lyle. Lolich fanned him. When Andrews suffered the same ignomy to end the inning, Lolich had notched thirteen strike outs over eight innings. Boston was running out of time.

As Reggie took center field in the last of the eighth, he couldn't help looking ahead to the Boston ninth. Jerry Adair would lead off followed by Yaz. George Scott was next, and if any of them reached, it would bring him up with the tying run on base. He wondered if Mayo Smith would stick with Lolich. If he went with a right-hander, Reggie would cross over to bat lefty, with a shot at the inviting right field bleachers. Then he turned his full attention to the scene in front of him.

Santiago came on to face the Tigers in the last half of the inning. He was in trouble before he even got adjusted to the mound. First Kaline walked. Then the usually sure-handed Adair bobbled a Horton grounder for an error. When Santiago failed to handle a Northrup nubber, the bases were jammed with Tigers with no outs.

Jose took a deep breath. He breathed a little easier when he forced Norm Cash to foul out to Gibson. Then he breathed a huge sigh of relief when he got Bill Freehan to ground into a double play to end the inning. The Red Sox had pulled their Houdini act one more time and remained within striking distance.

The Red Sox needed a break as they entered the ninth. Dick Williams was not superstitious, but he had noticed an omen in centerfield before the game began. Someone had placed a red broom, a dozen roses and a red sign reading "sweep" in the deepest reaches of Tiger Stadium. Boston would need all the help they could get in the ninth.

Jerry Adair set the spark with a lead off single to right. Then Lolich walked Yaz on four straight pitches. George Scott fought off a number of tough pitches and then rifled a single to center. Jerry Adair was running all the way and slid safely into home with the tying run.

This brought the switch-hitting Reggie Smith to the plate and manager Mayo Smith to the mound. Mayo Smith pulled out all the stops by bringing in twenty-game winner Earl Wilson for his first relief appearance of the year. Reggie showed his versatility by deftly dropping a bunt down the first base line. His sacrifice worked and the runners advanced to second and third.

Now all the wheels were turning. Manager Smith ordered pinch hitter Dalton Jones walked to load up the bases and set up a force play all around. Dick Williams countered by sending up lefty Norm Siebern to bat for Rico. All of this strategy went for naught when Wilson uncorked a wild pitch to score Yaz with the lead run. Gibson followed an intentional walk to Siebern by sending a drive that was deep enough to center to score the tagging Scott with an insurance run.

The Red Sox had only three outs to go and a two-run lead as the Tigers came to bat in the ninth. Santiago retired Wert on a nice catch by Yastrzemski to start the inning. Then his control faltered. He walked Lennie Green and McAuliffe to put the tying run at first. Williams brought in lefty Bill Landis to face aging slugger Eddie Mathews. Landis eased the tension by striking out the Tiger's veteran pinch-hitter. Williams wasn't taking any chances: he brought in Gary Bell to face the ever dangerous Al Kaline.

Reggie Smith felt quite comfortable in center field as he watched Bell take his warm up pitches. With his speed and reflexes, he was confident in his ability to get to any ball hit in his direction. He had played second, short and third in the minors and he had even started the 1967 season at second for the Red Sox, but center was home.

Kaline didn't wait for the suspense to build. He smashed Bell's first pitch on a dead line into center field. Both base runners were in full motion as soon as bat met ball. Smith was charging in from center field, but the hard liner was sinking fast. If it got by him, both runs would probably score and the game would be tied. Reggie turned on every ounce of his speed and snared the drive on the run at his knees. The Red Sox had pulled off another thriller and they had swept the Tigers.

In the clubhouse after the game, Yaz said, "At first, I didn't think Reggie was going to get it." Manager Williams echoed the compliment. "Reggie got a terrific jump on the ball," he said.

Reggie credited Yaz with an assist on the play. "If I trap the ball, it's a single. If it gets by me, Yaz is there to back me up."

Reggie would go on to make many similar catches during his seven-year career in Boston. But he never took to the city the way so many of his teammates did. Some attributed this to the racial tension that is often associated with Boston. Others felt that Reggie never really gave the city a chance.

Reggie was a Californian. The difference between Los Angeles and Boston is more than 3,000 miles. There was (and still is) a world of difference between the two cultures. Smith and his wife tried to make the best of it, but as soon as the season would come to an end, they would be California-bound.

.No one can argue with Reggie's numbers in a Red Sox uniform. He averaged over twenty home runs a year, he stole eighty-four bases for a team that didn't run, and he hit over .300 in three different seasons. And no one ever said that he couldn't play center field.

But Reggie's relations with the Boston press weren't great and he had a problem with a teammate from time to time. In 1972, an outspoken rookie, Carlton "Pudge" Fisk took both Reggie and Yaz to task publicly for their "lack of leadership." In his book *Yaz*, Yastrzemski says, "Reggie was more annoyed (sic: about Fisk's comments) than I was." According to Yaz, the three ball players sat down for five minutes with manager Eddie Kasko and resolved the whole thing.

Whether or not it was resolved to Reggie's satisfaction is unknown, but two years later he was traded to the St. Louis Cardinals. Smith was traded along with pitcher Ken Tatum for outfielder Bernie Carbo and Cards pitcher Rick Wise.

Smith played two and a half seasons in St. Louis. The change in scene apparently agreed with him as he batted over .300 in both 1974 and 1975. On June 15, 1976, he was traded to the L.A. Dodgers for three players including catcher Joe Ferguson.

Los Angeles was home for Reggie. Although he was thirty-one years old, he knew he had a number of good years ahead of him and he looked forward to playing in comfortable surroundings.

Smith played five and a half seasons for the Dodgers. During that time he appeared in three World Series. He rapped out three homers in the six-game series against the Yankees in 1977. His best season was probably 1978 when he hit .307 and tallied a career-high thirty-two homers.

The Dodgers' plans for 1982 didn't include a soon to be thirty-seven year old. Reggie looked to the north and signed as a free agent with the San Francisco Giants. He appeared in 106 games for the Giants and batted a credible .284. But when the season came to an end, his seventeen-year major league career was over.

Reggie was still in great shape; he had hit eighteen home runs for the Giants in 1982. He wasn't ready to give up the game and he followed the route of many of his contemporaries to Japan.

When Reggie's playing days in Japan were over, he kept up his ties with that country. For a number of years, he was in sales and marketing in the computer industry. Reggie's experiences in the orient were of great value and he was a frequent traveler to the far east.

By 1990, Reggie realized how much he missed baseball. He accepted an assignment with the Dodgers as their minor league hitting instructor, a position he still holds. In this role, he passes on the lessons learned in more than twenty years in organized baseball and looks for young players with the potential to match or exceed his .287 lifetime batting average. Since only about two percent of the players who sign a professional contract ever make it to the majors, few of these players possess the skills that Reggie did at the same age.

The year of the Impossible Dream did not affect Reggie the way it did so many of his teammates. Fellow Californians, Mike Andrews and Jim Lonborg moved their homes permanently to the Boston area. Reggie always called L.A. home. Teammates Carl Yastrzemski and Rico Petrocelli played their entire careers in a Boston uniform. Reggie wore three additional uniforms, all in a different league. Former teammates Russ Gibson and Dalton Jones are regulars at the Fantasy Camp reunion. Boston is not on Smith's travel itinerary.

Time heals many things. As the years pass, people mellow. Perhaps as time goes by, Reggie will come to value the magic of the 1967 Boston Red Sox and to remember his role in the proceedings with fondness.

Rico Petrocelli came into his own in 1967, anchoring the Red Sox infield and hitting a solid .259. (Photo courtesy of the Boston Red Sox).

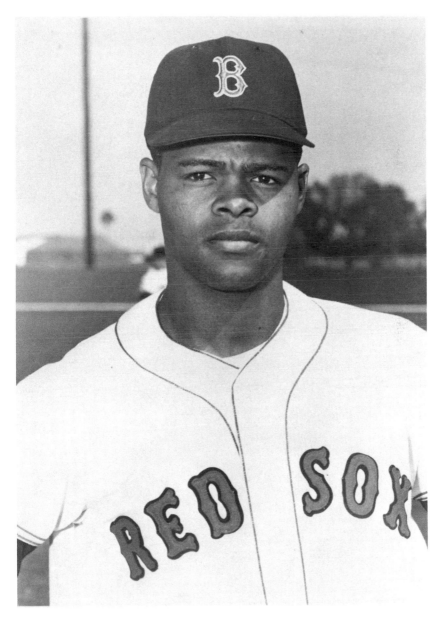

Reggie Smith overcame a slow start to finish at .246 with 15 home runs and 61 r.b.i.s. (Photo courtesy of the Boston Red Sox).

Jim Lonborg was the Red Sox "stopper" and led the American League with 22 wins and 246 strikeouts. (Photo courtesy of the Boston Red Sox).

Dick Williams was not universally beloved by his players or the umpires, but he was everybody's manager of the year. (Photo courtesy of the Boston Red Sox).

Until Conigliaro was beaned by Jack Hamilton on August 18, 1967, the Red Sox boasted the major's top outfield with Yaz in Left, Reggie Smith in Center, and Tony C. in Right. (Photo courtesy of the Boston Red Sox).

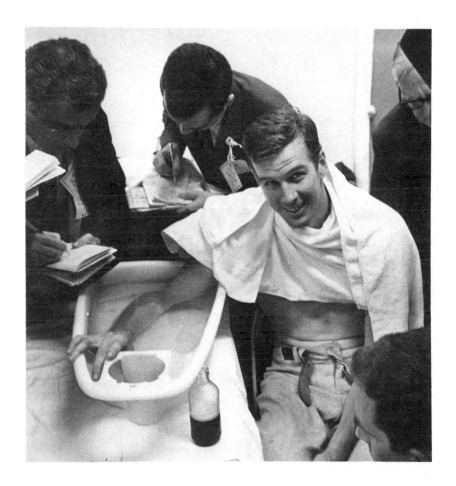

Lonborg's strong right arm gets a well deserved soaking; Lonnie logged 273.1 innings during the regular season and 24 innings in the World Series. (Photo courtesy of the Boston Red Sox).

Reggie Smith displays the speed that earned him the club's lead in stolen bases with 16 in 1967. (Photo courtesy of the Boston

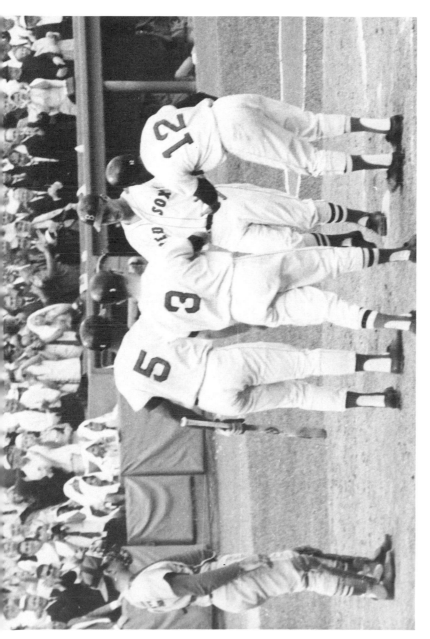

Carl Yastrzemski is congratulated by George Scott, Dalton Jones and Jose Tartabull as he crosses the plate following one of his league leading (tied with Harmon Killebrew) 44 home runs. (Photo courtesy of the Boston Red Sox).

Two future Hall of Famers, right fielder Al Kaline of the Detroit Tigers and Red Sox left fielder Carl Yastrzemski get together before an important game. (Photo courtesy of the New England

Rico Petrocelli squeezes the final out of the final game as Lonborg leaps and Yaz raises his arms in triumph. (Gerry Buckley photo courtesy of Dr. James R. Lonborg).

CHAPTER NINE

Boston Red Sox vs. Minnesota Twins

Saturday, September 30, 1967

After six years of frustration, Carl Michael Yastrzemski and the Boston Red Sox finally put it all together in 1967. After two outstanding years in the Red Sox' minor league system, Yaz arrived in Fenway Park in 1961 as the twenty-one year old designated heir to Ted Williams in left field. He played well as a rookie but his .266 batting average and eleven home runs didn't stir many memories of Williams. Although he elevated his game each year, the Red Sox continued their dismal performance and Yaz had a few problems with managers Johnny Pesky and Billy Herman. Things started to change for Yaz between the 1966 and 1967 seasons. Carl entered into a grueling physical regimen which put him in top form when he arrived at spring training. Also, Dick Williams relieved him of his duties as team captain, freeing him up to concentrate on his game and to provide leadership in a more comfortable way. The 1967 season was to be the greatest year of his career and in September he would have as good a month as any player in the history of the game.

The dramatic sweep of the Tigers placed the Red Sox in a flat-footed tie with the Twins for first place with a record of 86-66. Chicago was even with the leaders in the win column, but had one more loss to trail by one half game. Detroit now resided in fourth place, one game off the pace.

The Red Sox had ten scheduled games remaining to be played over the next twelve days. The next six were road games in Cleveland and Baltimore. The final four games were scheduled at home against Cleveland and the Twins.

Boston came into Cleveland's Municipal Stadium on a high and continued their clutch play. Lonborg got the nod from Dick Williams and Sudden Sam McDowell took the mound for the Indians on the eve of his twenty-fifth birthday. Both teams played long ball as a shower of one-run homers rained on the bleachers. Ex-Red Soxer Tony Horton had one of three Cleveland homers and Yaz, Petrocelli and Andrews added four baggers of their own.

When the homer barrage halted, the scoreboard read 4-4 after eight. George Culver had replaced McDowell for the Tribe and Yaz touched him for a single when two were gone in the eighth. After Scott had walked, the stage was set for more late-inning heroics. Reggie Smith delivered them with a sharp single to right field scoring Yaz with the go-ahead run. John Wyatt came on to close out the 5-4 win, picking up his tenth win in the process.

The pressure of continuous "must wins" games got to the Red Sox a little bit the following night. Starter Gary Bell pitched well for six innings back in his home park and the Red Sox held a 6-1 lead based on timely hitting. Then things started to unravel a little -- a misplay here, a miscue there -- and the next thing anyone knew, it was a tight 6-5 game. The unsung hero -- John Wyatt -- rode to the rescue again and the Red Sox held on to their share of first place. Bell got credit for the win running his record in Boston to 12-7.

Things really unraveled in the first game of the doubleheader in Baltimore on Friday. Most people would certainly consider giving up ten runs and scoring none in the heat of a pennant race an unraveling. That's exactly what the Red Sox did. Gerry Stephenson took the loss as the Red Sox were flat out inept.

Dick Williams elected to start Jose Santiago in the important second game. Used mostly as a reliever, Jose was making only his tenth start of the season, but he had come on strong in the second half to compile a record of 10-4. Santiago was a wise choice as he went the distance in a 10-3 victory. The offense was propelled by three hits each from Ken "Hawk" Harrelson and Joe Foy. The split of a doubleheader to the lowly Birds was disappointing, but the Red Sox clung to the top of the American League ladder.

The Red Sox lost their tenuous grip on the top rung the next day with a 7-5 loss to the Orioles. The lead in this one changed hands several times. Baltimore jumped out to a 4-0 lead, but Boston came roaring back to take the lead 5-4 as Yaz launched his forty-second home run. His three-week tear had propelled him into the league lead in five offensive categories: batting average, hits, runs scored, RBIs, and home runs.

Williams went to the John Wyatt well one more time in the eighth inning. Unfortunately, the well was empty this time as Brooks Robinson took John downtown for a two-run homer. The Red Sox were now in third place, one half game behind the Twins and one-thousandth of a percentage point behind the Tigers.

Jim Lonborg found himself in a familiar spot on Sunday in Baltimore: he was starting a must win game for Boston. In fact, Jim was shooting for his twenty-first victory and if he was successful, it would be his ninth win immediately following a Red Sox loss. He was opposed by Tom Phoebus, who was Baltimore's best pitcher with a 14-8 record.

Williams continued to search for the ideal combination as the team headed down the stretch. In this crucial game, he started Jerry Adair at second and he got Dalton Jones' left-handed bat into the lineup at third. His managerial midas touch paid off again as both of them responded with four hits for the day.

Lonborg pitched as well as he had pitched in any game all year that day. After six innings, he had given up only two hits and he had held the Orioles scoreless. With a safe 7-0 lead, Williams elected to pull him so he would have something extra for the last week of the season.

The Red Sox played the balance of the game like a racehorse with a twelve-length lead at the three quarters pole: they played well enough to win. George Scott joined Adair and Jones in the four-hit club as Boston held on for an 11-7 victory. Manager Williams was less than enamored with the performance of his bullpen.

The Red Sox were heading home in good position. While they remained one half game off the top, their four remaining games were all at home and they were nicely spaced over seven days. The fact that the next two games were against the eighth place Indians didn't hurt either.

Monday was an off day for the team, but when you're hot, you're hot. Boston moved back into a tie for first place without even lifting a bat as the pesky Angels defeated the Twins by a score of 9-2. Yaz took a little batting practice.

As luck and the pitching rotation would have it, Gary Bell was on the mound to face his old teammates on Tuesday night. He drew Luis Tiant (11-8) as his opponent. Surprisingly, only 16,652 fans showed up at Fenway.

Perhaps the fans who would have filled the other half of the park had a premonition. Gary Bell just didn't have it that night and he was gone after four innings. El Tiante was a complete mystery to the Red Sox on the other hand, and he brought a 6-0 lead into the last of the seventh. At this point, Yaz produced the one bright note of the evening as he powered a three-run homer 450 feet into the center field bleachers. The blast was home run number forty-three which tied him with Ted Williams for the most home runs by a Red Sox left-hander.

This highlight would have to suffice as Tiant dug a little deeper to hold on to the 6-3 win. The loss dropped the Red Sox back to third, one game behind the Twins and .001 behind the White Sox. Tomorrow would be another "must" game for Boston.

Dick Williams went with his ace Lonborg on just two days rest. Two days would prove inadequate for Lonborg. He skated through the first, but the Indians jumped on him for four in the second and he was gone early.

The Red Sox couldn't seem to get anything going against starter Sonny Siebert. They showed signs of coming to life in the sixth. With the score 5-0, Jerry Adair led off with a single. Yaz kept things going with a single of his own. Reggie Smith ran the count to 2-0 and the 18,415 faithful started to get into it.

Major league baseball is played at a different level of intensity than other sports at the end of a season. In some sports, the clubs at the bottom of the pack seem to play as if a high draft choice is their top priority. In baseball, the also-ran clubs challenge the contenders down to the last out. Cleveland manager Joe Adcock summoned reliever Bob Allen to complete the walk to Smith. Then he brought in his "horse", Stan Williams, who proceeded to strike out Jones, Scott and Petrocelli. The Boston bats went silent for the rest of the game. The final score was 6-0.

Many of the Red Sox players felt that the season was over for them following this disappointing loss. Some even began to pack so they could make a quick get away on the following Sunday. Although they were still just one game out of first place, the Twins only needed to win two out of their last three to win the whole thing and the White Sox were finishing up against the lowly A's and Washington Senators.

In his book *Yaz*, Yastrzemski recalls wandering around the locker room to thank the other players for their efforts. He recounts the following conversation with Lonborg, "Way to go, Jimmy, you kept us in it." "Thanks, Yaz, you did too," Lonborg responded.

But 1967 was a very unusual year. Shortly after the loss, the players remaining in the clubhouse learned that California had beaten the Twins. There was a faint glimmer of hope.

When Yaz returned to his home in Lynnfield, he told his wife, Carol, that the Red Sox were out of it. Still, he couldn't resist calling the Boston papers to check on the progress of the White Sox-A's doubleheader. After the A's won the first game, Carl began to rethink his position. When the A's won the second game, everyone had to rethink their positions.

Thursday turned out to be an off day for all of the contenders. The Tigers were scheduled to play the Angels but they were rained out. The four teams stood in place with one and one half games separating the top club -- Minnesota -- and the fourth place White Sox.

On Friday, the Red Sox were off again. The two off days served to build the tension surrounding the weekend showdown with the Twins who had already arrived in Boston to be well-rested for the next day. Jose Santiago was nominated to take his 11-4 record to the mound on Saturday.

There was some movement in the pennant race on Friday. The Chicago White Sox eliminated themselves by losing 1-0 to the seventh place Washington Senators. It rained in Detroit again and the Tigers faced back to back doubleheaders against the Angels on Saturday and Sunday.

The combinations of wins, losses and possible finishes among the three clubs seemed endless. One thing made it simple for the Red Sox: they had to win both games against the Twins.

No one felt this more strongly than Carl Yastrzemski. He had been preparing for this moment since childhood. Baseball had been his life for as long as he could remember. All those games with the Bridgehampton White Eagles -- playing with his father and his uncles -- were aimed towards this one moment. Yastrzemski had worked out like a man possessed during the off season to prepare for the 1967 season. He had spent day after day at the Colonial Hilton in Lynnfield, Massachusetts, rounding himself into the best shape of his career. And it had already paid off in increased power as his home run output shot up to forty-three versus sixteen the year before.

Yaz decided to return to the Colonial in Lynnfield for the Friday night before the opener against the Twins. Things were just too hectic at home. He tossed and turned for most of the night, retracing the path that led him to this point and anticipating game situations for the next day.

At about 6:00 a.m., Yaz gave up on sleep for the night and headed for the nearby golf course. As he walked the deserted links, he envisioned situations he might encounter and how he would respond. He had been on a tear for the whole month and the last ten games in particular. In these ten key games, Yaz had hit .444 and most of his sixteen hits had come at crucial times.

He truly believed that he would get a hit every time he came to bat.

Yaz was relieved when he could finally go to the ballpark. On this particular day, he really talked it up in the clubhouse. Now that he was out from under the captaincy, he could be himself and let his natural emotions out. He made a special point to seek out starter Santiago. Jose promised to keep Harmon Killebrew -- who was tied with Yaz for the home run lead in the American League -- from hitting one out. Yaz promised he would hit one out for Santiago.

The game had the festive air of a World Series contest. Vice President Hubert Humphrey was there to cheer on his hometown Twins. Senators Ted Kennedy and Ed Brooke were both on hand. A total of 32,909 fans were ready to react to every pitch.

The Twins started their big left-hander Jim Kaat who had been red hot for them in September. Minnesota held an 11-5 edge in the season series against Boston and they were anxious to put the Red Sox away in the first game. Kaat had looked like the twenty-five-game winner he had been in 1966 of late and he was the obvious choice.

Santiago started slowly for the Red Sox. As he told Cliff Keane of the *Boston Globe* after the game, he walked to the mound "feeling a little worried, as who would not feel worried in a game like that?"

Minnesota sandwiched a single, a walk and a single around a flyout to jump off to a 1-0 lead. When big Bob Allison singled to load the bases, things got more than a little tense. Jose reached back to retire Rod Carew and Ted Uhlaender without further damage and the crowd relaxed.

Kaat appeared more composed as he handled the Red Sox easily in their half of the first. The only damage done was a single by Yaz. Kaat's breaking ball looked tough and the inning ended with the Twins up 1-0.

Santiago found his rhythm in the second. As he told Keane, "I had good stuff and I no worry." The Twins were retired without scoring in the top of the frame.

Kaat looked simply awesome. The Red Sox touched him for a couple of hits but the 6' 5" hurler had his strike out pitch working. After two innings, the Red Sox had no runs and Jim Kaat had three strike outs.

Santiago mowed the Twins down in their half of the third. The game was starting to shape up as a pitcher's duel, but the complexion was about to change.

Kaat began the third by striking out Santiago for victim number four. After two pitches to Mike Andrews, Kaat wig-wagged to the Twins dugout. Something was wrong. As it turned out, Kaat had pulled a tendon in his left arm and the Twins needed bullpen help in a hurry.

The Twins summoned Jim Perry who brought an 8-7 record and an ERA of 2.96 to the mound. Perry was given extra time to warm up to compensate for the injury. He then disposed of Andrews and Adair and the inning was over. But the Red Sox were glad to see the last of Jim Kaat.

Santiago encountered a little trouble in the Twins' fourth. A Ted Uhlaender fly ball was played into a triple by rightfielder Hawk Harrelson and the Twins had another runner in scoring position with only one out. Jose managed to strike out Jerry Zimmerman. Then he induced Jim Perry to fly out to Reggie Smith and Boston was out of the jam. Perry sailed through the Red Sox lineup in the fourth inning. Santiago matched him in the Twins' fifth and the string of zeros continued.

The Red Sox finally got something going in the fifth. Reggie Smith started off with a double to left center. Williams then inserted Dalton Jones as a pinch hitter for Russ Gibson. Jones responded with a little dribbler to second baseman Rod Carew. It is often said that over the course of a 162-game season, the bad hops even out. If this is true, the Red Sox had saved one for the right occasion. Somehow the ball hopped up and hit Carew on the left shoulder and there were runners on first and third.

Perry opened up a little daylight by striking out Jose Santiago and Mike Andrews. Now it was up to Jerry Adair. As he had so often during that season, Jerry came through with a clutch single and the game was tied at one. This brought Yaz to the plate. He grounded sharply between first baseman Killebrew and Carew. The ball eluded Killebrew but Carew made a nice effort to snag it. Unfortunately for the Twins, pitcher Perry had neglected to cover first. Carew held onto the ball in frustration as he watched Yaz reach first and Dalton Jones cross the plate with the go-ahead run.

The Twins struck back in the top of the sixth. A walk to Bob Allison followed by singles from Uhlaender and Rich Reese knotted the score at two. The next thing Santiago knew, the bases were loaded with Twins and the dangerous Zoilo Versalles was up. Versalles was having a terrible year -- he would end up hitting .200 -- but he had been the American League MVP in 1965 and he was a dangerous hitter. Jose came in with a terrific sidearm curve and Versalles popped it up to end both the inning and the threat. Santiago would say later, "That was my best pitch of the game."

Since Rich Reese had pinch hit for Perry in the top of the sixth, the Twins had to bring in a new reliever: Ron Kline. Kline was given a rather unceremonious welcome by George Scott. He drilled Kline's first pitch to the far reaches of the center field bleachers tor the Boomer's first homer since August 19. The inning came to a close with the Red Sox clinging to a 3-2 lead.

Santiago cruised through the Twins order in the seventh and Red Sox fans were on their feet for the seventh inning stretch. They must have willed some more good luck since dame fortune was about to smile on them again.

Mike Andrews began things with a checked swing tapper that pitcher Kline couldn't handle. Then Adair sent a one-hopper directly back to Kline. Ron wheeled to throw to second to start the double play. Much to the fans' delight, shortstop Versalles dropped the ball.

In perfect drama, this brought Yaz to the plate again. Twins manager Cal Ermer signalled the left-handed Jim Merritt in from the bullpen to face Boston's hottest hitter. Yaz studied pitchers constantly. He knew Merritt had given him nothing but sliders in

Minnesota, but he was hoping for a fastball in Fenway. When the count went to 3-1, Yaz sat on his fastball. Yaz got his wish and a fan in the right field bleachers got a very valuable souvenir. Carl had done it again with a three-run homer at the crucial moment.

That achievement symbolizes Yaz's season as well as any single moment. Most fans believed that Yaz would homer in that at-bat. Yaz believed he would do it. Most fans and players hope for a home run. On that turn at bat, on that day, in that special year, everyone **knew** that Yaz would hit a home run.

Carl remembers the crowd reaction in his book. "It started from the bleachers -- those stands 380 feet away that I never thought I'd ever reach -- and a roar started. It built as I circled each base, continued as the '3' went up in the scoreboard, to show we had a 6-2 lead, and the noise didn't end for three minutes. It continued long after I had gone into the dugout."

When the Red Sox returned to the field for the top of the eighth, the fans gave them another standing ovation. The cheers were meant for all twenty-five team members, but they were mostly directed towards left field, towards the man they call "Yaz".

When Santiago returned to the mound, he had already thrown 120 pitches to the plate. After Jose walked lead-off hitter Bob Allison, Dick Williams came to the mound and waved Gary Bell in from the bullpen.

Santiago wanted to try to go the whole way but he recognized the wisdom of his manager's move. Williams quoted Jose as saying, "All right with me. I tired." He headed to the dugout amid yet another standing ovation from Boston's faithful.

Gary Bell was the right man at the right time. He retired the Twins without a murmur and the Red Sox were three outs from a gigantic win.

The Red Sox offered no resistance in the last of the eighth inning and the stage was set for the Twins' last stand.

Gary Bell retired the first two Twin hitters in the ninth and the fans were on their feet again. The celebration was postponed for awhile when Cesar Tovar touched Bell for a double. Big Harmon Killebrew stepped to the plate. Bell tempted him with a 1-0 fastball and "Killer" hit it over everything. It was last seen heading in the general direction of the Massachusetts Turnpike. Now the score was 6-4 and Red Sox fans were more than a little concerned. Bell ended the suspense by enticing Tony Oliva to line out. The Red Sox were alive to fight another day.

Carl Yastrzemski was as satisfied with this victory as he had been with any in his career. He had produced three hits including the decisive home run. He was certain that they would win the next day and he was sure that he would play a major role.

Yaz did indeed play a major role the following day. When Sunday's game was over, he had achieved an incredible record over the twelve final, crucial games. Yaz had gone twenty-three for forty-four for an unbelievable average of .523. He had driven in sixteen runs in the twelve games, scored fourteen and banged out five home runs. But even those awesome numbers don't begin to tell the story. Hit after hit had been a critical one and homer after homer had been a game winner. Most observers call it the greatest exhibition of clutch hitting in baseball history.

Yaz went on to star in the World Series that followed. He had ten hits in the seven game series and batted .400. His two homers in the second game carried the day for Boston. When you combine the last twelve games and the Series, Yaz was thirty-three for sixty-nine for an out-of-this-world average under pressure of .478.

Carl would play another sixteen seasons for the Boston Red Sox. In some ways, 1967 became his blessing and his curse. The fans expected a repeat of that performance, but it was a performance that would never be duplicated by any player.

In the pitcher-dominated season of 1968, his numbers fell precipitously. His average dropped twenty-five points to .301, but it was still good enough to lead the league. However, his home runs diminished to twenty-three and his RBIs fell from 121 to seventy-four. Dogged by injuries and targeted by opposing pitchers, it was a disappointing year all around.

In 1969 his power returned -- his homers were back up to forty and his RBIs got up to 111 but his average fell to .255. In 1970 his numbers were almost as good, and in some cases better, than 1967 (.329 - 40 - 125), but the Red Sox were never in contention and his accomplishments went relatively unnoticed.

Over the next several years, Yaz settled into something of a routine. He became a .280 type hitter who would hit fifteen or so homers and knock in 80-85 runs. He gradually came to spend more time at first base than left field. In many ways, he was happier with his relatively low profile out of the spotlight. Yaz never thought of himself to be a superstar. He certainly didn't have a superstar's dimensions at 5' 11" and 175 pounds. He came from a hard-working background and he thought of himself to be an above-average, blue collar ballplayer.

Boston fans had a love-hate relationship with Carl Yastrzemski. They loved him for 1967 and they loved the fact that he was in the lineup day after day. They hated the fact that he couldn't duplicate 1967 and they hated the fact that he was not Ted Williams. Yaz was largely indifferent; he just wanted to be Carl Yastrzemski.

Carl and the fans had a reconciliation of sorts in 1975. By then he was thirty-six and after fifteen years in town, he qualified as an institution. Besides, the golddust twins of Fred Lynn and Jim Rice were in the spotlight and Carl could do his workmanlike job without being the center of attention. Since he had been through pennant races before, he could provide veteran leadership by example and skip the "rah rah" stuff.

Yaz's numbers were modest in 1975 -- .269 - 14 - 69 -- but he contributed key hits and he was a stalwart at first base. He moved back to left field for the League Championship Series against Oakland and he fielded flawlessly. His .455 batting average was a big factor in their three-game sweep and his play evoked memories of a younger Yaz in 1967.

Yaz was a key contributor in the classic seven game World Series against the Cincinnati Reds. He banged out nine hits and averaged .310. Unfortunately, he had the distinction of making the last out as the Reds squeaked out their fourth win. However, the fans had come to view him as human and they had begun to accept his shortcomings.

Boston tailed off in 1976 and 1977, but Yaz actually improved with age. His home run output was back in the twenties and his RBIs were over 100. He and the Boston fans had settled into the kind of comfortable relationship that results over years of being together.

Yastrzemski still hungered for a World Championship and 1978 looked like it could be the year. Boston was loaded with power; their ninth hitter, Butch Hobson, socked seventeen home runs with eighty RBIs. Dennis Eckersley, Mike Torrez and Luis Tiant gave Boston their best starting pitching in years and Bob Stanley came out of the bullpen to pick up fifteen wins. In late July, the Red Sox had a 14-game lead over the Yankees.

Many old-time Red Sox fans feared a collapse and a collapse is exactly what they got. When the Yankees took four straight in Fenway in early September, the panic was official. With eight games to go, Boston had actually fallen two games behind the Yanks. But this team still had a little left and they managed a win on the last day of the season to force a playoff with New York.

The one-game playoff was scheduled for Fenway: Torrez vs. Ron Guidry (25-3). Yaz had turned thirty-nine in August. He realized that this was probably his last shot. He really wanted this one and he got off on the right foot with a homer in the second. After Boston fell behind 5-2 on the infamous Bucky Dent three-run home run and a one-run homer by Reggie Jackson, they came storming back. Yaz sent Jerry Remy home on a single and subsequently scored to cut the lead to 5-4.

As fate would have it, Yaz came to bat with two outs and one runner on in the last of the ninth with the Yankees clinging to their 5-4 lead. He took a mighty swing at a Goose Gossage fastball and lifted a towering popup in the general direction of third base. When the ball settled into Graig Nettles' glove, the season was over and Yaz's dreams of a World Championship were dashed.

Carl Yastrzemski played five more years for the Boston Red Sox. He was used largely as a designated hitter and his average settled down in the range of .270. He could still hit for power on occasion and as his twenty-second season came to a close, he had clouted sixteen home runs in only 131 games.

The year 1983 was to be his last season. Along the way, he had managed to become the first player in American League history to hit 400 home runs and gather 3,000 hits. It had become clear that Yaz had become one of the game's greats through durability and hard work.

Yaz actually had second thoughts about retiring in 1983 since he was hitting over .300 in July. But the Red Sox fell out of contention and his average fell along with the team. Carl Yastrzemski day on October 1, 1983, was one of the more dramatic events in Fenway Park history. It was the day that Carl and the fans realized they loved one another and that they were free to show it. Yaz let them know by circling the park one last time and touching as many fans as he could.

When it was all over, Carl had played in over 3,300 games and registered over 12,000 official at bats. He had come to the plate over 14,000 times for the Boston Red Sox. His lifetime statistics placed him in the top ten in major league history for games, at bats, hits, doubles, RBIs and walks. Not bad for a blue collar guy.

In July of 1989, Yaz was inducted into baseball's Hall of Fame in Cooperstown, New York. He had been elected in his first year of eligibility. He had been named on 94% of the ballots, the sixth best average in history. Carl Yastrzemski had earned election to the Hall of Fame based on his accumulated accomplishments over twenty-three seasons. But in no small part, he had earned election based on his incredible season of 1967.

In his biography, Carl Yastrzemski talks about what 1967 meant to him:"You can't kill what we had and what we did just because we lost one game in October. It remains a part of people to this day. The call it the Impossible Dream or the Miracle of Fenway. For me it always went beyond a slogan. It wrapped me up forever with New England. No matter what, I would always be a part of them, the fans, the team, the city. It became our permanent connection to each other, like a family tie. And nothing could ever break that. Not to a Yastrzemski."

We love ya, Yaz!

CHAPTER TEN

Boston Red Sox vs. Minnesota Twins

Sunday, October 1, 1967

Jim Lonborg, a lanky, twenty-four-year-old right handed California native pitched the most important game of his young career in this vintage matchup with the Twins at Fenway Park. The drama as to who would prevail for the American League pennant had been played out throughout September. Coming down to the last game of the season, the Detroit Tigers could ensure a tie and force a playoff by sweeping the pesky California Angels in their doubleheader that day. The winner of the Red Sox-Twins contest was assured of at least a tie and would emerge as the outright winner if the Tigers stumbled in either game. Lonborg, a native of San Luis Obispo, California, and a pre-med graduate of Stanford University, was the undisputed ace of the Red Sox staff with twenty-one wins already to his credit. However, he entered the game winless against the powerful Twins, a team that had always given him trouble. Lonborg couldn't have known it as the sun came up over Boston Harbor that morning, but he was about to achieve the most important victory of a distinguished career that would span fifteen seasons in the major leagues.

Fall comes early to New England. October 1, 1967, was no exception as the day broke with a crispness more associated with football than this day's premier event. Lonborg thought it would be a good day for pitchers as he made his way to Fenway. The air was crisp but mild and the sun was warming but not too bright from a pitcher's point of view. Lonborg remembers that "it was a great day on the mound; it was a nice cool fall day."

Lonborg was well rested for the day's epic contest. He had lasted only two innings before taking an early shower in Wednesday's game against the Red Sox jinx team, the Cleveland Indians. In his typical forthright candid manner, he recalls, "I didn't do well against the Indians on Wednesday." With three full days of rest, he felt strong -- but not too strong, he hoped.

Lonborg had looked for an edge in preparing for the big game and he thought he had found it by spending Saturday night in Ken Harrelson's room in the Sheraton Boston. In Lonborg's words, "I was a bachelor at the time and had an apartment in town but didn't think it was a good idea to stay there that night because of all of the excitement going on with my single roommates."

Lonborg's thinking went like this: he had a better road record during the season so by treating it as an away game, he would give himself an edge. He followed the routine right through to ordering his regular pregame breakfast from room service. Lonborg reflects that "I just thought it would be different if I pretended I was on a road trip . . . having room service meals . . . coming out of the hotel . . ."

It wasn't that Lonnie was superstitious as much as he was analytical and competitive. He considered every angle of the issue in order to gain the maximum leverage. That was partly his nature and partly his academic training as a biology major pre-med at Stanford. In any event, it helped to make him the successful pitcher he had become.

Lonborg was really up when he awoke Sunday morning. "We had so much going for us in terms of energy. We had a sense of momentum. Like we couldn't be denied. When you think about it, we were so lucky really to even have a chance on Sunday of still winning the pennant. We were losing Saturday's game against the Twins until the last of the fifth when we got two runs. Jim Kaat blew out his elbow and then we unloaded on them."

The final game at Fenway Park in recent years had been traditionally witnessed by relatives and close friends of the players plus a few optimistic fans who had purchased their tickets in the euphoria of the earlier April. This fateful day was unlike any season closing game in Red Sox history. Fenway's capacity was listed at slightly in excess of 33,000, but on this Sunday there had to have been at least 36,000 souls crammed into every nook and cranny. You could have cut the pre-game tension with a knife.

Lonborg began throwing gently on the sidelines to Russ Gibson. Manager Dick Williams had been going with catcher Elston Howard of late but decided to go with Gibson on a hunch. Jim wasn't about to second guess Williams -- his hunches had gotten them this far -- and besides, he was equally comfortable with Gibby, Howard or the third catcher, Mike Ryan.

In many ways, Jim Lonborg and Dick Williams represented the odd couple. Lonborg was thoughtful and well-spoken; Williams was acerbic and outspoken. Lonborg enjoyed *Scientific America*; Williams read *Male Magazine*. But Lonborg knew that Williams had made him into a better pitcher. Even if you hated the S.O.B., you had to realize that he goaded you into showing him that you were better than he thought you were.

While the Red Sox were assuming the mantle of the "Impossible Dream" team, a takeoff on the then current broadway musical, Lonborg was more akin to another broadway hit. That same season, "A Man For All Seasons" was enjoying a successful run based on the life of the late Sir Thomas Moore. Lonborg was close to a Renaissance Man. He had entered Stanford University -- the Harvard of the west -- on an academic scholarship. His first love at that time was medicine.

The son of a professor at California Polytechnical Institute, he had grown up in a loving environment which emphasized the whole person. If there were any sports anticipated at Stanford, they were expected to be on the hardwood floor and not on the diamond. But Lonborg's upper body began to fill out and his skill on the mound developed along with his physical growth. A summer in the fast college league in South Dakota convinced Lonborg and the Red Sox that he had the makings for a professional career.

As Lonborg made his way to the mound that day, he knew he was ready. He had told his teammates the day before "this is the first **big** game of my life." He had meant it and he really wanted this one.

Lonborg felt as if he didn't really get into his rhythm right away. When he had been **on** that year -- and he had been **on** a lot -- his fastball moved in on a right hand hitter, his curve ball broke right at the left hand hitters and his sharp slider gave them both fits. In the early going, he wasn't quite loose and the ball didn't go **exactly** where he wanted it to.

His teammates were tight as well. Lonborg had walked the dangerous Harmon Killebrew on four pitches. Before the series even started, Williams and the Red Sox had decided that they weren't going to let Killebrew beat them even if they had to walk him four times each game. Lonborg remembers, "We weren't ever going to let Harmon hurt us with one swing of the bat... we figured that even if we walked him, it would take two or three major hits because of his size to get him around the bases." Following the walk to Killebrew, Yaz misplayed Tony Oliva's line drive and Scott compounded the felony by butchering the relay intended to get Killebrew out at the plate.

You could almost feel the bubble burst collectively for 36,000 fans. Twenty-one years of waiting for a pennant can make even the most partisan fan into a pessimist.

Dean Chance had started the mound for the Twins and he was no slouch. He had brought a 20-13 record into the game with him and he looked almost unhittable through two innings. He had beaten the Red Sox four times already in 1967.

Disaster struck again in the top of the third. Yastrzemski employed his kamikaze style in pursuit of a Cesar Tovar single into left but this time it backfired on him. The ball got by him and eluded his pursuit long enough for the lumbering Killebrew to score all the way from first. It was beginning to look like if Killebrew couldn't beat them by tattooing the left field wall, then he could beat them on the base paths!

The crowd grew even quieter. Two errors and two unearned runs. Worst of all the invincible Yaz had proven that he was only human. Perhaps the magic had evaporated? Perhaps lightning wouldn't strike again. As the autumn shadows inched their way across the playing field, it was almost as if the curtain was slowly setting on this improbable drama.

Jim Lonborg remembers this as perhaps the darkest point of the game. Five errors against the White Sox in the second game of the season was one thing, but two errors in the first three innings of the most important game of the season was quite another. It brought to mind the old baseball adage: if you have to lose, make the other team beat you, don't beat yourself.

But Lonborg was feeling better about his pitching rhythm. When he came off the mound trailing 2-0 in the middle of the sixth inning, he still hadn't given up an earned run. Even better, he had really found his rhythm. His three pitches were all moving and he was able to locate them just where he wanted them.

At that point, Lonnie had logged a fraction over 270 innings in 1967. The fact that he was as strong as he was at this point in the last game of the regular season was no accident. Right after the end of the 1966 season, he had gone to Venezuela to pitch Winter Ball for a couple of months. His expressed purpose was to work on his curve ball in tough spots like 2-1 and 3-2. And it had worked. From South America he went directly to the ski slopes where he spent two months working on his conditioning. (The irony of his choice for a conditioning locale would not be apparent until Christmas of 1967.) When Lonborg reported to Winter Haven in February of that year, he was in the best shape of his life. That rigorous program was serving him well on that afternoon of October 1, 1967.

Lonborg was due to lead off the last of the sixth. At that point, Chance looked almost unhittable. He had given up only two hits and nary a walk. The silence of the crowd was almost eerie. They were disappearing in the lengthening shadows along with the Red Sox' chances.

The mood seemed to be "well, here's one automatic out -- are we ever going to get a run off this guy?" Lonborg was proud of his skills as a hitter. All pitchers are (at least pre-D.H.). But the reality was that he was bringing a .141 average to the plate. Lonborg recalls with some pride, "I could hit Chance. He had this funky windup where he would turn around and you wouldn't see his head. I won a few games that year with my bat. Won my twentieth hitting that triple off Kansas City pitcher Catfish Hunter. I faked a bunt, swung away and hit the ball over the rightfielder's head."

Ever the thinking man, Lonborg considered his options as he studied the field from the on deck circle. His calculation of all of the combinations and permutations paid off. By the time he reached the plate, he had determined that Cesar Tovar was a mite deep at third base. The perfect symmetry of a bunt might be the solution to the problem.

Lonborg could fly before his conditioning mishap (read: ski injury) and fly down the first base line he did after he had perfectly calibrated the flight of the ball and the angle of the bat. Third baseman Tovar did not grasp the principles of empirical research nor did he grasp the sphere dropped down by Lonborg. Instead he studied it like some prehistoric relic and looked for the hole it might have emerged from so he could crawl into it.

Lonborg's brilliant play inspired the crowd and seemed to breathe new life into his teammates. Jerry Adair singled. Dalton Jones followed with a single.

If you see the '67 Red Sox as high drama brought to life, you knew you would see Carl Yastrzemski step to the plate with the bases loaded in this spot. Carl Yastrzemski had over 12,000 official at bats during his 23-year career with the Red Sox. It is important to remember that for every 100 times he came to the plate, Yaz failed to hit 72 times. But you knew he would get the needed hit in this spot. In this year -- his year.

If you thought he would hit a grandslammer, you didn't know Yaz. He said after the game, "I wasn't going to try for a home run . . . he gave me a pitch I could have hit out of the park, but

I hit for a single." Yaz was such an extreme competitor that he wouldn't chance glory at the risk of a rally-killing pop-up. His single into center scored Lonborg and Adair to tie the game.

Hawk Harrelson came up with Yaz on first and Jones on third. Chance nearly sawed his bat in half with a 3-2 slider, but Hawk managed a ground ball to Zoilo Versalles at short. Then the inexplicable happened. Versalles threw home to try for a play on Jones who was nearly stepping on home plate when Zoilo released his throw. Runners on first and third, no one out and the Red Sox up 3-2. The Twins seemed to be coming apart at the seams!

Relief pitcher Al Worthington contributed to the comedy of errors by first wild pitching Yaz to third base and then home for the fourth run as Harrelson advanced to third. After a Scott strikeout and Petrocelli walk, Reggie Smith hit a ground ball directly at Harmon Killebrew at first. Grown men and women don't believe in gremlins but one seemed to be loose in this inning. Perhaps the extraterrestrial who had caused Johnny Pesky to double-pump while Enos Slaughter was racing in to score the winning run in the seventh game of the 1946 Series had decided to even the score. Whatever the cause, Killebrew bungled what should have been a routine play. The "Killer" played it like a hockey goalie and while he didn't get credit for a "save", the Red Sox got credit for another run as Harrelson raced in from third. The Red Sox were up 5-2. Worthington finally retired the next two hitters, including Lonborg, to bring the inning to a merciful end from the Twins' point of view.

In the normal course of events, a 5-2 lead after six innings with a strong pitcher on the mound would appear safe. But 1967 was anything but normal. Besides, this was a team without the precedent of victory. Twenty-one years is a long, long time between pennants. Would the Red Sox find a way to snatch defeat from the jaws of victory?

Lonborg and his teammates were not thinking that way at all. Lonborg reminisces, "People tend to forget that the 1966 team started to come into its own after the All Star break. We had a lot of young guys who were starting to get it together. We had something like the second best record in the league over the last half of the season."

In addition, the Toronto alumni -- Russ Gibson, Mike Andrews and Reggie Smith -- were used to winning. And to Dick Williams winning was everything. He didn't even like to hear the word 'lose'.

The Red Sox had something else going for them as they attempted to hold a 5-2 lead over the last three innings of this their most important game: Jim Lonborg. Lonborg is as charming and kind a man as you will ever meet. But he is also about as intense an individual as you will ever meet. A dental school professor recalls that "he was as dedicated and conscientious as any student I ever had in thirty years of teaching. It was as if he applied the perfectionism of pitching to the study of dentistry." His power of concentration is incredible. The author, a patient of Dr. Lonborg's, once coughed during a complex procedure and Lonborg went straight into orbit. It was as if he had left the living to go into a state of total concentration.

Jim Lonborg is also an extremely competitive individual. As he faced the prospect of retiring nine more Twins, he applied every ounce of his considerable concentration. In 1965 and 1966, Lonnie had compiled a mediocre record of 19-27. Some of it was his inexperience, some of it poor support from a lacklustre team. But a large part of it was his failure to move the hitters off the plate by throwing inside with malice. To establish the inside quarter of the plate as his territory. To reclaim the outside quarter of the plate for his curve ball.

The Red Sox had counselled him on this subject. Sal Maglie, the Red Sox pitching coach, had continually urged him to employ the "brush back" pitch. Maglie had been so proficient at the art during his days with the Brooklyn Dodgers and later with the New York Giants that he was known as "the barber." Old Sal had shaved more than a few hitters in his day and he was fond of the term "chin music." And Dick Williams had used his sharp needle on Lonnie on more than one occasion. Williams really knew how to get under a guy's skin.

But most important of all, Lonborg had decided to get tough. He is a gentleman by nature but he is driven to excel and he would never be happy to be mediocre at anything. He had worked hard at establishing his new image right from opening day. He had begun marking the inside of his glove to record every "hit". When he took the mound at the top of the seventh against the Twins, his glove reflected nineteen "scores".

Lonnie breezed through the Twins' order in the seventh without a scare. He was 271 innings into the season but he seemed to be getting stronger as the game wore on. Six more outs, he thought as he walked to the dugout. Get me some more runs!

But the Red Sox squandered their opportunity to pad their lead in the seventh and Lonborg walked to the mound to start the eighth inning with a three-run lead. These Twins, it turned out, were not inclined to go gently into the rapidly gathering night. Happily for Lonborg, the Red Sox defense would rise to the occasion and save the day. Rich Reese led off with a pinch-hit single. Cesar Tovar followed with a shot right at second baseman Adair. Adair fielded it cleanly, brush-tagged Reese and threw quickly to Scott at first for the double play. Two down and no one on! Adair took a spike wound for his trouble and was replaced by Mike Andrews at second.

Then the Twins erupted again. Killebrew and Oliva put together back to back singles. This created Yaz's chance to return to center stage. Bob Allison hit a smash into the dreaded corner beside the left field wall. It had double written all over it. But in his trademark, Yaz aggressively cut it off and came up firing to second. The throw was right on the money and Allison was an easy out to end the Twins threat and the inning.

For Jim Lonborg this was the first point that he felt that victory was assured. "As a pitcher to go in seconds from a situation with runners on first and third . . . the potential winning run at the plate . . . to a situation where you're out of the inning

. . . at that point I was certain that we would win. We had made the big play all year and you felt that if we had to do it one more time we would. Yaz's play made the difference."

The Red Sox couldn't do anything with Mudcat Grant in the last of the eighth and suddenly the Red Sox were three outs away. Lonborg was confident that he could find the strength in his strong right arm to nail down the victory.

But there was one more gremlin to deal with. At the last moment, a Ted Uhlaender ground ball hit something and caught shortstop Petrocelli right below the right eye. Rico shook it off: this was no time to miss an opportunity for immortality. Rod Carew's grounder to Andrews at second produced an instant replay to the Adair double play in the previous inning. Andrews took a rolling block from Uhlaender but was bailed out by Scott's scoop save at first. Two down ... one out to go!

Pinch hitter Rich Rollins represented the only barrier to the Red Sox' first share in the pennant since their tie with the Cleveland Indians in 1948. Lonborg looked in, went into his big windup and came inside with a pitch which nearly sawed Rollins' bat in two.

Lonborg recalls, "I remember that my last pitch of the game was a fastball to Rollins. At the time I was just throwing fastballs, one after the other. I was really pumped up and I was in my groove. I didn't have to go with much of anything else. We had runs to work with. It wasn't a matter them of having to trick somebody at the plate. It was just a matter of going straight in at the hitter."

For sheer drama, the sky-high popup that Rollins hit towards Petrocelli at short can only be compared to one other batted ball: the fly ball that Roy Hobbs hit off the light tower in "The Natural". Rollins' ball seemed to go up forever. As it reached the peak of its arc, it seemed to have become suspended for a split second. For that split second Red Sox fans throughout New England -- the nation really -- held their collective breaths. They seemed to be saying in unison "this can't be happening; this is only a dream and I'll wake up in a second." Then the ball began its downward descent, gaining in acceleration just like a roller coaster. Suddenly, it was in Petrocelli's glove and time stood still for another split second. An alert cameraman near the Red Sox dugout captured this scene with one single frame of film. It shows Lonborg poised to celebrate on the mound . . . Rico grasping the ball as if it were his first born . . . Yaz beginning his dash in from left field . . . and . . . most importantly, over Yaz's shoulder the fabled scoreboard reading "Boston 5, Minnesota 3". For this single frame, all was right with the world. It was like everybody's first Christmas. The gorgeous blonde of your dreams really did love you. And yes, Bobby Kennedy would make it to the White House. For one brief second, it seemed that you could tilt at windmills and win. And then the celebration began.

Lonborg remembers it as the happiest moment in his baseball career. Pure unadulterated joy and celebration. Players and fans together. An unthinkable scene in the current day.

Mike Andrews and Rico Petrocelli hoisted Jim upon their shoulders and the trio was carried around the field by the surging crowd. It was uplifting at first for the winning pitcher but it soon became downright scary and he had to be rescued by the police.

"The first person I saw rushing toward me was Scotty. And then Gibby was there and Dick and all the guys. Then very quickly as I looked around there were all these strange faces, but they were happy faces. Everybody was yelling, jumping around and enjoying the moment to the utmost. Some of the players were smart enough to run for the clubhouse straight off, but I was enjoying the occasion. I guess I was more personally involved than anyone else."

As the crowd on the field swelled with each passing moment, Lonborg began to have second thoughts about his decision not to run for cover.

"When we started moving in the middle of the crowd initially, I thought we were moving toward the dugout. By then that's exactly where I wanted to go. Next thing I looked up and we were headed for the right field foul pole. Now some of the faces don't look familiar at all. My shoelaces disappeared, my sweat shirt was being torn off, my hat was long gone. Finally, Boston's finest came out and rescued me from those happy but wild fans."

Pandemonium reigned in the Red Sox clubhouse. The obligatory shaving cream was everywhere and every visitor had a beer in his hand. The champagne would come later. Tom Yawkey made a dramatic entrance and tearfully embraced winning pitcher Lonborg.

After about thirty minutes, the celebration wound down so that everyone could listen to the second game of the Tigers-Angels doubleheader. With a 6-4 first game victory, the Tigers needed a sweep to force a one game playoff on Monday. Williams had already decided that Lee Stange would go for the Red Sox.

The Tigers took an early 3-1 lead. As the game droned on, the Angels started to come on and the Tigers began to fade. "Go get 'em, Rig," Yaz encouraged California manager Billy Rigney. Finally, the waiting was over. The Tigers had lost 8-5 and the Red Sox were the undisputed champions of the American League for the first time in twenty-one years. Williams had kept his promise that they would win more than they would lose and he had rode home a 100-1 longshot.

Lonborg remembers October 1, 1967, as the highlight of his major league career. "When you combine what we went through to get there, the obstacles we overcame and the drama of the setting . . . nothing can compare."

Lonnie went on to cover himself with more glory in the World Series against the Cardinals. He pitched a one-hitter in game two and a three-hitter in game five. After his first two World Series games his ERA stood at a sparkling 0.50. While he ran out of gas in game seven, pitching on only two days' rest, Lonborg was the hands down choice for the Cy Young award in the American League. *The Sporting News* also selected him as Pitcher of the Year and the Boston baseball writers named him Most Valuable Pitcher.

The following Christmas Lonborg suffered an injury that would have great impact on his major league career. While his training regimen of skiing had stood him in such good stead for the '67 season, it nearly finished him that Christmas as he suffered torn ligaments in his left knee on the slopes.

Lonborg struggled to regain his Cy Young form in 1968, 1969 and 1970. He even accepted a demotion to the Triple-A farm club in Louisville at one point to try to pitch himself into shape. He had changed his motion to compensate for his leg and it hurt his arm in the process. He managed only a total of seventeen victories over the 1968-70 seasons.

When Lonborg showed signs of promise in 1971 with ten victories, the Red Sox quickly shipped him off to Milwaukee. It was a disappointment to Jim. "I was newly married and thought of Boston as my home. But the Milwaukee club was a class operation."

After fourteen wins with Milwaukee in 1972, he found himself traded again. This time he was traded to the Philadelphia Phillies in the National League. "I was fortunate. The Phillies were a fine organization. Very much like the Red Sox in many ways."

Red Sox fans may not be fully aware of it but Lonborg enjoyed a number of successful seasons in Philadelphia. In fact, he won seven more games in a Philadelphia uniform (seventy-five wins) than in a Red Sox uniform (sixty-eight wins). His high point with the Phillies was an 18-10 record in 1976. He had learned to pitch with his head -- the same scientific approach that had lead to his successful bunt to lead off the sixth inning on October 1, 1967 -- even though some of the strength in his arm had deserted him.

The Phillies released him in June of 1979. But Lonborg felt he still had some baseball left in him. He had gone to a lot of effort to get into shape for the season and he hooked up with the Town Team in Scituate, Massachusetts. "I enjoyed it but those guys came right up there swinging at me. I never got a chance to set them up!"

Lonborg transferred his earlier interest in medicine to dentistry. He enrolled in the Tufts Dental School in Boston and drew on his baseball earnings to carry his family through four years of schooling. He applied the same perfectionist tendencies that made him a successful pitcher to his new field and more than held his own against fellow students freshly out of school.

Jim Lonborg's dental practice in Hanover, Massachusetts, is a thriving one. He lives in nearby Scituate with his lovely wife, Rosemary, and their six energetic children.

One story about Jim Lonborg the health provider and caregiver paints an accurate picture. When the author had an abscessed tooth on the Fourth of July in 1989, Dr. Lonborg graciously examined me in his living room and provided fast relief. He is as effective in his practice of dentistry as he was on the mound on October 1, 1967.

One last anecdote remains to be told. It tells a lot about what kind of year 1967 was like. It tells a lot about the Red Sox ball club. And it tells a lot about Jim Lonborg.

Lonborg was perhaps the last player to leave the clubhouse. Hours had passed since the game had ended and the quiet of Fenway was disturbed only by the sounds of the post-celebration cleanup. Only one other man remained in Fenway.

Lonborg made his trek to the top of Fenway. He found his way to the office of the man who **was** the Boston Red Sox: Thomas Austin Yawkey. He found Mr. Yawkey sitting in solitary reflection in his office. Lonborg had barely escaped from the fans with his life but somehow he had ended up with the game ball. He walked over to Yawkey, handed him the ball and said, "if anyone deserves this, you do."

Dreams do come true.

CHAPTER ELEVEN

Boston Red Sox vs. St. Louis Cardinals

Game 7 of The World Series

Thursday, October 12, 1967

As the sun rose on Columbus Day, 1967, Dick Williams faced the most important game of his brief managerial career. In spring training the brash Williams had said, "We'll win more than we lose". Not even the cocky Williams had dared to dream that this would mean twenty-two more wins than losses, clinching the pennant by one game on the last day of the season and coming within one game of the first Red Sox World Championship in almost fifty years! Williams had the ace of his staff, Jim Lonborg, ready to go to the mound in this winner-take-all final contest. Unfortunately, through the quirk of the schedule, "Gentleman Jim" was going on only two days of rest. He was also pitching his fourth "must-win" game in just twelve days. Williams knew he was taking a gamble by starting the over-worked mainstay of his staff. But Williams had come within one game of a championship by playing his hunches all year. The thirty-eight-year-old native of St. Louis had started the season with a one-year contract and a three-year lease on the furniture in his rented apartment. Williams had put together thirteen years in the big leagues through cunning and gut instincts and he had complete confidence in his intuition. "Red" Schoendienst would go with his "horse", future Hall-of-Famer, Bob Gibson, who had three day's rest. Williams would counter with the guts and

competitive spirit of Lonborg. Just let Lonborg get through five or six innings with minimal damage and the rookie manager knew he would think of something. Besides, there really was no one else.

In many ways the 1967 World Series was an anti-climax for the Boston Red Sox. Their impossible dream had already come true on October 1 when they clinched the American League pennant. No one ever expected them to be playing for the World Championship. Plus, the Series really is a week and a half of parties and celebration.

The Red Sox entered the Annual Classic as 3-1 underdogs to the National League Champion St. Louis Cardinals. And well they should have. The Cardinals, led by wily manager, Red Schoendienst, had finished ten games atop the strong National League.

Schoendienst was Dick Williams' superior in several respects. He was just finishing his third full year at the helm of the Cardinals and he was six years older than Williams. Red had played nineteen years in the big leagues including three World Series. He was a starter at second base for most of those years and his batting average nearly always hovered near .300. Schoendienst began and ended his career with St. Louis; he had a brief stop in New York with the Giants and a longer successful stint with the Milwaukee Braves.

Schoendienst also knew how to deal with adversity. In 1959 he had been stricken with tuberculosis and faced months of hospitalization. At age thirty-six, his big league career appeared over. But Red refused to give up and achieved a miraculous comeback with the Braves in 1960. Traded to the Cardinals in 1961, Schoendienst batted .300 that season and .301 the next as a part-time second baseman and oft-used pinch hitter. Yes, Red could handle a tough spot.

The Cardinals were led by MVP first baseman, Orlando Cepeda. The "Baby Bull's" numbers: a .325 batting average, twenty-five home runs and 111 runs batted in nearly matched Yaz's stats. Cepeda fielded flawlessly at first base. Red Sox fans shuddered at the prospect of his right handed power and Fenway's friendly left field wall.

The rest of the Cardinal infield was well-balanced. Julian Javier was a steady glove and a solid .280 hitter with speed and power. Dal Maxvill at short had a weak stick (.228) but he made up for it with his slick fielding. St. Louis native, Mike Shannon, was in his sixth season with the Cards and he had made a nice transition from the outfield to third base in 1967.

The St. Louis outfield was their jewel. It featured two future Hall-of-Famers and one star who would become the scourge of baseball owners. The latter was Curt Flood, who would later pioneer in challenging the players' rights to free-agency. Ironically, Flood would fail in his first test of baseball's version of slavery and never benefitted from the fruits of his groundwork.

Labor relations were far from Flood's mind in 1967 and he would have a "career year". Curt batted .335 and anchored the Cardinal outfield in center field.

Left field was patrolled by Lou Brock, one of the great base stealers of all time. All Lou did in 1967 was lead the league in at bats (698), runs scored (113) and stolen bases (52). Schoendienst hoped that Brock's base running antics would prove a distraction to Red Sox pitchers.

Right field was home for the enigmatic Roger Maris. Roger astonished the baseball world by smashing sixty-one home runs in 1961 to break Babe Ruth's record of sixty set in 1927. What is even more astonishing is the considerable evidence to suggest that Roger was basically a solid, journeyman ballplayer who caught fire for one year. The next year his home run output dropped to thirty-three and would never approach even that level again in his next six seasons. Roger performed credibly for St. Louis in the field and batted a respectable .261 with nine home runs. He knew something about catching lightning in a bottle.

The St. Louis pitching staff featured four starters all with earned run averages below 3.00. Bob Gibson was the anchor. He had been troubled by injuries in 1967 and had an off year (for him) with a record of 13-7. He appeared to be rounding into form as the series approached.

Another future Hall-of-Famer, Steve "Lefty" Carlton chipped in with a 14-9 record. Nelson Briles had the year of his major league lifetime with a 14-5 record although most of his forty-nine appearances came in relief. Dick Hughes had the only good year of his brief three-year career with a record of 16-6 and an ERA of 2.67. Joe Hoerner and Ron Willis provided depth in the bullpen.

On paper, the St. Louis Cardinals were clearly stronger than the Boston Red Sox. If the series went the maximum of seven games, four of the games would be played in Fenway and three of the games at Busch Stadium in St. Louis. None of the games would be played on paper.

Nineteen sixty-seven was the next to the last year that each league's representative to the World Series was determined based on the results of the full season. The division playoffs were introduced in 1969 and this system has been in place ever since. Winning the playoffs to get to the Series is like a victory in a mile run. Winning the pennant over the regular season is like winning a marathon. It was with the joy and fatigue of the long distance runner that the Red Sox began the 1967 World Series.

GAME ONE

The Series opener was played before a capacity crowd at Fenway on a sparkling fall day. The crowd responded all day as if they were just happy to be there. As if winning was too much to hope for. Perhaps they didn't know how to behave at a World Series game after twenty-one years of frustration. The Red Sox played pretty much the same way.

In defense of the Red Sox, St. Louis starter, Bob Gibson, was flat out overwhelming. Gibson had only pitched in 175 innings that year and he was in mid-season form. He "put on a clinic" on the mound.

In his 1990 autobiography, *No More Mr. Nice Guy*, Williams says of Gibson's game one performance, "That was one of the best parts of the series, watching Gibson protect the mound like it was his own home, throwing inside and hard and keeping each of our hitters worried about becoming another Tony Conigliaro." Nice analogy, Dick.

Williams started Jose Santiago who was simply the best pitcher available. Jose had come on strong in the second half of the season and finished with a record of 12. He was, in fact, the Red Sox counterpart of the Cardinal's Nelson Briles.

The Cards drew first blood in the top of the third. Roger Maris knocked in Lou Brock to begin this series which would be his last moment in the sun. Roger would go on to bat .385 and knock in seven runs in the seven-game series.

The Red Sox got on the board in the bottom of the third through an unexpected source. Much to the surprise of the assembled multitude, especially Mr. Robert Gibson, Jose Santiago homered into the left field net. Since Jose had only one other home run during his eight-year big league career, we can only assume that the afore-mentioned Mr. Gibson had suffered a momentary lapse in concentration.

Santiago staggered through seven innings like a middleweight fighter. He gave up ten hits and three walks. But he persevered until Messrs. Brock and Maris repeated their earlier feat to put the Cards up for good, 2-1 in the seventh inning.

The Red Sox appeared relieved that they had acquitted themselves well in the opener. Tomorrow would be another day and game two starter, Dick Hughes, was no Bob Gibson.

GAME TWO

Dick Hughes was no Bob Gibson but Jim Lonborg went Gibson one better. If Gibson was overwhelming in game one, Lonborg was just plan unhittable. Well, almost unhittable.

Lonborg set the Cards down like ten pins over the first four innings. In the last of the fourth, lightning struck again. Captain

Carl took Dick Hughes downtown and the Fenway crowd finally came alive.

Lonborg continued unhittable nursing a 2-0 lead into the last of the seventh. Yaz then struck one more time to put the game on ice with a three-run homer.

The lingering suspense was whether or not Lonborg could preserve his no-hitter. This dream was shattered when Julian Javier cleanly doubled into left center with two out in the eighth. But Lonborg finished up with a one hit shoutout and the series was tied at one.

ON TO ST. LOUIS

As the series moved on to St. Louis for games three, four and five, Dick Williams was going home. Williams was born in St. Louis on May 7, 1928. He grew up in St. Louis, living there until his family moved to Southern California while he was in junior high.

Williams was a child of the depression: literally and figuratively. He worked for everything he ever had in his life. When Williams' family could not afford to buy him a bat he finagled a broken bat from the Cards' star, Pepper Martin and taped it up. When his throwing arm went bad, he made himself into an indispensable utility man and a world class bench jockey.

GAME THREE

Williams was going home and the series was tied. But even Dick Williams couldn't will Gary Bell into going beyond the second inning of game three. Gary just did not have it and left for a pinch hitter after giving up three runs in his brief stint.

Gary Waslewski (remember that name) came in to hold the Cards at bay through the fifth inning. When Dalton Jones singled home Mike Andrews in the top of the sixth to make it 3-1, there was some hope. But Brock and Maris combined again in the bottom of the inning to make it 4-1. The teams traded runs as the Cards prevailed 5-2 behind Nellie Briles' seven-hitter.

Williams was distressed by the lack of fire in his team. During the third game Nelson Briles had nailed Yaz in the leg with a pitch that was clearly in retaliation for his two homers in game two. After the game, Williams told reporters, "The St. Louis Cardinals are as bush as the name of the beer company that owns them." Never let it be said that Williams would miss any opportunity to motivate his team.

GAME FOUR

Game four appeared to be another "must win" game for the Red Sox. The last thing they wanted to do was go down three games to one. But go down 3-1 they did as Williams' incendiary remarks failed to strike the desired sparks.

Bob Gibson was even better in game four than he had been in the opener. He scattered five hits and walked only one in nine complete innings.

Jose Santiago finally ran out of gas. He started for the Red Sox and never got out of the first inning. Jose gave up six hits and four runs: all of them earned. In a curious move, Williams relieved Santiago with Gary Bell who had been shelled out as the starter the day before. Penance perhaps?

Bell didn't embarrass himself this time but reliever Jerry Stephenson gave up two runs in the bottom of the third and it was all over but the shouting. The way Gibson was pitching, a six-run lead was as sure a thing as a Democratic Mayor in Boston. The two teams went through the formality of playing innings four through nine but the game was not as close as the final score of 6-0 suggested.

It was widely agreed that the Red Sox flirtation with destiny was finally over. The club had clearly peaked in game two and they would simply show up for game five.

GAME FIVE

Anyone who thought that did not know Jim Lonborg. Or Carl Yastrzemski. Or Dick Williams, for that matter. This team wasn't through just yet.

In the diary that he kept all season, coach Bobby Doerr noted "Now we're down three games to one, and everyone realizes that we can't lose again. But we've come back all year and I think we will again."

All Lonborg did was throw his third superb game in nine days. All three games were money games: had-to-win games. And all three games were tightly contested from beginning to end.

Steve Carlton started for the Cards and pitched well. The only run that Carlton allowed came on a single by Joe Foy, an error and a single by Ken Harrelson in the third.

Jim Lonborg, however, had pitched even better. Through eight innings he had held St. Louis scoreless on just two hits.

The Red Sox eked out two all important runs in the top of the ninth. St. Louis manager, Red Schoendienst, elected to walk Rico Petrocelli to load the bases to get to Ellie Howard. The cagey veteran, one of five future Hall-of-Famers in the starting lineups that day, dropped a single down the line into right field to bring in two runs.

Roger Maris homered off Lonborg in the ninth to end Jim's series scoreless streak at seventeen and two-third innings but nothing could detract from his achievements. In two key games, Jim had held the mighty Cards to only four hits and just one run.

And the Red Sox were still alive.

BACK TO BOSTON

Dick Williams selected his starter for the crucial sixth game of the series based on two factors: principle and hunch. Williams had a few choices available to him. Lee Stange had started twenty-four games during the regular season and had a strong

ERA of 2.77. But Williams thought he took too long between pitches and caused the fielders to lose their concentration.

GAME SIX

Williams startled most of the baseball world by naming little-used Gary Waslewski to start game six. Waslewski had only appeared in twelve games with the Red Sox for a total of forty-two innings during the regular season. His was the most surprising choice to start a critical game for the Red Sox since Joe McCarthy picked Denny Galehouse to start the 1948 payoff game against Cleveland. We all know how that turned out! Williams made his decision partly because he had promised Waslewski the sixth game start after a great stint in game three. Dick Williams never goes back on his word. Williams also made his choice based on the hunch that Waslewski would rise to the occasion. As it turned out, Williams had rolled another seven.

Gary Waslewski would only win nine more games over his next five big league seasons. But Gary Waslewski would come through for Dick Williams on October 11, 1967. He held the Cardinals to four hits and two runs over five and one-third innings. That was all Williams wanted from him, or, as it turned out, needed from him.

While Waslewski dazzled the Cardinals, the Red Sox bats came to life. Rico homered in the second. Yaz, Reggie Smith and Rico all went for the downs in the fourth.

The Cards fought back to tie it 4-4 in the sixth but the Red Sox were indomitable. Jones, Joe Foy, Andrews and Yaz all chipped in with hits in the seventh to put the Red Sox up 8-4. Gary Bell caused some anxiety for the capacity crowd in the last two innings but hung in to there ensure the win.

The Red Sox had dodged one more bullet and awaited their date with destiny.

GAME SEVEN

Columbus Day is a major holiday in Boston. All of the schools and businesses are closed. There is a parade in the city and smaller celebrations throughout greater Boston.

This holiday spirit added to the festiveness of the occasion. Every fan in New England waited expectantly as game-time neared.

Fenway was crammed to the rafters with 35,188 spectators. This did not include the mass of fans sitting on the base of the billboard far beyond the center field bleachers.

Most of the Red Sox' hopes were pinned on the tired right arm of James Reynold Lonborg. Not counting winter ball nor spring training games, at that point Jim had thrown 291 innings of baseball. That translates into perhaps 4,000 pitches.

In an interview with Will McDonough of the *Boston Globe*, Lonborg would admit "I felt loose but I knew I wasn't really strong." Somehow Lonborg managed to hold the potent Cards at bay in innings one and two. Through a combination of guts and guile, he kept them off the board and gave his teammates a shot at drawing first blood.

Bob Gibson matched Lonborg's performance inning for inning. And his extra day of rest made him clearly the stronger of the two. If the Red Sox were to have a chance in this game, some-one -- Yaz? Scott? Rico? -- would have to take Gibson downtown early. But Mr. Gibson would not be denied on this day.

The Cards got to Lonborg in the third. The weak-hitting Maxvill led off the inning with a triple which hit three quarters of the way up the bleacher wall in center field. The Red Sox ace bore down to retire Gibson and the dangerous Brock and it appeared that he might work his way out of the jam. Curt Flood ended this hope with a dying quail single into center to score Maxvill with the initial run.

Red Sox nemesis, Roger Maris, kept things going with a hard grounder into right field which eluded the usually sure handed George Scott at first. Any question that Lonborg was tired was laid to rest when he bounded a curve ball by Elston Howard, allowing Flood to score from third.

Lonborg got out of the third without further damage but he was clearly laboring. Lonborg would recall "The first couple of innings I thought I was going to be all right. But around the third or fourth I knew I was struggling."

If anything, Gibson appeared to grow stronger as the game went on. Bobby Doerr's diary entry reads, "Gibson was on top of his game again: outstanding fastball, good quick curve, fine control." Over the first four innings, Gibson was simply perfect. At the end of four, the Red Sox line score read: No runs, no hits, no base runners left on.

The Cardinals got to Lonborg again in the fifth. Red Sox fans greeted Bob Gibson with a generous round of applause when he came to the plate to lead off the inning. Gibson rewarded the classy crowd with a shot off the left field wall to the right of the flag pole which caromed into the center field bleacher seats. All true Red Sox fans recognize that pinball shot as a Fenway Park home run. Take that, Jose Santiago.

While Gibson had used power to put his signature on the series, Lou Brock then used speed to ensure that his accomplishments would live on in legend. Brock worked Lonborg for a walk. Then he stole second. Then he stole third. Then he tagged up and scored on Maris' line shot to Ken Harrelson in right. It seems poetic justice that Gibson's athleticism and Brock's speed would seal the verdict for St. Louis. Red Schoendiest's hope that Brock's base running would be a critical difference had come to pass.

Red Sox partisans grew very quiet as the game reached its halfway point. As legitimate Red Sox fans, they had arrived hoping for the best and prepared for the worst. The worst seemed to be transpiring before their very eyes.

But this Red Sox team had pulled off more escape acts than the legendary Houdini. They hadn't earned the label the "Cardiac Kids" for nothing. They had one last gasp left in the repertoire.

George Scott led off the fifth against Gibson: raw power against raw power. Scott had been disappointing in the series. When he stepped into the batter's box he was but five for twenty-three with only one extra-base hit. But Scott was always a long ball threat and he caught every bit of a Gibson fastball driving it into the deepest part of Fenway. The ball bounced around in the right center field triangle 420 feet from home plate and Scott was hell bent for third. When Julian Javier's errant relay throw landed in the Cardinal's dugout, Scott came on to score the Red Sox' first run of the game.

Gibson bore down to get out of the inning without further damage. But the Red Sox were now within a grand slam home run of victory and hope burned eternal.

The game, the series and the season turned on the decisions made by Dick Williams over the next ten minutes. The Red Sox year had officially begun 230 days earlier on February 25, 1967. Over that time, Dick Williams had made thousands of decisions. Many of his decisions were gutsy, some of his decisions were courageous. This time he failed to make a decision. He simply let Jim Lonborg walk out to the mound to begin the sixth inning.

Lonborg recalled later, "Dick (Williams) was thinking about taking me out in the sixth but I wanted to pitch. That's the funny thing about this job, you always want to go on." The mark of a great pitcher is that he always believes he can get the next hitter out. The mark of a great manager is knowing when to take the ball from a great pitcher.

Bobby Doerr's seventh game journal entry: "I have to believe if Jim had three day's rest, we might have won it. He's been outstanding in his last three games, but today he just didn't 'snap' the ball the way he was in his two previous starts in the series."

Williams' indecision came back to haunt him in the Cardinal's sixth. Tim McCarver of television broadcasting fame doubled off the tiring Lonborg. Joe Foy failed to handle a Mike Shannon one-hopper and two were on with no outs and the pesky Julian Javier coming to the plate.

Dick Williams went to the mound to confer with Lonborg. Williams had one more opportunity to make a tough decision in 1967. Jose Santiago was ready in the right field bullpen. Williams elected to leave the pressure on Lonborg's broad shoulders and returned to the Red Sox dugout along the first base line. The only sound audible throughout New England over the next several minutes was the sound of Javier's bat sending Lonborg's 1-2 pitch soaring into the left field net for a 7-1 Cards lead. Lonborg somehow finished the inning through sheer courage. Then he walked off the mound with tears streaming down his face.

When quizzed about his indecision after the game, Williams replied, "He was my best and he had pretty good stuff, so I went with him. He's been great. Javier hit that homer and we thought he might be bunting. He fooled us."

The Red Sox refused to go quietly. Petrocelli doubled in the eighth, moved to third on a Gibson wild pitch and scored on a ground out. But a 7-2 lead would be too much to overcome. Bob Gibson would see to that.

The crowd had one last hurrah left. When Carl Yastrzemski came to bat in the ninth, 35,184 loyalists gave him one of the greatest ovations ever heard in Fenway.

Bob Gibson was not to be denied his moment on this Columbus day. He took the final bow with his celebrating teammates. He had won his third victory of the series with a three hit, ten strikeout, 7-2 win.

Could the Red Sox have won if Williams had lifted Lonborg after five innings? Maybe, maybe not. Four different Red Sox relievers combined to shut down the Cardinals over the last three innings. After the game, Gibson acknowledged that he was "dead tired" and couldn't have pitched another inning.

In *No More Mr. Nice Guy*, Williams recalls his thoughts on the eve of his 1972 Series appearance with the Oakland A's. He remembers, "Yes, I was happy about making it to my second Series in five years as a manager. But no, I didn't want to go through another 1967 Series, where I'd suffered not only the pain of losing but the far worse pain of wondering whether I'd done enough. In 1967, I was as awed as the players, and perhaps sometimes I managed like it."

Is this Dick Williams' way of saying that he erred by leaving Jim Lonborg in too long? If so, it is pretty oblique for a guy who happily recounts his confrontations with Yaz in 1967 and who holds nothing back in his recollections of the late Tony Conigliaro. And the man who once said, "talking to George Scott is like talking to cement." The headline in the next day's *Boston Globe* over Carl Yastrzemski's byline read, "We'll Be Tough For 5-10 Years." Carl went on to say, "...we're going to be pennant contenders over the next five to ten years." Carl Yastrzemski and the Red Sox would next appear in a World Series in 1975.

This is the last entry in Bobby Doerr's 1967 diary: "There were some tears in the clubhouse afterwards, but there was also a lot of pride and good feeling. This had been a truly amazing year. I'm sure that what happened this year will stay with us and the fans a long, long time."

Sweet dreams.

EPILOGUE

Red Sox Fantasy Game

"Boston" vs. "Pawtucket"
Winter Haven, Florida

Sunday, February 7, 1988

Dreams die hard. For some former members of the 1967 Impossible Dream team, the dream never dies.

Each year, in early February, many of the members of the '67 team gather in Winter Haven, Florida, to participate in the Red Sox "Fantasy Camp". This concept was pioneered by former members of the Chicago Cubs in 1983, and now every major league team has its version.

The idea is that die-hard fans of the Red Sox pay a king's (or queen's) ransom to live the life of a Major Leaguer for one week. During the week, the "campers" use the spring training facilities of the Red Sox, train under the eyes of former major leaguers, and play live games against one another.

The Fantasy Camp is not operated by the Boston Red Sox. It is organized and run by a profit-making group: The Sox Exchange of Montpelier, Vermont. The Sox Exchange ran their first camp in 1984, and the week has expanded and prospered each year since.

Obviously, not every former '67 Red Sox player attends the camp each year. However, a surprising number do. Rico Petrocelli, Dalton Jones, Gary Bell, and Russ Gibson all are regulars. You'll probably find Darrell Branden, Dennis Bennett, and George Thomas there. Jim Lonborg, Mike Andrews, and George Scott have all been there at one time or another. Coach

Bobby Doerr has become a much-beloved participant in recent years.

For the players, the week is a reunion. They come to see old friends and to relive the dream. And they come to **finally** win the last game of the season.

The Fantasy Camp culminates with a series of games between the veteran Red Sox and the campers. The Red Sox veterans always win. At least, they almost always win.

I found myself at the Fantasy Camp in Winter Haven in 1988 based on the advice of my dentist. Of course, my dentist is Dr. Jim Lonborg.

I had told Dr. Jim that I intended to go to the camp after I made my fortune. He said, "Take my advice. Do it now while you can still run. If you wait until you can afford it, you'll pull a muscle on the first day and sit out the whole week."

Seemed like good advice to me. I waited until the Fantasy Camp trip came up on the Channel 2 Auction and bid seventy-five percent of the retail price. The next thing I knew I was on a plane en route to beautiful downtown Winter Haven, Florida.

I really didn't know what to expect of the week. I had trained rigorously to get in shape by growing a mustache. It turned out to be one of the greatest weeks of my life. One or two disappointments, but overall fantastic.

The first night turned out to be a disappointment. Over 100 participants, including eighteen former Red Sox players, had gathered at Buddy LeRoux's luxurious Holiday Inn from all over the United States. The evening's activity? Watching the Super Bowl!

Most of the campers and players were consumed by the football game. For a few of us, this was sacrilegious. The difference between the two games can be summarized in a classic quote from Bill James, baseball statistician extraordinaire: "You don't see anyone keeping score at a football game."

Any disappointment of Sunday night was more than offset when I stepped into the Red Sox clubhouse at 7:30 a.m. on Monday. There, over my locker was affixed a small hand-lettered strip: "CREHAN 1". So what if there were five other campers wearing number one on their uniform? This was a fantasy camp after all! If Bobby Doerr could share number one with Bernie Carbo, I could be gracious as well.

Bernie Carbo turned out to be the first ballplayer I met. The first day was spent working out-- fielding, batting, throwing -- so the players could divide us into six reasonably-balanced teams. Bernie sidled up to me in the outfield and introduced himself. Right, Bernie, you really have to introduce yourself to me. Inside-out swing into the centerfield bleachers, game six is saved! Headline: "Carbo Traded--Lee Retires in Protest." Sure, Bernie, you really have to tell me who you are.

Bernie put his arm around me and began to give me some advice. This is it, I thought. The tip I always needed to hit .300. Before I knew what was happening, I realized that Bernie was giving me advice on the art of making love to a woman. Forget the fact that I already knew every tip he offered me, I'll never forget a word he said!

Apparently, I projected as a good listener because Bernie picked me for the team he was managing with Russ Gibson. Neither one of them could ever remember my name. All week I was "Yogi". I never did ask whether it was for my Hall of Fame potential or my clutch-hitting. Some questions are better not asked.

Dr. Jim had warned me that many of the players had sharp tongues. When I stepped into the batting cage, George Thomas called out, "Says here, Herb, on your form that you're forty-three?" Trying to be nonchalant I replied, "Right, George." From Thomas, "Herb . . . you been sick a lot?" Gales of laughter from the other veterans gathered around the cage. Welcome to the big leagues.

We started our "season" on Tuesday with a game against the Bobby Doerrs/Darrell Brandons. The Carbo/Gibson entry consisted of a plumber, a chemical engineer, a policeman, a pharmacist, and a photographer among others. Clearly, this mix would take time to jell as we went down to ignomious defeat.

Bernie was undaunted. "We'll get 'em tomorrow," were his inspirational words. Gibbie grunted in agreement.

But Wednesday was no better. We continued to play like plumbers, engineers, policemen, etc. It was during this game that Bernie began referring to us as his "chihuahuas". At first, I thought it meant that we were playing like dogs. But it became clear that Bernardo meant it as a form of endearment. You've never met anyone quite like Bernie Carbo.

After our loss to the Petrocelli/Monboquette entry, Bernie decided that drastic measures were in order. At the camp-wide meeting on Thursday morning, he called all of his "chihuahuas" to the front of the group. He informed one and all that we were going to break our losing steak and string of bad luck by drinking a Bud at 8:30 a.m.

What a guy, that Bernie! No matter that we were all fined five dollars at that evening's kangaroo court. The money went to the Jimmy Fund, and we swept a doubleheader.

In the morning game, Jerry Moses tried to psyche out the "chihuahuas" by lining us up at attention for the Star Spangled Banner. Then he had his third baseman, Bill Bob Grogan, play the Star Spangled Banner on his kazoo. But we were above head games. Bernie had brought us to a competitive peak (or high), and we were not to be denied. Score one for the Carbo/Gibson entry.

We really hit our stride in the afternoon game. Much to the chagrin of Frank Malzone and George Thomas, Neil Kennedy pitched a no-hitter. Your faithful servant made his one outstanding play of the week to end the game and preserve the no-hitter. My fielding gem was captured by the camp photographer and is preserved for posterity in the Red Sox Exchange brochure. It appears over the caption, "Herb Crehan will continue for years to re-live this play in '88."

Our winning streak was snapped at two by the charges of Bill Lee and Dalton Jones. It was clear that the week had taken its physical toll when my throw from third base took four bounces to reach its destination. Enough of the regular season. Bring on the Red Sox veterans for the World Championship!

On Saturday, all six camper teams were scheduled to play the Red Sox in a series of three-inning games. On Saturday we were rained out. We did what all ballplayers do on a rain-out: hung around the bars and went to the movies.

Russ Gibson had the best line. He told me: "This is the only weather they let me play in. They didn't want the regular catcher to get hurt on the slippery field."

The sun came out on Sunday morning, and our big day had arrived. At the first Fantasy Camp, the game was played by regular major league rules and the campers lost 15-0. Since then, the rules have been modified as follows:

*

The Red Sox get only two strikes per at bat and only two outs per inning;
*

The campers get five outs per inning;
*

The Red Sox may not walk-they must hit; and
*

No stealing or advancing on passed ball or wild pitches is allowed.

In spite of this equalization, the closest the campers had ever come was an 0-1 loss in 1987. The "lifetime" series stats read: Red Sox 10 wins, Campers 0.

The day is intended pretty much as an orchestrated event. Everyone gets at least one at bat. The campers get a hit or two. The Red Sox win 3-0 or 4-1. Everyone shakes hands and goes home happy. Until the "chihuahuas" had their day.

By the time we took the field, three of our counterparts had gone down gracefully. Next! But the veteran Red Sox had not prepared for our secret weapon: No-hit Neil Kennedy. On this day, Gary Bell was no match for Neil Kennedy.

I had never met Neil Kennedy before that week. Nor have I ever seen him again. For all I know, he is Joe Hardy of "Damn Yankees" fame.

My game day program tells me that he works in insurance in Vermont. There is also one other revealing fact: Neil Kennedy is a Yankee fan!

When we came to bat in the top of the first, I must acknowledge that we were all filled with fear. Then we watched Gary Bell warming up on the mound. At that point, we knew how the St. Louis Cardinals felt when they faced Bell in Game Three of the World Series. He was tossing up grapefruits!

Our first hitter was shoeless Joe, a.k.a., Neil Kennedy. Poetic justice. Neil swung with all of his strength and topped a grounder down the third base line. Bell approached the ball like it was a loaded grenade, about to explode. He threw to first with as much accuracy as if the ball had been marinating for twelve hours. It skidded by Jerry Moses at first base after taking four hops. The official scorer's decision? Base hit! This was a fantasy camp.

Our sagacious manager, John Gounaris, sent Tommie Parsons in to pinch-run for Kennedy. Tom had confided to me before the camp began that he had never played baseball before in his life. He was very nervous. It turned out he worried needlessly. Most of us performed as if we had never played the game either.

Our self-appointed player-manager, John Gounaris, was next to the plate. He demonstrated his wisdom by taking four misdirected pitches from Bell, earning a free ride to first. Don't look now, but the campers had a rally going!

Some of us on the bench felt that Bell was toying with us. Others felt he was having trouble shaking off the effects from the bright lights of the exciting Winter Haven night life. No matter: the pros sent Darrell Brandon down the line to right to warm-up for relief.

Our next hitter was Ed Shaeffer, a fifty-seven-year-old banker from Little Falls, New Jersey. While a fifty-seven-year-old banker may not seem like the ideal candidate to face a former major league pitcher, it turns out that Ed was at his third Fantasy

Camp. He had already logged two hits in previous games against the pros. Ed turned on a Gary Bell cupcake and drilled it into left field!

The speedy Tommie Parsons wheeled around third and turned on the after-burners heading home. He slid under the throw while the campers and the crowd went wild.

Visions of a rout dissipated as Chip Orcutt from Belmont, Massachusetts, grounded into a double play, erasing Shaeffer at second. Even though campers Craig Maine, Dave Lutz, and Dennis O'Brien went down without bringing Gounaris in from third, the "chihuahuas" took the field with a 1-0 lead.

I know that the game-day program says that Kennedy is from Chelsea, Vermont, and works in insurance. And I really don't believe that he is Joe Hardy, reincarnated. But in my mind's eye, I will always picture him as a flinty Vermont farmer, throwing baseballs against the farm door in the receding sunlight. A Yankee fan preparing for the day when he would make his dream come true: to beat the Red Sox.

Apparently, Kennedy looked like the reincarnation of Roger Clemens on February 7, 1988. Darrell Brandon did lead off with a "seeing eye" single that just eluded the legendary Ed Shaeffer at third. Our fearless leader, Bernardo, was next up for the Red Sox. Bernie grounded sharply to big Dave Lutz at first. Lutz played the grounder nicely and retired Bernie unassisted as Brandon moved to second. Under the rules in effect for the pros we had two down.

Jerry Moses was the next hitter. Moses grounded into the hole at shortstop where Craig Maine made a nice play and flipped to first to nip the runner by half a step. Wait a minute! The ump had called him safe! Then we remembered. Dick Radatz ("the Monster") had recruited and paid for the umpiring. We were going to play nine against twelve: the nine Red Sox on the field and the three umpires.

With runners on first and third, Kennedy really had to bear down. And bear down he did. He forced the ever-dangerous Dalton Jones to ground to first base where Lutz made another unassisted putout. **SCORE AT THE END OF ONE: Campers 1, Red Sox 0**

Our pre-game fear returned when we saw that Darrell "Bucky" Brandon had replaced Gary Bell. In his pre-camp counseling, Lonborg had warned me, "Whatever you do, don't hit against Bucky Brandon. The rest of us don't want to be embarrassed, but we don't mind seeing you get your bat on the ball. Bucky is different. He wants to strike everyone out. He's tough." Hitting against Bell had been like hitting against your father when you were age ten. Hitting against Bucky would be another story.

Our lead-off hitter, Paul Chiofar, a cop from California, was quickly struck out by Bucky. As I moved to the on-deck circle, I asked Paul what Bucky had. That's what we "pros" always ask a retired hitter. Paul replied, "I don't know. I couldn't see it."

The hitter before me was Albert Karam, a fifty-five year old state assemblyman from Elmira, New York. Al hit a pool cue shot down the first base line and was easily put out. He mumbled something as he walked by me on his way back to the dugout.

As I stepped into the batter's box, I was as frightened as I have ever been in my life. I could only think of two things: Lonborg's words, and the fact that this game was being videotaped. I barely saw Brandon's first pitch, but I saw enough to know it was low and inside. I let it go. "Strike one!"

Radatzized again.

I dug in for Brandon's second pitch, and my worst fear was realized: his second pitch was coming directly for my head. At what seemed like the last possible moment I bailed out, ending up flat on my back in the batter's box. The umpire's call of "ball one" was small consolation. I asked for time, stepped out, and said to the catcher (Paul Medici from Hanover, Massachusetts, a camper who was helping out the tired pros by catching), "Should I have gone down?" He replied, "I would have if I were you."

I set myself up once again, more determined than before. I was just happy to have survived. I fouled Brandon's next pitch back to the screen. Brandon's fourth offering was high and the ump saw it the same way I did. Two and two. The next pitch was the highlight of my batting career. I managed a ground ball which was only ten feet foul of the first base bag. Brandon's following delivery was inside until at the last minute it broke with the most hellacious curve I have ever seen. Somehow I got the end of my bat on the ball and sent it in the direction of the Red Sox dugout. "Now he's really mad. He didn't think you could hit that one," the ump said. I swung right through Brandon's next pitch, and my glorious time at bat was over.

In Jim Bouton's book, *Ball Four*, he talks about the ballplayers' fear of embarrassment. Bouton maintains that baseball players love to win but their desire to avoid making a fool out of themselves is even stronger. I had not made a fool of myself.

Tom Parsons followed me and hit a ground ball to Jerry Moses at first. Jerry played the grounder like a catcher, letting Parsons' ball get by him. Tom never played baseball in his life, and he's on base for the second time in two innings.

Our next hitter, Steve Berg from Rockland, Massachusetts, grounded to Moses at first as Parsons moved to second. Our next hitter, Dave Peters, a pharmacist from Long Valley, New Jersey, struck out to end the inning.

Rico Petrocelli led off the last of the second with a sharp single. Was this the beginning of the end for the upstart campers? But Kennedy dug a little deeper as he faced the pesky Denny Doyle. Denny was a little bantam of a guy who rode us all unmercifully all week. I still wish I had asked him why he couldn't turn the double play in game seven of the 1975 World Series. It's too late now, and it was soon too late for him. Popeye Doyle popped up to Arnold Preston, our ace first baseman.

Bill "Spaceman" Lee was next to face Kennedy. I had looked forward to having a conversation with Lee before the camp. Then I got there and found out you don't talk with Bill Lee. You listened to Bill Lee. We were all delighted when "Space" grounded meekly to Arnold Preston at first base. Arnold was a sixty-year-old plumber in real life, but he played that ball as if he were a sixty-year-old carpenter. The Red Sox were retired again, and it was as if Kennedy had the ball on a string. Kennedy throws to home, the Red Sox hit to first, and the batter is out.

At this point, the crowd was really getting into it. The "fans" the campers had brought along were on their feet, and our fellow campers were really urging us on. We learned later that the Red Sox' wives were also rooting for us. Their general theme was "let's teach these guys some humility." It may be that the only two people cheering for the pros were Charlie Moss, the Red Sox trainer, and Russ Gibson's son. **SCORE AT THE END OF TWO: Campers 1, Red Sox 0**

Neil Kennedy led off the top of the third like a pitcher: He struck out. John Gounaris was easily retired on a ground ball to Dalton Jones at third. Jones was not as sure-handed on Ed Shaeffer's grounder, and our veteran third sacker was on for the second time. Chip Orcutt followed with a line single into right center. Shaeffer's fifty-seven-year-old legs let him down, and he was thrown out at third on a nice relay from Rico. Actually, he could have been out at shortstop, he was so far from third when the throw came in. Craig Maine struck out to end our half of the third and the high drama was about to begin.

The fearsome Bucky Brandon led off for the Red Sox. Kennedy threw his first side-arm pitch wide. STOP THE VIDEO. The Red Sox have batted out of order, and the ball game is over. The campers win 1-0!

But our manager, John Gounaris, must have been busy writing his memoirs. Nobody noticed that Russ Gibson with his lifetime average of .228 in the dugout, and Paul Medici, their borrowed catcher, never hit. The Red Sox were so desperate they skipped from their seventh hitter to their lead off hitter, and we never noticed.

The immortal Neil Kennedy would not be fazed by this small bit of chicanery. He forced Brandon to line to our chemical engineer--center fielder, Dennis O'Brien--and we were one out from our impossible dream.

Our mentor, our leader, our idol, Bernie Carbo stepped to the plate. Would Bernie do us in or would he go in the tank so we could win? Did Bernie even remember who we were? I saw Bernie have his first beer sometime around 9:00 a.m., and it was now after 3:00 p.m.

I flashed the two-out sign to the outfielders from my position at second base. All the great ballplayers want the ball hit to them in a spot like this. I am not a great ballplayer. I prayed that the ball would not be hit to me.

My prayers were answered. Bernie got under a fastball and hit it a mile high towards Craig Maine at short. The videotape highlight film has Craig's catch in slow motion. In slow motion, the execution is kind of ugly. In person, it was the prettiest thing I've ever seen.

Pandemonium broke loose on the field. Pandemonium was our pet chihuahua and team mascot. Just kidding, Bernie. I don't know how the Red Sox would have felt if they had beaten the Cards in game seven, 1967, but they couldn't have felt any better than we did. We embraced one another as if we hadn't seen our loved ones in over a week. Come to think of it, most of the guys hadn't seen their loved ones in over a week.

The pros were very gracious as we went through with the hand-shake ritual. Dennis Bennett tried to steal my watch. Bill Lee did steal my watch. The highlights film shows a "freeze frame" of Bernie Carbo hugging me at the end of the line. It's too bad you can't hear his words as well. He is saying, "What was your name again?"

Capturing the essence of Bernardo Carbo, a very complex man, in a few sentences is tough. It truly is akin to catching lightning in a bottle. I will simply close with the last sentence from my fantasy camp baseball card, "Bernie Carbo changed my life." I'm not certain that it was for the best, Bernie, but you certainly did have an impact.

"Chihuahua" power, Bernie. "Chihuahua" power.

INDEX